BACKPACKING

Revised Edition

R. C. Rethmel

Burgess Publishing Company
426 South Sixth Street • Minneapolis, Minnesota 55415

Printed in the United States of America
Library of Congress Catalog Card Number 70-187156
SBN 8087-1824-X

1   2   3   4   5   6   7   8   9   0

Preface

Backpacking has been an intriguing subject, and a favorite outdoor activity, to the writer for many years. Most of us have a certain "explorer instinct." We would like to know and see what is beyond the next bend in the river, or over the next mountain, or in the canyon far below. A backpacker can find out for himself and enjoy the healthful exercise, the fun of camping out, and many other benefits in doing so.

An experienced backpacker can go into a remote area for a week with a thirty to thirty-five pound pack on his back and live very adequately, shut off from all outside communication. In fact, in many cases he will live more comfortably and eat equally as well as others who take to the highway with a full trailer-load of equipment, in spite of the fact that the highway travelers will probably make daily stops to replenish certain foods and supplies. Specific information on just how the backpacker keeps down the weight of his pack, however, is not very plentiful. Therefore, the primary purpose of this book is to set forth this information in terms that the average hiker can understand. A particular effort has been made to be very specific rather than to discuss the various applicable subjects in general terms.

My background includes a long term as a Boy Scout and Scout leader, as well as present participation in Boy Scouting activities. For many years I have made frequent backpack trips into the Gila Wilderness in southwestern New Mexico and into some of the other wilderness areas. On many of these trips I have been organizer and leader of small groups of adult sportsmen. Checklists and pretrip plans, as well as notes made during and after pack trips, have led to the publication of this book.

Please keep in mind as you read through this book that the material herein applies specifically to backpacking. Otherwise you may "squirm" a bit in your chair when you read such recommendations as to take little or no extra clothing for a week-long backpack trip, to use a five ounce sheet of plastic for rain protection (under some conditions), or to use certain freeze dried foods which may cost fifty cents or more for one ounce. In some instances the material may apply to other types of outdoor activity also, but that is only coincidental. Clothes, food, and equipment which you would normally use for other kinds of camping will frequently not be suitable for backpacking. With some foresight, however, certain clothing and equipment that you may purchase for backpacking can be used for other purposes.

For those readers who are "old hands" at backpacking, it is hoped that you will be broad-minded about the amount of detail included in this book. After reading the book you may feel that your experience dictates that some procedure or technique should be approached differently. Perhaps you have a favorite food recipe or an item of equipment that you think is especially good for backpacking. If you have comments of any kind, either general or specific, I would appreciate receiving them in a letter or note addressed to me at P.O. Box 1526, Alamogordo, New Mexico 88310.

Well, we were going to talk about backpacking — so pull up a log, get a little closer to the campfire, and we will get started.

Alamogordo,   R.C. (Bob) Rethmel
New Mexico

Contents

Part   Page

1. AN INTRODUCTION TO BACKPACKING 1-1
2. EQUIPMENT 2-1
3. CLOTHING 3-1
4. FOOD AND RECIPES 4-1
5. MENUS AND FOOD LISTS 5-1
6. COOKING 6-1
7. SAFETY 7-1
8. ON THE TRAIL 8-1
9. IN CAMP 9-1
10. PREPARING FOR A BACKPACK TRIP 10-1

Tables

1. Some Suppliers of Backpacking and Mountaineering Equipment 2-2
2. Recommended Personal Equipment 2-14
3. Recommended Common Equipment 2-14
4. Optional Personal Equipment 2-15
5. Optional Common Equipment 2-15
6. Some Sources of Special Foods for Backpacking 4-2
7. Information on Some Foods for Backpacking 4-3
8. Measuring Units (Approximate) for Foods Used in Backpacking 4-12
9. Equipment Required for Meals 6-11
10. Wind Chill Factor 7-3
11. Weight Summary 10-12

Appendices

A. Suppliers Specializing in Backpacking and Mountaineering Equipment A-3

Some Suppliers of General Camping Equipment Who Carry Some Backpacking Equipment   A-3

B. General Sources of Special Foods for Backpacking A-3

C. One-Man Backpack Tent A-4

D. One-Wheel Duffel Carrier A-7

E. Wilderness and Primitive Areas in National Forests A-9

F. Sources for Maps, Trail Information, and Backpacking Information. A-12

G. Organizations Which Promote Conservation of Natural Resources A-13

H. Survival A-14

I. Sub-Zero Camping A-20

OTHER LITERATURE A-26

INDEX A-27

1

Introduction to Backpacking

WHY GO BACKPACKING?

People go backpacking for a variety of reasons. Backpacking can take you into beautiful scenery that may lie just a few miles beyond the roadhead. It can provide an inexpensive vacation. It is certainly healthful exercise, if you are in reasonably good physical condition to start with. Entire families, frequently with children as young as eight or ten years of age, have backpacked into some of our forest and wilderness areas. In addition to the objectives of photography, rock collecting, fishing, relaxation, or whatever else you may be after, there is a tremendous satisfaction in being able to carry your "house" on your back for a week and to live comfortably in the woods, shut off from all outside communication. It takes skillful planning, and this too is part of the fun in backpacking. If you want some unusual fishing, wildlife study, or just plain solitude, you leave a lot of the competition behind when you pack into areas where only your two feet can carry you.

Persons interested in technical mountain climbing find that backpacking is useful and necessary in carrying their climbing gear and supplies to a base camp, from which they will do their climbing. Sportsmen use backpacking equipment and techniques in getting to good hunting and fishing grounds, which are frequently more than a day's travel from the roadhead. Thus, to some persons backpacking is simply a necessary means of moving equipment and supplies into an area in order to accomplish another, more primary objective. Many others find backpacking in itself an enjoyable and exhilarating sport, especially when done in an area that is isolated and attractive from a scenic standpoint. For those in Boy Scouting and Girl Scouting, backpacking brings together the basic skills which they have learned and puts them to good test.

In this "modern day civilization" it is possible for a person to go from the cradle to the grave and hardly draw a deep breath. He may never have a problem in seeking shelter from the elements or a need to build a fire from natural materials and cook his own food. You can go through life and never experience the fatigue and pleasure of real physical exhaustion. A drink from a cool mountain stream on a hot day, the smell of a pine forest, and the taste of a fresh caught mountain trout are pleasures that are available to practically everyone in reasonably good health, if they will but make the effort and take the necessary initiative. Psychologically it is good for us to have new problems and new experiences that are different from the pattern of our everyday living. We all need some adventure in our lives, if only for a few days each year. Backpacking is a wholesome, invigorating activity that will provide a physical and mental atmosphere which is a pleasant change from our daily routine.

Trail trips, using riding horses and pack horses or mules, are common, especially in the West.

These certainly have a very important place as a means of seeing and enjoying our wilderness and forest areas. Without them many persons would never know the pleasure and general well being that comes from packing into a remote area. They do have certain limitations, however. On the average pack trip by horse, reasonably good trails must be followed. If you want to explore a deep and rugged canyon, or some other difficult terrain, the horses must frequently be left behind. There is also the matter of water and forage for riding and pack animals. Along some of our well-used wilderness trails, forage, in particular, can be a problem. Even though you may be a good rider, unless you have had considerable experience with horses and pack animals on trail rides (wrangling), their care is best left to experts. When the night is dark, the grass is thin, and a horse starts getting visions of the home pasture, he can travel surprisingly far, even if he is hobbled. Throughout a horseback trip, constant consideration must be given to the care and well-being of the horses, and this detracts considerably from the time that is left for other pursuits. Therefore, such pack trips are frequently made up of formally or semiformally organized groups of ten to twenty persons or more, plus hired guides and wranglers. The privacy and individual decision that is inherent to a small party of backpackers is impossible on such trips. The techniques and experience required, however, dictate that most persons must join such a group if they are to participate. By no means a small consideration is the cost, usually ranging from $20 to $30 per person per day. However, these remarks are not intended to discourage you from taking such a trip. If a trail trip by horse is your chosen way of seeing a remote area, then by all means take it. A well-conducted trail trip will be an experience which you will long remember.

PHYSICAL CONDITION

In a discussion of backpacking, the matter of physical condition usually comes up. If you have no serious defects, you can walk. If you can walk, you can hike. If you can hike, you can backpack. It then becomes a matter of pace, the type of terrain to be attempted, and the size of pack you can carry. To a considerable degree, from this point on your technique and "know-how" are deciding factors in how long you can stay out (on the trail) and how comfortable you will be (whether you will enjoy the trip or will decide to give up backpacking).

BE PREPARED

On a backpack trip into a remote area, you must not only be a hiker but you (or other members of the group) must be a camper, cook, doctor, pathfinder, and many other things. On an automobile camping trip, or on any other trip that keeps in touch with civilization, forgotten items of equipment can be bought at the nearest store. If your equipment needs repair, you require medical attention, you need a change from your own cooking, or you require some other service, you can usually buy that service. Your money won't help you on a backpacking trip in a wilderness area. You are on your own.

YOUR EQUIPMENT

You will find numerous references in this book to specific brand names of equipment and food. These are brands which the writer has personally used on backpack trips and found to be satisfactory for the job. It is not meant to infer that there is not another product which may be equally as good. You may wish to try other brands or your own substitute equipment, and that is certainly your choice to do so. However, before taking off on an extended backpack trip it is recommended that you thoroughly try out all such equipment and food at home, or on a very short backpack trip, just in case they do not work out as planned. This cannot be emphasized too strongly.

PACK WEIGHT

As for every other kind of outdoor activity, there are equipment, clothing, and techniques which are especially pertinent to backpacking. This book sets forth information on these and other applicable subjects that will enable you to properly prepare for a backpack trip and to hit the trail with confidence. It would not require nearly so much skill and planning for a backpack trip if the matter of weight did not need to be continually considered. The pack weight, in turn, is interrelated with equipment, clothing, food and technique. Your equipment and clothing can be perfect for backpacking but, if you plan for and take the wrong foods, your pack weight will grow out-of-bounds. Those persons who like to "throw a few things together and take off" when they go camping had better prepare themselves for a drastically different approach if they plan to do some serious backpacking. Assuming that you or the group leader has the necessary "know-how" to plan and conduct an interesting and safe backpack trip, then the single most important factor affecting your enjoyment of the trip is the weight of your pack. Consider it carefully.

You should not plan to carry a loaded pack totalling more than thirty-five pounds. This applies to the average adult male backpacker, with average experience, for a trip lasting up to a week or ten days. A forty pound pack may feel quite comfortable when walking around in the living room or in the backyard at home for a few minutes, but five or six hours on a mountain trail can be quite different. If you have a special purpose for going into the wilderness, say for commercial type photography, and you choose to carry ten or twelve pounds of photographic equipment, then it is going to be difficult to keep the total pack weight under thirty-five pounds. However, the average backpacker should not be carrying this much special purpose gear. If you are of small body build, or not accustomed to backpacking, you should eliminate all nonessential equipment and clothing to keep the total pack weight between twenty-five and thirty pounds. The irony of it is that the experienced backpackers will have least difficulty in keeping their packs light, while the beginners (who are most apt to really suffer from a heavy pack) will find it more of a problem. However, it can be done, even by those who are relatively inexperienced — so let's see how.

2

Equipment

IMPROVISE

You can easily spend several hundred dollars on special equipment for use in backpacking. On many items, however, you can improvise or "make do" with equipment that is already around your home or with substitute items that are locally available. A list of some of the firms that sell special equipment for use in backpacking is given in Table 1. It is recommended that you order the catalogues of some of these suppliers and browse through them. This "window shopping" won't cost anything, and it will add to your knowledge to read through these catalogues. This book will outline what is desirable in the way of effective and lightweight backpack equipment, but it will also give particular emphasis to pointing out acceptable substitutes for special (and frequently expensive) equipment. If you keep on with backpacking, you will probably want to replace some of these substitute items with better equipment. It is recommended that you do this gradually, however, and gain some experience and knowledge as you go along, so that you can spend your dollars more wisely.

SLEEPING BAGS

Backpacking requires the expenditure of a lot of physical energy. If you are to recover this energy and be prepared to start each day with renewed strength and enthusiasm, then you must sleep soundly and comfortably at night.

Nothing is more important on a backpack trip than your bed. It is one of those factors, like food, that can mean the difference between an enjoyable trip and one where you wish you had stayed home.

Warmth in a sleeping bag is a primary consideration. Warmth, in turn, is determined by the amount of air confined by the filler material of the sleeping bag. The more fluffy a sleeping bag, the warmer it will be because it will confine more air. This air, heated by your body inside the sleeping bag, is what keeps you warm. The best filler material for a sleeping bag, where weight is important, is northern domestic goose down. A sleeping bag containing 2-1/4 pounds of goose down will keep the average person warm at temperatures of 25° F. or slightly below. It will require eight to ten pounds of wool blankets to give the same comfort, or about four pounds of dacron filler material. Individuals differ considerably in their ability to sleep warm, and this must always be taken into account.

The shape of the sleeping bag is important. It should preferably be of the "mummy" type for backpacking. A rectangular shaped sleeping bag has more room in it than is necessary to confine your body, and thus it weighs more than a mummy shaped bag which will provide the same warmth. With a rectangular shaped sleeping bag you can turn your body during the night without turning the bag at the same time. With a mummy type bag you turn the sleeping bag with

TABLE 1. SOME SUPPLIERS OF BACKPACKING AND MOUNTAINEERING EQUIPMENT *

Supplier No.	Name	Address
1	Holubar	Box 7 Boulder, Colorado 80301
2	Thomas Black and Sons	930 Ford St. Ogdensburg, New York 13669
3	Trailwise	1615 University Ave. Berkeley, California 94703
4	Recreational Equipment Co.	1525 11th Ave. Seattle, Washington 98122
5	Moor & Mountain	14 Main St. Concord, Massachusetts 01742
6	Camp and Trail Outfitters	21 Park Place New York, New York 10007
7	Leon R. Greenman	132 Spring St. New York, New York 10012
8	Himalayan Pak Co.	807 Ocean View Ave. Monterey, California 93940
9	Kelty Mfg. Co.	P.O. Box 3645 Glendale, California 91201
10	Camp Trails	3920 West Clarendon Ave. Phoenix, Arizona 85019

Note: Suppliers 1 through 7 list a wide range of equipment, clothing, and some foods.

Suppliers No. 8 through 10 list primarily backpacks and accessories.

A very comprehensive list of trail equipment, suppliers, and prices can be obtained from The Appalachian Trail Conference, 1718 N Street N.W., Washington, D.C. 20036. Ask for the booklet on Hiking, Camping, and Mountaineering Equipment.

*Also see Appendix A

your body when you want to turn during the night. Once you get used to this, it is no disadvantage. Most mummy type sleeping bags have an attached "hood" which can be drawn around your head and neck, leaving only the face exposed. On a cold night this is important because it prevents the escape of warm air from the sleeping bag. Such sleeping bags usually come from the manufacturer with a tie tape threaded around the circumference of the hood. When you are snug in the sleeping bag you reach up from the inside with your hands and tie a nice bow knot in the tie tape. However, this frequently presents a problem later on. When you wake up, either during the night or early morning, and sleepily reach up to quickly undo the bow knot in the tie tape, you may find that it has relapsed during the night into a good solid knot. Not being able to see the knot you are trying to untie makes the job no simple matter and being somewhat captive inside that sleeping bag may give you claustrophobia real fast. The

solution is to use one of the small spring-loaded drawstring clamps in the tie tape, as stocked by several suppliers in Table 1. They weigh only about 1/4 ounce. They are simple to use and effective.

The construction of the sleeping bag is important. A "sewn-through" construction between the layers of cloth which contain the down or other filler material will result in cold spots and a less effective bag for a given amount of insulation material. A baffle or overlapping tube construction will eliminate these cold spots, and such construction will be found in the better sleeping bags. Don't try to drive any "hard bargains" in purchasing a sleeping bag for backpacking. A good sleeping bag, purchased from a reputable manufacturer or supplier, is a wise investment, a pleasure to pack, and a joy to use. With reasonable care it will last for many years.

Be sure to get your sleeping bag long enough. If you are six foot or taller in height, this requires special consideration. If you should pur-

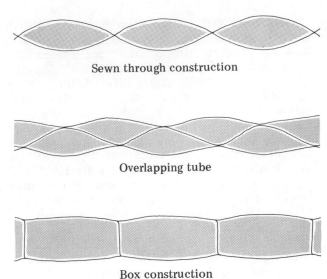

Sewn through construction

Overlapping tube

Box construction

SLEEPING BAG CONSTRUCTION

chase a sleeping bag that is too short, you will regret every night that you spend in it.

Whether to get a zipper on your sleeping bag is frequently a question. A mummy sleeping bag is not difficult to get into and out of, even though it has no zipper. A zipper will add to the cost of your sleeping bag, and it will add a little weight. It is also a potential area for leakage of warm air to the outside. If a zipper is used, a short length one will usually suffice, except for perhaps a husband-wife team who buy two sleeping bags with a specific plan to zip the two together and thus make one large bag. If you do plan on a zipper, be sure and get a good one and also make sure that the zipper area is protected with a well-designed, well-insulated flap. In warm weather a zippered bag can be partially unzipped for cooling. However, most mummy bags have a sufficiently wide opening at the top that the bag can simply be pushed down on the top side for a similar effect.

If you plan to use a liner in your sleeping bag, you should purchase a bag with tie tapes or fasteners installed on the inside for holding the liner in position. A liner which is not anchored in place will get twisted and uncomfortably wrapped around the body. A liner will add somewhat to the warmth of a sleeping bag, depending upon material, and will aid in keeping it clean. However, many persons feel that wearing a pair of pajamas will accomplish essentially the same job as a liner and generally be more comfortable than a liner. Do not wear any articles of daytime clothing in your sleeping bag unless they are clean and dry and needed for warmth. The wearing of such clothes at night should be considered as an emergency measure. If you choose a good sleeping bag for the temperatures

you expect to encounter, it should normally not be necessary to wear clothing for warmth while sleeping. If your sleeping bag must be used for somewhat colder weather than it is designed for, a dacron jacket and pants underwear suit is sometimes a good solution.

To be prepared against rain, you should carry a separate waterproof tarp or tent. The cover of a sleeping bag should never be waterproof. Your body gives off moisture, up to one or two pints during the night. This moisture must be able to escape through the sleeping bag cover. If the cover is waterproof, the moisture cannot escape and you will become damp and chilled. There is a big difference between water repellent and waterproof material. A water repellent cover will allow moisture to escape and is generally satisfactory. So-called "canopies" that are pictured at the head end in some sleeping bag advertisements, particularly for the large rectangular sleeping bags, are worthless insofar as furnishing any protection from weather is concerned.

A stuff bag is useful as a carrying pouch for down sleeping bags. A stuff bag normally is about ten or twelve inches in diameter and about eighteen to twenty inches long. To use such a bag, rather than rolling a down sleeping bag into a bundle, simply "stuff" it into the carrying bag, handful by handful.

The quality of filler material, the amount of filler, and the quality of construction and workmanship are the primary factors in determining the price of a sleeping bag. Common inexpensive filler materials are kapok, orlon, celacloud, and a long list of others which can be quite confusing to many people. Most of these fillers have a tendency to mat and pack into lumps, thus losing their insulating value. Some attract vermin. Sleeping bag materials which are especially suitable for backpacking bags are Dacron, duck down and goose down.

DACRON FILLED BAGS. DuPont Dacron "88" (polyester fiberfill) is one of the best of the synthetic filler materials. It is resilient and somewhat fluffy. It will not pack into lumps. Not too many suppliers carry mummy shaped bags with Dacron filler material, but some do. A well-constructed mummy shaped bag, containing about 3-1/2 pounds of Dacron and having a total weight of about six pounds, will keep the average person warm at temperatures down to about 35° F.

FEATHER AND DOWN FILLED BAGS. To achieve the light weight desired in a sleeping bag used for backpacking, some manufacturers use a mixture of down and small curled feathers as a filler material. They are not as effective as an all-down bag, but for moderate weather they will do the job. Such a bag will usually be a pound or two lighter in weight than a Dacron filled bag, for an equivalent comfort range. Duck down is sometimes used as an insulating material rather than goose down. For an economy sleeping bag it is generally satisfactory. Avoid any sleeping bag which uses reprocessed down. Check the label.

DOWN FILLED BAGS. The most effective filler material available for sleeping bags, for the weight, is northern domestic goose down. A sleeping bag containing a filler of 2-1/4 pounds of goose down and having an overall weight of about 3-1/2 to 4 pounds will keep the average person warm at temperatures down to about 20° F. Such bags are available at prices starting at about $65. For the person who plans to do considerable backpacking, such a sleeping bag is recommended. Except in special cases, where very cold temperatures are expected, a bag containing 2 to 2-1/2 pounds of down is most suitable. For very cold temperatures two bags, one slipped inside the other, is frequently a better choice than a single bag. In that way the sleeping bag is not too hot for normal spring, summer, and early fall use, and you have the use of two bags instead of one. If a member of the family wants a very cold weather bag, say for hunting, then he has a suitable combination by placing one inside the other.

OTHER SLEEPING GEAR

ROUGHING IT. A bed made on the bare ground will not provide the comfort that most people need for a good night's sleep. Most of us require something a bit softer. There was a time when a person could take an axe or hatchet and cut limbs from live trees in order to make a bough bed. That time is past. Don't do it. Leaves, grass, and other similar materials can also be used to provide a foundation for your sleeping bag. However, the time required to gather such materials and the likelihood that you won't find them when and where you want them add up to the fact that you should plan to carry a pad or mattress of some sort on which to lay your sleeping bag. It should also be pointed out that most bough beds, as well as beds made from other natural materials, would look pretty sad in comparison with a good air mattress or foam pad. Especially after such beds have been slept in for four or five hours, they leave much to be desired. Try to imagine too, some nice, large, sticky, stained areas on your good sleeping bag, caused from the pitch in the pine or balsam boughs.

AIR MATTRESS. The average person will sleep comfortably if his head, shoulders, and hips are properly supported. Your legs can extend past the edge of the mattress onto the ground and it will make little difference. A mattress about twenty-five by forty inches (inflated) and weighing under two pounds is good for backpacking. For short backpack trips the added weight of a full length mattress may not be important, but on longer trips it will be. An air mattress made of plastic material will be lightest in weight for a given size. Such a mattress will also be the most subject to tears and pinholes from twigs, pine needles, sharp stones, and other material lying on the ground where you choose to make your bed. You should go over the ground very carefully (on your hands and knees) before you put down your air mattress and remove all such objects. It is a good idea to use a ground cloth under an air mattress; this will give some protection against puncture and abrasion from materials on the ground. A heavy plastic sheet will usually make a suitable ground cloth. If you use a plastic air mattress, be sure it is in new condition. After they have been lying around for a few months (even though they are not used much), plastic air mattresses will start to develop pinholes that will about drive a person crazy trying to keep them patched. The best air mattress for backpacking is made of coated nylon fabric. The Stebco is a good air mattress of this type. The Stebco "backpacker" is about forty-eight inches long and weighs twenty-eight ounces. It is carried by several suppliers listed in Table 1. It will take a lot of fairly rough treatment. Air mattresses made from other materials are available but most of them are too heavy for regular use in backpacking. Always carry a patch kit so that you can make any necessary repairs on the spot.

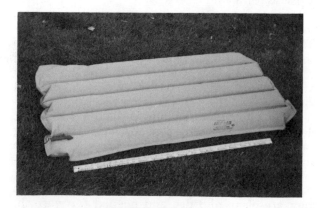

BACKPACK AIR MATTRESS. This is the Stebco "Backpacker," made of coated nylon fabric.

When you inflate your air mattress for the night, don't blow it up too hard. It should be fairly limp. When you lie on it and you can just barely feel your hip touch the ground at one point, it is about right. Lay it out so that the valve end is near your head. Then you can easily reach over and let a bit of air out if it is too hard. Or, if it is too soft, roll off to one side and blow it up a little. When you first wake up in the morning, reach over and open the air valve while you are still lying on your mattress. This will save a little time later on in getting the air out. Lying on the hard ground will also provide additional incentive for getting up. In packing your air mattress, try not to fold it in the same pattern each time. This will cause the mattress to weaken along the seams where it is repeatedly folded.

FOAM RUBBER PADS. The polyurethane foam pads are quite popular among backpackers. They are lighter in weight than most air mattresses of equivalent size and comfort. They provide better insulation from the cold ground than an air mattress, and there is some advantage in that they are not subject to puncture, as is an air mattress. Their primary disadvantage is that they are bulky to pack. One must apply a lot of pressure in rolling up a foam pad to have a reasonable size roll for packing. A satisfactory hip length pad, about twenty-four by thirty-six inches in size, weighs as little as eighteen ounces. The polyurethane foam pads are of open cell construction and will absorb water, but that is ordinarily no great problem. A waterproof cover may be made or purchased, if desired.

RAIN PROTECTION

You can protect yourself from rain in a number of ways. The kind of protection you plan for will depend largely on the type of country, the season, and the frequency of rain expected. If you are camping in desert regions, or if it is the time of year when little or no rain is expected, you can probably get by with the simplest kind of protection or possibly none at all. If you are going into high mountains in the summer or in another area where rains are frequent, you will probably want to plan some substantial protection.

TENT TARPS. A canvas tarp is generally too heavy for backpacking. A coated nylon tarp or poncho is fine, being both lightweight and durable. The least expensive form of protection is a plastic sheet. It can be pitched over a ridge line, in pup tent fashion, and weighted along the ground edges with rocks. A nine by twelve foot sheet of plastic, weighing as little as five ounces,

will give protection. However, they are not at all durable. They must be kept away from bushes and sharp objects or they will tear easily, but with some precautions they will last for a week-long backpack trip. You should buy a new sheet for each trip. Heavier plastic sheets, of 2 or 3 mil thickness, can be used and will be more durable.

ON THE TRAIL. If you are thoroughly acquainted with the area you are packing into and know that rain at that particular time of year is highly improbable, you may prefer not to take a raincoat. In case of rain, you could get under a plastic tarp and wait it out. Nondurable plastic raincoats, weighing about nine ounces, are available in many local stores. For occasional protection where the trail is good, and relatively free of brush that will tear such a raincoat, they may be satisfactory. On trips where rain is expected, better protection will be provided by a hip length rain jacket and rain pants or chaps. (The latter are two individual "legs," fitting over the trousers and hooking to the belt.) Rain pants or chaps are particularly good where low brush or weeds bordering the trail may thoroughly wet the trouser legs during or after a rain. Still another possibility is a poncho. Some ponchos are made to go over the pack as well as the hiker. Ponchos do not come in a "tailor fit." They are loose and "floppy." Some are suitable for pitching over a ridge line to form a lightweight shelter at night. Coated nylon raincoats or ponchos will be fairly light in weight and rather durable, compared to plastic. Rubber slickers are generally unsatisfactory for backpack trips. They are too heavy.

Condensation inside close-fitting raincoats and jackets is something of a problem, depending upon the length of time they are worn, temperature, degree of exertion of the wearer, etc. Since ponchos are fairly loose fitting, there is not so much of a problem, but it is by no means eliminated.

Never lay a poncho, plastic tarp or similar rain protection directly on your sleeping bag and then go to sleep in the bag. The protective cover should always be pitched over a ridge line and maximum ventilation provided, even though the size of the cover may limit the peak height when pitched to 1-1/2 to 2 feet. There must be free circulation of air under any such waterproof covering, or excessive condensation will result.

TENTS

A tent cannot be considered an essential item of equipment for most mild weather backpacking. For cold weather backpacking, or for severe weather that may occur at any season in some of the very high mountains, a tent may be

BACKPACK TENT. Instructions for making this tent are given in Appendix C.

desirable. There are some good commercial light-weight tents, made especially for backpacking and mountaineering, weighing from two to five pounds for a one-man size. These are usually made of coated nylon or other lightweight cloth that has good water repellency, wind resistance and high tear strength. They are not made of completely waterproof materials because to do so would bring on the familiar problem of condensation when a person was inside the tent. Absolute protection against rain is usually accomplished by a separate waterproof fly, pitched over the main tent. Suppliers of back-packing and mountaineering equipment usually carry such tents. The cloth is fairly expensive; therefore a good tent is rather expensive.

In some areas of the country, at certain seasons, insects are such a severe threat to a good night's sleep (and your comfort in general) as to call for special measures. With a little ingenuity it is not difficult to make a one-man tent, suitable for most backpacking, which will provide protection from insects, rain, reptiles, and rodents. I frequently use such a one-man tent that I planned and fabricated, and which meets these requirements. Detailed instructions for making the tent are given in Appendix C. This tent is essentially a cover for your sleeping bag, with some additional room at the head end for a few items of clothing or equipment. The tent is about eight feet long, twenty-eight inches high at the head end, and seventeen inches high at the foot end. It weighs about one pound, including a lightweight plastic fly which provides rain protection. With such a tent you dress and undress outside. There is not room inside. You slip into your sleeping bag at the same time you slide into the tent. However, it answers the re-quirement for a lightweight, inexpensive shelter. If you expect to encounter much rain on your trips, a flysheet made from one of the light-weight coated cloths (such as polyurethane coated nylon) will make a durable fly. If the tent fly is to be in place for long periods, it is best to pitch it on a separate ridge line, directly over and about one foot above the tent ridge line, for maximum ventilation.

It is not necessary to carry or make poles for this tent in most situations. The ridge line is fastened at the head end about four feet off the ground, using a tree or bush, and sloping to a stake or rock several feet out from the foot end. You have perhaps had the experience of search-ing through a grove of trees to find two trees which were the right distance apart, with level ground between, so you could rig a ridge line for a tent that had a level ridge. If so, you can appreciate the advantage of a tent with a sloping ridge, that requires only one small tree or bush for anchoring the high end of the sloping ridge line.

FIRE MAKING EQUIPMENT

It is important to check on the area into which you plan to backpack to make certain that open wood fires are permitted. In some instances a fire building permit may be required. If wood is available and wood fires are allowed, you will probably want to take some fire build-ing equipment. The name "country matches" or "kitchen matches" is usually applied to those matches having a "handle" about 2-1/2 inches in length. You should carry about four country matches for every fire you intend to build, in waterproof containers. To save time a few fire-making aids, such as a plumber's candle, inflam-mable pellets, etc., are also recommended. Another fire aid, which is especially good in damp, muggy weather, is a short length of gum rubber hose with a metal tubing on the end. With this you can direct a draft to the fire just where you want it. It is usually better than fan-ning the fire with your hat or a plate or blowing on it in the usual fashion.

CANTEEN

On most backpack trips in the western states you should carry a canteen. Running out of water can be one of the most serious problems you will meet in desert or wilderness camping. Unless you are thoroughly familiar with the trail and know positively that there will be good drinking water at intervals of an hour or two along the trail, then by all means carry a canteen. It can save your life. A quart size can-teen for one person will usually do the job, and a quart of water will usually last a person for four to six hours of hiking under ordinary condi-

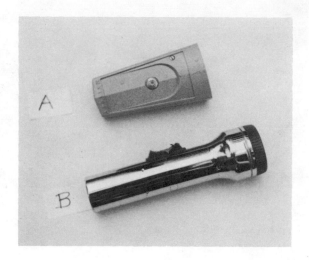

PLASTIC CANTEEN. This is a good, durable, one quart canteen, weighing 4-1/2 ounces.

MALLORY FLASHLIGHT. The Mallory flashlight (A) is shown in comparison with an ordinary two cell "C" size flashlight (B).

tions. If you are in doubt, carry two quarts. In the one-quart canteens, a plastic type is available which is the lightest in weight. It will also stand a lot of fairly rough treatment. If streams, springs, or other water sources are going to be more than five or six hours apart, you should consider a different route.

ROPE

This is a necessary item of equipment on most backpack trips. About fifty to sixty feet are required for a clothesline and about the same amount for a ridge line if you want to put up a plastic tarp or similar covering for rain protection. Heavy rope is not necessary. Parachute cord, about 1/8 inch in diameter and having about 550 pound test strength, is light in weight and will do the job. A 150 to 200 pound test nylon cord is lighter yet and completely satisfactory for all the usual backpacking needs.

KNIFE

A good pocketknife, with a sharp blade, is an essential item of equipment. If you are fishing, or intend to be cleaning fish, a knife with a long tapered blade is better than a short blunt blade. Knives with bottle openers, screwdrivers, punches, etc., attached are satisfactory for general usage, but they are not usually essential for backpacking. It's your choice.

FLASHLIGHT

A large flashlight is not required. With few exceptions, camp should be made, the evening meal prepared, and dishes washed before dark. If

you start each day at daylight or soon after, you will be ready for your sleeping bag after you have sat around the campfire for an hour. There is no need to tramp around the woods at night, and it is not advisable. The requirement for a flashlight is therefore simple. You need the light to find your way from the campfire to your sleeping bag. You can undress and get ready for the sleeping bag in the dark except for an occasional beam of light to untie a shoe or stow your clothes. It all adds up to about one to five minutes of intermittent light required each night. A standard "D" size two-cell flashlight can be used (weight about ten ounces with batteries). The smaller "C" size flashlight can also be used and will weigh less (about five ounces with batteries). The recommended flashlight, however, is a good two-cell penlight. Many ordinary penlights are so cheaply constructed and unreliable as to be worthless. The Mallory is a good flashlight, using two penlight batteries, with a total weight of about 3-1/2 ounces. Two long-life penlight batteries will usually be adequate for a backpack trip of a week's duration. If you use ordinary batteries, rather than the long-life kind, you should carry two extra batteries for each three or four days of the trip. Always carry a spare bulb. Batteries will usually burn out gradually, but a bulb will give no warning. Do not dispose of batteries by throwing them in the fire. They may explode.

SAW

A small saw can be a very handy item of equipment. Saws are available which consist merely of a ring on each end of a flexible sixteen

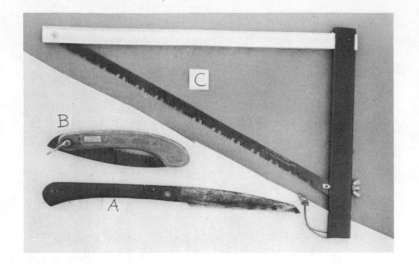

SAWS. Two jacksaws are shown, one open (A) and one closed (B), weighing 4 ounces and 7 ounces, respectively. The Sven saw (C) weighs about 17 ounces. The saw readily breaks down for packing, all three parts being carried inside the handle.

to twenty-four inch blade and weigh about one ounce. Such saws can best be used by finding a limber, green stick, about 3/4 inch in diameter, and a little longer than the saw blade, and using this as a saw handle. Using your knife, notch this stick about one inch from each end. Slip one ring of the saw into one of the notches, put a bow in the handle, then slip the other ring into place in the other notch. Securing the rings in place at the notches with cord or wire will keep them from slipping out of the notches when in use. Some of these ring saws are nothing more than gadgets. If you should decide on this type, get a good one and try it out at home. A more convenient saw is the jack saw. These usually have an eight or ten inch blade that folds into an attached handle. One lightweight saw of this type weighs as little as four ounces. Such a saw is useful in cutting such things as skillet extension handles, dingle sticks (used for hanging cooking pans), tent stakes, walking staffs.

TAPE

There always seems to be a need for a roll of tape around camp. Waterproof tape can be used to repair torn plastic tarps, raincoats, air mattresses (small holes), and for temporary repairs to waders. A roll containing several yards of 1/2 or 3/4 inch tape for each person is recommended. Another handy tape is rip-stop tape for repairing tears in clothing, etc. One foot of rip-stop tape per person should be sufficient.

PLIERS

A pair of needle nose pliers is frequently useful. They are handy in moving pans on and off the fire, unless you have a pan gripping tool. They can be used in first aid for removing splinters and thorns. In dishwashing they can be used to dunk eating utensils in a pan of hot water for rinsing. If you are fishing, needle nose pliers are almost a necessity for removing fishhooks (preferably from the fish).

TOILET ARTICLES

SOAP. There are a number of good bar soaps available, which will lather well in hard water, that can be used for your personal bathing as well as washing dishes. "Vel" brand soap is an example. With frequent bathing, about two ounces of soap per person per week is required for personal use. The same bar can be used for dishwashing. Germs are not carried by a bar of soap, so don't worry about using the same bar for this dual purpose. Packing of liquids should be avoided in backpacking whenever possible, and this certainly applies to liquid soaps. It is downright disheartening when someone accidentally knocks over an unstoppered bottle of liquid soap and you watch the week's supply soak into the ground.

TOWEL, WASHCLOTH. One small towel and washcloth per person should be sufficient. A large bath towel is too heavy and bulky. If you don't have a small one, make one from a towel remnant. If it should get too dirty, rinse it out and hang on the line to dry overnight.

TOOTHBRUSH, PASTE. You will want a toothbrush, but toothpaste is not considered essential on a backpack trip. You can satisfactorily brush your teeth with a half teaspoon of salt. Rubbing the bristles of your toothbrush against a cake of soap will also provide a good cleanser for your teeth. This may not sound very appealing, but it works. Try it at home. It will leave your mouth clean and refreshed. If you must carry toothpaste, be sure that it is a very small tube or one which has been mostly used up. A full large-size tube of toothpaste weighs about eight ounces, and there is no need to carry that much weight just to brush your teeth a few times.

You may have heard of backpackers sawing off the handles of toothbrushes. In case you should get the notion to saw off the handle of your toothbrush in order to save weight, you may be interested to know that a full size toothbrush, about six inches long, weighs only 3/8 to 1/2 ounce. If you saw off the entire handle, about four inches long, you will save only 3/16 to 1/4 ounce, which isn't much — even to a backpacker. Also, after the handle is sawed off, there would seem to be some doubt as to how useful the toothbrush would be. The plastic holders (carrying cases) for toothbrushes are something else. The usual plastic case toothbrush holder will weigh 3/4 to 1 ounce. You can save essentially all of this weight by using a small, pint-size plastic bag to contain your toothbrush, or simply wrap the bristle end in a small square of aluminum foil.

TOILET TISSUE. This is best carried in roll form, just as it comes for household use. It should be packed in a small plastic bag and kept out of the rain and away from anything damp. This is very important. The requirements are about 1/3 ounce of toilet tissue per person per day. As bought in the store, a full new roll is about 4-1/2 inches in diameter and weighs eight ounces. One-third ounce is equivalent to about a nine-foot strip of the common household variety.

COMB. A comb is advisable, but a hairbrush is not. You can usually get along without brushing your hair for the length of a backpack trip. Toilet kits should be left at home.

SHAVING GEAR. On most backpack trips, the usual rule is to "let 'em grow." Shaving gear means added weight and some nuisance in heating water, as well as carrying a basin for the water. It frequently turns out that even those persons who carry shaving gear don't use it. If some members of the group decide that they want to carry such gear, it is best to get together on the equipment required so as to save weight. Battery and spring-wound shavers are available. It's your decision.

SUN PROTECTION. Besides wearing a hat, you should have a good cream to protect your face and hands from sunburn and to keep your skin from getting too dry and uncomfortable. Glacier cream, which is stocked by several of the suppliers listed in Table 1, is good to use on face, hands, and lips. It is packaged in a sturdy

tube which will not break or split in your pocket or pack. Another good protective cream is A-Fil, available from most pharmacies.

INSECT REPELLENT. Depending upon the season and the type of country, you may want some protection against insects. A stick or cream (in a tube) insect repellent is again preferable to a liquid with a bottle container or a cream in a jar. A common stick repellent is 6-12. The Cutter brand insect repellent is also good.

DITTY BAG ITEMS

There are a number of small, lightweight items, generally classed as "ditty bag" items, that are frequently worthwhile. Some of these are:

SEWING KIT. A single needle and a few feet of strong cotton or nylon thread should suffice. You can also use fish line for thread. Don't worry about the color. An emergency sewing job can be done over again when you get home. The needle can double as an item of first aid equipment, and a good way to carry it is taped to the inside of the lid of the first aid box.

SAFETY PINS. A few medium-size safety pins are useful. In addition to their ordinary uses, they are smaller than clothespins and equally suitable for hanging socks or towels on a line to dry.

WIRE. Several yards of light-gauge wire, commonly referred to as "stove wire," is frequently useful. This flexible wire is recommended for bails on cooking pans, as discussed in Part 6 on Cooking, and a few feet should be carried as a spare bail.

PENCIL, NOTE CARDS. If you want to make some notes during the trip, a short wood pencil (with a metal protector for the tip) and some three by five inch note cards, or a small notebook, should be carried. A ball-point pen will be heavier than necessary and most of them will not write well on a greasy or slightly soiled surface, which is apt to be the case for note cards carried in your pocket and worked on when your hands are sweaty, etc.

MAP AND COMPASS

On most trips into wilderness areas you will be following trails, usually Forest Service trails. If you lose the trail you should backtrack until you find it again. The best maps are usually sketches of the area, the trails, and prominent features, which you draw yourself, with the aid of a topographical map and preferably some per-

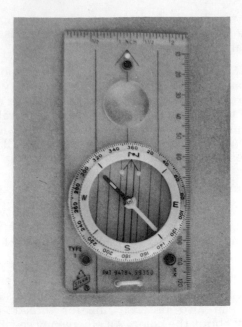

A good compass, with attached base plate, direction-of-travel arrow, and a ruler for measuring map distances. This type is most useful for orienting a map, taking a field bearing, and following that bearing. A course is set and followed by degrees. Compass variation (true north versus magnetic north) is very important, and you should know what it is for the area you are in. On U.S. Geological Survey maps the compass variation is marked on the bottom of the map.

son who has been in the area. If you carry a map, don't carry a thirty inch by thirty inch map when the only area you are interested in is a five inch by five inch section. Cut the section out with a razor blade and reinsert it later, using transparent Scotch tape. It is a good idea to follow your progress on the map and to know your position at all times. You may be leaving the trail at times, but it should not be under circumstances that there is any danger in finding it again. Attempting shortcuts or going cross-country in the wilderness is not recommended.

The maps put out by the U.S. Geological Survey will be found very helpful in most backpacking. These maps show all of the important natural features, as well as main trails. Elevations are shown by contour lines and this is an important feature when traveling in rugged terrain. For the Western states an index of the maps, as well as the maps themselves (costing about fifty cents each), is available from the U.S. Geological Survey, Denver Federal Center, Denver, Colorado. Other useful maps are published by the U.S. Forest Service and are frequently available at no cost. The writer has always found members of the Forest Service to be very helpful in furnishing information on forest and stream

conditions, trails, and in supplying similar data important to the planning of a backpack trip.

You may carry a compass for months or even years and never use it. Yet, it should be considered an essential item of your equipment when you are going into a remote area or an area with which you are not completely familiar. Choose a good compass. Become thoroughly acquainted with it in "practice exercises" in a familiar area. If the end of the needle which points north is not unmistakably marked, then you should make a small note as to which end of the compass needle (such as the "red" end) points north. Use transparent tape and tape this note to the bottom of the compass. A liquid-filled compass is recommended.

FIRST AID KIT

GENERAL CONTENTS. The following items are recommended for a first aid kit, as a minimum:

1. two three by three inch sterile gauze pads
2. ten yards of one-inch sterile gauze
3. 1-1/2 yards of 1/2-inch adhesive tape
4. 1/2 ounce tube antiseptic first aid cream
5. ammonia inhalant, one or two small vials
6. one dozen Band-Aids, assorted sizes
7. small booklet on first aid
8. Aspirin tablets (about one dozen)
9. Halazone or iodine water purification tablets

OPTIONAL ITEMS. If a wound occurs on a part of the body which is thickly covered by hair, it may be desirable to remove some of this hair before dressing the wound. Also, the suction cup on a snakebite kit will not work too well if that part of the skin is covered with hair. Such hair can be readily removed with a sharp single edge razor blade (no soap or water needed), by holding the blade almost parallel to the skin. A needle is useful in removing slivers and in a real emergency can be used with thread to temporarily draw together the edges of a very bad cut. Benadryl tablets are usually good for bee, wasp, scorpion, and other insect bites. They will counteract the allergic reaction that many people have to such bites. (If in doubt, get your doctor's advice before you plan to use these tablets.) Therefore, these additional items, a needle, a single edge razor blade, and about ten Benadryl tablets, are also suggested. All of the items listed can be easily packed into a small metal first aid box, having outside dimensions of 1-3/8 inches by 3-3/4 inches by 5-1/4 inches and weighing about 7-1/2 ounces when filled.

OTHER FIRST AID ITEMS. A few other items in the first aid category that are considered desirable to be carried, not necessarily inside the first aid kit, are:

1. Milk of magnesia tablets. These are good for constipation and upset stomach. The tablet form, usually mint flavored, is easy to pack and easy to take.

2. Moleskin patches. A moleskin patch, applied to a tender spot on the foot or toe at the first sign of tenderness, will usually keep such a spot from developing into a blister and thus giving real trouble. Some hikers, knowing the spots on their feet that are likely to give trouble, apply these patches when first starting out.

3. Salt tablets. You need to replace the salt in your body that is lost through perspiration, if you are to feel well. Salt tablets are frequently more convenient than drinking salt water. Be sure to get the coated kind to avoid nausea. Enseals, put out by the Lilly Co., is a good brand.

4. Muscle ointment. For sore shoulders and other sore muscles, a 1-1/2 ounce tube of Ben Gay, Deep Heat, or similar preparation is helpful.

SNAKEBITE KIT. In many areas of the country, a snakebite kit should be carried. Suction type kits are the most common. The Cutter snakebite kit is a well-known brand of the suction type. There are many others. On some extended trips, an antivenin kit may be desirable; however, expert instruction should be obtained in its use, and you should know the horse serum sensitivity reaction of the snakebite victim before using it.

THE PACK

The type of hiking, the load to be carried, and the expected terrain are primary considerations in choosing a pack. Most backpacking for pleasure involves carrying twenty-five to thirty-five pound loads for substantial distances, over reasonably good trails. For this type of hiking a large rectangular pack frame, with fitted packsack, is best. An important feature of a pack frame is its size. It should be as large as possible, commensurate with the body build of the user. This is not so you can carry an extra heavy load, but rather because a normal load distributed over a large area of your back is much more comfortable than the same load applied to a small area of your back.

The pack frame may be constructed of wood or of metal tubing. Tubular aluminum frames are most commonly used, although magnesium tubular frames are also available and are somewhat lighter. The frame should be constructed to hold the pack bag with its load away from the wearer's back and permit circulation of air in this area. On most pack frames there are two wide canvas back panels wrapped around the vertical frame members so that the pack load bears on the hiker's back through these panels. The panels should be adjustable up or down on the frame to fit the individual, with the lower panel resting on the slope of the buttocks. The pack frames made by Camp Trails of Phoenix, Arizona and by the Kelty Co. are of the tubular metal type and are very good frames.

Shoulder straps should be attached high on the frame. They should be wide where they bear on the shoulders and narrow where they pass under the arms. The straps should ride close to the neck, never far out on the shoulders. They should always be firmly attached to the frame, rather than having a "floating" arrangement which will allow the pack to move either up or down or from side to side. Padded shoulder straps will be found on most of the good pack frames. If the shoulder straps on your pack frame are not padded, you can buy the shoulder pads separately and install them on the straps.

When carrying a good pack frame that is properly loaded, the center of gravity of the load will be very nearly over the hiker's hips. The hiker will feel comfortable when walking in essentially an upright position, bending forward only very slightly to balance the load. In order to keep the center of gravity of a substantial load close to the back, the frame and the load on it needs to be high, wide and not very deep (toward the rear). A waist belt is an important part of a good pack frame. It will help to keep the frame and load close in to the body and will take a part of the load off the shoulders. A waist belt must be tight when in use. Padded waist belts will be found on the better pack frames. It is important to keep the belt that holds up your trousers free of canteens, sheath knives and similar equipment which will interfere with the waist belt.

The pack load should ride close to the back and high on the back but not be top-heavy. Where the terrain is very rugged or steep climbing is to be done, the center of gravity of the load needs to be kept low, so as not to throw the wearer off balance. In most backpacking over reasonably good trails, the heaviest items in the load need to be near shoulder level. This is accomplished by mounting the packsack high on the pack frame and by packing light objects in the bottom of the packsack, heavier objects near the top. The sleeping bag is usually lashed to the lower part of the pack frame.

A good pack bag is an important complement to a good pack frame. The better pack bags have outside zippered pockets, frequently two on each side and one at the rear. These pockets

"Skyline" pack frame and pack bag

The Kelty pack

Both the Skyline and the Kelty are good packframe-packbag combinations. These packframes are made of tubular aluminum, with contoured construction to fit the back and to provide good distribution of the pack load. The Skyline is made by Camp Trails of Phoenix, Arizona, makers of the well known "Cruiser." The Kelty is made by Kelty Co. of Glendale, California.

The Trapper Nelson

Army packboard

For serious backpacking these packs have been largely replaced by the contoured, tubular aluminum packframes, which have better weight distribution, waist belts, and other desirable features. The Army packboard will carry large and odd shaped loads and is sometimes useful in hunting, in packing out a quarter of game. For normal backpacking it leaves much to be desired.

provide ready access to certain items such as knife, pliers, canteen, salt tablets, trail snacks, raincoat, first aid equipment, camera, etc., that may be needed during the day. Some pack bags are constructed so that the main compartment is partitioned, with the lower compartment reached through a zipper extending across the full width of the bag. Coated nylon is usually used as a material in making the better pack bags. When you buy a new pack bag, check over the inside of the pack bag pockets for possible loose ravelings of thread along the seams. When these get stuck in the zipper, in camp or along the trail, it can be very annoying. In general, the manufacturing processes used in the better pack bags eliminate this problem.

An accessory sometimes used with pack frames is a tumpline. This is a strap that generally fastens near the bottom of the frame and has a padded area that bears on the top of the head. However, unless your head and neck are thoroughly accustomed to use of a tumpline you probably will not find it very comfortable if used for more than a few minutes at a time. It is not recommended for the average backpacker. Somewhat more useful accessories, for some situations, are clamps which mount along the vertical frame members (tubular frames) for lashing various items of equipment. A removable shelf, which mounts to the lower part of the pack frame, is also available.

SUMMARY OF RECOMMENDED EQUIPMENT

Now that we have discussed equipment, let's see what it adds up to in an actual backpack trip. First we will consider only that equipment which is considered necessary to do the job, provide reasonable comfort and assure your well-being. Recommended items of equipment, adequate for a backpack trip lasting up to one week or more, are used in making up the lists in Tables 2 and 3. Equipment is considered in two categories. First, the personal equipment, which are those items which are for your personal use and benefit only, each hiker taking his own. Secondly, the "common equipment," which are those items shared by the group as a whole. You probably won't have all the items that are recommended in these lists. Where you have a different or substitute item, make the proper allowance for weight.

OPTIONAL EQUIPMENT

This is the point where many backpackers get "carried away." They take too many things that they think they might need and then never use. Consider your optional equipment carefully. If you are not sure you are going to need it (excepting first aid and emergency items) better leave it at home. Following are some optional

The "belt pack" is useful for day hikes. When you know absolutely that a few small items of equipment and your lunch and canteen will suffice for the hike you are taking, this is a good way to carry your few items of gear.

Belt pack being worn by author

Belt pack

TABLE 2. RECOMMENDED PERSONAL EQUIPMENT

Item	Approximate Weight (Ounces)
Sleeping bag (down filled, baffle construction, mummy shaped, for temperatures down to 20° F.)	64
Ground cloth (plastic sheet)	4
Rain protection (light plastic sheet, about eight by ten feet)	5
Polyurethane foam pad, hip length	21
Flashlight (Mallory type)	3
Canteen (one quart, plastic, filled with water)	37
Rope (thirty feet, nylon cord, about 150 pound test)	1
Toilet articles (small towel, washcloth, toothbrush, comb, sun protective lotion, insect repellent)	5
Knife (folding pocket knife)	2
Pack frame and bag	72
Total	214

TABLE 3. RECOMMENDED COMMON EQUIPMENT

Item	Approximate Weight (Ounces)
First Aid Kit	8
Other first aid items (water purification tablets, milk of magnesia tablets, moleskin patches, salt tablets, snake bite kit, etc.)	5
Fire starting equipment (one week supply; four country matches per meal, 1/2 fire cube per meal)	5
Bar soap (two ounces per person per week)	2
Toilet tissue (two ounces per person per week)	2
Tape (1-1/2 ounces per person per week)	1½
Pliers (small, needle nose)	4
Map, compass	3

Note: The total weight of common equipment is obtained by adding the above list, after mulitplying items fourth, fifth and sixth by the number of persons in the group. The weight of these items is to be shared by all members of the group.

equipment items that you may want to consider:

CAMERA. A camera is not an essential item of equipment but on many trips it will be desirable. A 35mm camera and case weigh about twenty ounces. One way of saving weight on this item is for several or more hikers to go together, and the one with the camera can simply take duplicate or extra shots where desired. The others sharing in the camera shots take a corresponding weight of the "cameraman's" share of the common equipment.

FISHING EQUIPMENT. If you are going into an area where there are lakes or trout streams, you will probably want to take some fishing equipment. This will usually be either a fly rod, spin cast rod or spinning rod, and a reel to match, plus a small box of lures and some extra line. Don't go overboard on accessories. A landing net is nice, but it isn't essential. Neither is a creel. If you intend to wade streams you will want a pair of tennis shoes or lightweight waders. Besides the pleasure of catching fish from wilderness streams or lakes, the weight of the fishing equipment will probably more than make up for itself by the lighter food load (meat) that will need to be carried.

OTHER OPTIONAL EQUIPMENT. Depending upon the nature of the trip, you may want to take other special equipment, such as for rock hunting. The question of guns frequently comes up when planning a backpack trip. With very few exceptions, guns should be left at home. They are not needed for protection. Unless the trip is for hunting and all members are trained in gun handling, guns represent a safety hazard.

SUMMARY OF OPTIONAL EQUIPMENT. As for recommended equipment, the optional equipment items are divided into two categories, personal equipment and common equipment. Some of the above items, as well as a few other items of personal equipment to be considered, are listed in Table 4. Table 5 lists some items of optional common equipment that you may want to consider.

TABLE 4. OPTIONAL PERSONAL EQUIPMENT

Item	Approximate Weight (Ounces)
Fishing equipment (rod, reel, small box of lures, maximum weight)	18
Tent, with plastic fly (see Appendix)	15
Sleeping bag liner	12
Pliers (small, needle nose for fishing)	4
Paperback book (for possible bad weather)	5

TABLE 5. OPTIONAL COMMON EQUIPMENT

Item	Approximate Weight (Ounces)
Camera (weight is for average 35mm)	20
Jack saw	4
Wood pile cover (plastic sheet, about six by eight feet)	4
Rope (150 pound test, thirty feet length)	1
Plastic wash basin	5
Metal mirror	2½
Miniature playing cards (for bad weather)	1½
Nail file	¼
Survival Kit (see appendix H)	5 to 12
Other. This is up to you, but remember, you have to carry it.	—

3

Clothing

GENERAL

For mild weather backpacking you will need very little special clothing. Usually some of the clothing that you already have will do the job, except for possibly hiking shoes or boots. This does not mean that "any old thing" will do for clothes on a backpack trip. It will not. With some searching and a little ingenuity, however, you can usually find clothes among those you already have that will suffice. Never take any worn-out article of clothing (or equipment) on a backpack trip with the idea that it will "probably last" and after the trip you can throw it away. Every item should be in good condition, and there should be no doubt about it. Various articles of clothing are discussed in the following paragraphs, pointing out the important requirements of each item. Your outer clothing should give you maximum protection from the sun. You will take less risk with heat exhaustion, save on drinking water, and avoid sunburn if you keep this in mind. Sunburn on a backpack trip is serious, and every precaution should be taken to avoid it. Sunburned shoulders, especially, can be a catastrophe. Therefore, long-sleeved shirts, long trousers and a broad-brimmed hat are advisable. At the same time you will get more protection from nicks and scratches caused by rocks and bushes and from poison ivy, etc. Long-sleeved shirts and long trousers also offer significant additional protection against snake-

bite, compared to bare skin, where rattlesnakes (or other poisonous snakes) may be encountered. All clothing should be a little loose fitting rather than a little too tight.

Clothing must breathe. This is demonstrated when you wear a pair of rubber hip boots or a rubber slicker on a warm day. Your perspiration cannot escape to the outside and evaporate. Depending upon the amount of exertion, humidity, and other factors, your clothes soon become damp and uncomfortable. Keep shirts and other clothing clean, insofar as practicable, and keep them dry. When clothing becomes sweat or rain soaked it loses a lot of its insulating value. You can easily become chilled when you allow your clothing to get damp.

In general, girls and women wear the same type of outer clothing on backpack trips as men. Long-sleeved shirts, long trousers and a brimmed hat are recommended.

If you are backpacking into high mountain country or if the trip is to be made in winter, special clothing and rain gear will probably be necessary, as well as special techniques. Weather in high mountain country is frequently unpredictable, at any season. Before going into such country you should have had ample experience at lower elevations. You should also not attempt high mountain backpacking unless there are capable persons in the party who are thoroughly experienced in the special equipment and techniques required.

HAT

Any comfortable hat, reasonably soft and flexible, with a broad brim, should be satisfactory. An old felt hat is OK. A few holes punched or cut in the crown will make it cooler. An ordinary straw hat (not stiff) is good if rain is not expected. The "Crusher" hat, sold by some of the suppliers listed in Table 1, makes a good hat for backpacking. It weighs about three ounces. Hats made from preshrunk, water repellent, poplin material are frequently good. To keep from losing your hat in a brisk wind, it is easy to attach a chin strap. Punch a hole in the brim just above each ear and thread a leather thong around the back half of the brim circumference on the top side, down through the holes, and tie or use a slide fastener to tighten under the chin. If you expect rain, better carry a plastic rain cover for your hat if you want to protect it. You will usually need to roll the brim of the hat up in back (or turn it down) to keep the top of your pack from bumping against your hat as you hike along the trail. (This can be very annoying.)

CRUSHER HAT. Note that the top of the pack is well above the hat. The "Crusher" hat, worn here, is soft and flexible. The annoying "bumping" of the rear part of the brim against the pack, that occurs with many broad brimmed hats, is avoided.

SHIRT

Choose a shirt with a loose weave and soft finish. When you perspire, you will be more comfortable in such a shirt than you will in one made from tightly woven, hard finish material. A thin cotton flannel shirt is good for mild weather hiking. Some hikers will prefer wool, in all weather. Others find that wool causes their skin to itch and to become very uncomfortable. In cool, wet weather, wool has an advantage in that it will keep you warm even though it is wet. Light colors are cooler in hot weather than dark colors. A plaid design will not show dirt as easily as a solid color. If you are backpacking during hunting season, bright colors are important from a safety standpoint. If the shirttail is worn outside the trousers in very hot weather you will be cooler because of the added ventilation provided. For wearing outside the trousers, a square cut shirttail is more convenient than the long tapered shirttails. Shirts should have long sleeves. Two generous size pockets, with button tops or flaps, will prove useful. Before starting out, check all buttons and resew those that are loose.

TROUSERS

Khaki trousers and some blue jeans are satisfactory. Unlike the shirt, trousers should be of rather tightly woven material, with a hard finish. A canvas trouser like those commonly used in duck hunting, however, is too stiff and uncomfortable for long hikes. Trousers should not be form fitting but comfortably loose. Long trousers, without cuffs, are advisable. They should have full width legs, not the narrow kind. Don't hang any more items of equipment on your belt than necessary, especially if you use a waist strap on your pack. Equipment on your trouser belt is going to interfere with its use. Even without equipment on your belt, your trousers are going to tend to "sag" as you hike along, unless you keep hitching them up or pull your belt quite tight. A good solution to this problem is to wear heavy duty suspenders, in addition to a wide belt, to keep your trousers in place. Even if you don't normally wear suspenders, you will probably find them useful and comfortable in backpacking. Trousers should be a little short rather than too long and should fall two or three inches above the heel on your boot. Don't load the pockets down with equipment. If you have a packsack with outside pockets you can put most of the items in those pockets that you would normally want to carry in your trouser pockets, and they will be almost as accessible. Otherwise put such items in a small bag near the top of your pack.

On most backpack trips you will be doing a lot of bending, stooping, squatting and stretching, and this is a major reason why trousers, as well as other clothing, should be comfortably loose rather than tight. If you need to do a considerable amount of wading to cross fairly deep streams that lie in your route, there is another good reason why trouser legs, in particular, should be wide rather than form fitting. You will want to take off your trousers in wading the deep streams which may come up to your waist. If you have narrow leg trousers you must take off your shoes each time you come to such a place, in order to get your trousers off. This takes time, and struggling with wet knots in wading shoe strings is no fun. With wide-leg trousers, they will slip on and off over your wading shoes without removing the shoes, and save a lot of time and patience.

SHOES

The shoes and socks that you wear on a backpack trip are your most important items of clothing. Choose them carefully. Tender and sore feet can make you thoroughly miserable. Blisters or a bruised Achilles tendon (the tendon at the rear of the heel of your foot) can put you completely out of business. Problems with your feet and shoes that never occur in the walking required by your usual daily routine will show up on a backpack trip. If you take the matter of footwear too lightly you can easily ruin a trip, both for yourself and your companions.

A leather boot, extending above the ankle, but not over six inches high, is recommended. An eight inch height may be satisfactory, but the higher the boot the more tendency there will be toward some restriction of the calf muscles. Also, with a high boot there will be some sagging of the leather at the ankles and a tender or bruised Achilles tendon is more apt to occur. A good boot should give your feet ample support and protection against rocks (cushion the foot and protect ankles against bruises), give good traction, keep out dirt, and be comfortable on your feet. They should not be insulated. Insulated boots are too hot for normal weather use. The insulation will soon become sweat soaked, and you will be hiking with wet feet. A lined boot is not necessarily an insulated boot and may be quite satisfactory. Rubber footwear and canvas footwear are not recommended for hiking.

A shoe with a welt construction will usually be found to have a more secure sole, after a few weeks of hard usage, than one without a welt. Rocky trails call for a good substantial sole and a sturdy construction. Provided they have sturdy construction and sufficient cushion for the feet, your boots for hiking should not be one ounce heavier than necessary, however. If you have an average stride, you lift each boot and set it down again about 1100 times in traveling one mile. If your boots are a few ounces heavier than necessary, this represents a lot of useful energy going to waste. For example, if each boot is four ounces heavier than necessary, this amounts (energy-wise) to walking one-quarter of the distance traveled with a one pound weight strapped to each ankle (as compared to using a proper weight boot). Also, it takes a lot more energy to carry extra ounces on your feet than in the pack on your back.

Whether the boots have a moccasin style foot or a lace to toe style is generally a matter of personal preference. Either rubber or composition soles and heels should be used. Leather soles and heels do not give satisfactory traction on rocky trails. In fact, under many conditions they are dangerously slippery. Several of the suppliers listed in Table 1 carry mountaineering and trail boots that are very good for normal hiking use. Many of these use Vibram or Roccia lug soles and heels which are long wearing and give good traction under most conditions. To provide maximum footing safety, most shoes used in technical rock climbing do not have a welt. Hiking shoes, however, are in a different category insofar as this feature is concerned and a welt sole is advantageous. The Kletterschuhe is a general type of lightweight technical rock climbing shoe, mostly foreign made, a few of which are satisfactory for general trail use. Many Kletterschuhes, however, are of such light weight and construction that they will not stand up well when used for hiking.

The better heavy duty hiking boots will have a large, flexible outer tongue which is permanently fastened on either side to the boot. This tongue keeps water (to some extent), small sticks, stones, dirt, etc., out of the boot. Under this outer tongue will be found a separate, heavy, padded, inner tongue. This padded tongue keeps shoelaces from cutting into your sock and foot, when snugly laced, and prevents chafing of the foot in that area. A good, heavy duty hiking boot will also be padded at the ankle and around the top edge, where chafing is likely to occur. A hard toe cap is frequently used in the construction of such boots. It is certainly not essential that you have a special mountaineering boot or trail shoe in order to go backpacking. Whatever boot you choose, it should have the general characteristics mentioned, however.

Be sure to get your hiking boots large enough. When trying them on always wear the heavy

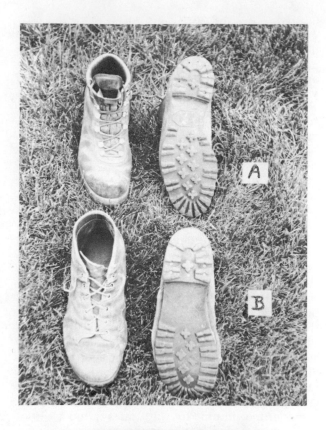

HIKING BOOTS. Boot (A) is the "Bighorn." Boot (B) is the "Cortina." The Bighorn is a heavy duty, rugged boot, weighing about 4-1/4 pounds for size 9-1/2. It has a separate, well-padded, inner tongue; padded top edge; welt sole and similar features. The Cortina is popular with many hikers who want a lightweight, medium duty boot. It weighs about 3-1/4 pounds per pair (size 9-1/2). Both boots have the Vibram lug sole.

This is the Eddie Bauer K-4 hiking boot for ladies. A pair of size 7½ hiking boots weighs 2 lbs. 7 oz. Quite a few suppliers carry only men's or boy's hiking boots and many women frequently buy and use them. However, it is best for women and girls to choose and wear a hiking boot that is made over a women's last, as these boots are.

This is the Maine guide shoe, made by L.L. Bean of Freeport, Maine. It is a very good lightweight trail shoe. A pair of size 9½ boots weighs 3 lbs., which is about the lightest weight boot available that is comfortable to the feet and offers the necessary protection for normal trail use.

socks, or combination of socks, that you intend to wear when hiking. If you order your hiking boots through the mail, always send along an outline of your foot. Again, this outline should be made with your hiking socks on, and by tracing the outline onto a piece of paper with your full weight on the foot. Your feet cover more area when you are standing on them than while sitting. They are also bigger in the evening than in the morning, so take your measurements in the evening. It is not uncommon for a person to have one foot larger than the other, so use the larger foot, if this is the case. It is always better for hiking boots to be a little too large rather than a little too small.

Do not wade water with leather boots. Most leather boots are water repellent enough that you can go through wet grass or even a few puddles, but wading streams is something else. If your trail is going to be crossing streams, you should consider carrying a pair of tennis (canvas) shoes to use for this purpose. It is not advisable to cross streams in your bare feet. Your feet will be uncomfortable, your footing unsure, and you run the risk of a cut from stones or other material in the stream bed. A plastic bag, to put wet tennis shoes in after use, will keep them from dampening other equipment in your pack. If you are only going to be crossing a few streams, one (large size) pair of tennis shoes may suffice for the group and could be considered as an item of common equipment. After one man gets across the stream, he can throw the shoes back for the next man, and so on. Or, they can be retrieved with a hand line. If there are only a few "mild" stream crossings along your route, a rubber soled shower slipper or canvas hospital slipper may suffice for crossing such places and will weigh less than tennis shoes.

It is frequently difficult to locate the right length of shoelace for hiking shoes or boots and often they are not rugged enough. If they have a wrapped end, there is usually a problem in threading them through the eyelets on your boot if you make them shorter and cut off the ends. Some hikers prefer nylon laces; however, the smooth finish on many nylon laces has a tendency to make the lace come untied. A good quality leather lace is fairly strong, can be cut to any length, and will still thread through an eyelet. In lacing your boots, lace them snug but not tight. Tie them at the top with a square knot (again, a snug knot, but not tight), and a couple of loose overhand knots on the top of that. You should then have several inches of shoelace left over, but not enough to step on while hiking. Do not wrap the laces around your leg if they are too long, or tie them in big bowknots. Cut them off. Before you start on a backpack trip, take

the laces out of your shoes and give them a hard yank. If they break, or appear weak, replace them.

Do not start a hike with new boots or shoes. They should always be well broken in. They should not be so old that there is any doubt about their lasting the trip, however. Don't take any pair of shoes on a hike that you had planned to throw away soon. Regardless of whether the shoes are new or not, it is a good idea to take a few preliminary hikes of a few miles to check them out and toughen up your feet a bit. There are several ways to break in a new pair of hiking boots. One way is to simply start wearing them for brief periods at home. To start with you probably won't want to wear them for more than five or ten minutes. Increase this period by about five minutes each day until you can wear them comfortably for an hour or more. Then start taking short hikes, over uneven terrain. It takes about a month to break in a new pair of hiking boots by this method. If you must break in your boots quickly, one good approach is to stand for a minute or two in about six inches of water with your boots on. Then go hiking until the boots dry on your feet.

Inner soles made from felt, nylon mesh, and other materials are available; these will provide additional cushion for your feet on rocky trails. If you have flat feet, and many people do, it is a good idea to wear arch supports.

When you go to bed at night, stow your hiking boots in a place where they will be protected from dew or frost, as well as rain. If your boots should get wet, do not try to dry them out near an open fire or near a similar heat source. They will become stiff and very uncomfortable to wear. You can easily ruin a good pair of leather boots by forced drying. Using dry socks, and a change of socks, you can walk the dampness out of your boots, with much better results than forced drying.

Clean up your boots and apply waterproofing occasionally. For boots made of chrome-tanned leather, and for suede material, you should use a silicone or wax waterproofing. For oil-tanned leather a grease waterproofing should be used. Use all such compounds in moderation. Using too much waterproofing compound, or too frequent applications, will soften the leather too much.

SOCKS

The socks that you wear with your hiking boots are very important. They should either be new or in new condition, without darns or patches. On a hiking trip don't try to get by with old, well-worn socks or the thin socks that

NET UNDERSHIRT

The fishnet construction holds your outer shirt away from the skin. In cold weather your outer shirt and jacket should be closed at the neck and wrists (elastic or knitted cuffs on jacket and preferably a hood) to prevent the escape of warm air at these points. The air pockets provided by the net construction will then be heated by your body and will aid in keeping you warm.

In hot weather your shirt neck should be open and your sleeve cuffs loose, to allow maximum air circulation. The net construction, holding your outer shirt away from the skin, allows perspiration to evaporate without soaking the shirt. This is important in keeping your body cool. Wearing the shirttail of your outer shirt outside the trousers will provide still more circulation.

DOWN VEST. The down vest shown, made by the author, provided an interesting week-end project. It weighs ten ounces. In combination with a flannel shirt and light wind breaker jacket it keeps the wearer comfortable at temperatures down to 20°F. (in low humidity). It was made from a kit (precut materials) purchased from Frostline Co., Boulder, Colorado.

you usually wear with street shoes. Socks made especially for hiking boots are available from several of the suppliers listed in Table 1. A single pair of thick wool socks can be worn; however, most hikers agree that wearing two pairs of socks (simultaneously) gives better results than a single pair. These can be two pairs of medium weight wool socks, but the usual preference is for a thin inner sock (next to your foot) of cotton, and a thick outer wool sock. Wool socks have the advantage that when they get wet they do not feel wet in the way that cotton socks do. Also, the moisture in wool socks will more readily evaporate than with cotton socks. Try different combinations of socks on your hikes and see which provides the most comfort. Always carry a duplicate set of socks, in whatever combination you prefer, on your backpack trips. At the end of each day it is a good idea to rinse out the socks you have worn that day and dry them overnight.

If your feet sweat a great deal, it is advisable to carry more than one extra change of socks. Stop and change them during the day when they become sweat soaked. Pin or tie the sweat soaked socks to the outside of your pack so that they will dry as you hike along. The use of a good foot powder is usually a help to persons whose feet perspire a lot.

When you take off your socks run your hand carefully over the outside to detect and remove any tiny stones, twigs, burrs, balls of thread, and so forth. Then turn the sock inside out and repeat the process. Also check the inside of your boots for such tiny particles, which can easily cause a blister or tender spot on your foot.

HANDKERCHIEF

A handkerchief is not generally essential. This is usually used for blowing your nose, and it is hoped that you won't start a backpack trip with a cold. A handkerchief will soon get dirty and carrying dirty laundry in your pack is not recommended. A small package of Kleenex or some toilet tissue will do the same job. If you usually use your handkerchief or bandana for wiping your hands and face on, as many hikers do, a ten inch square of old, thin toweling carried in your hip pocket will do a better job.

If you use disposable tissues, put them in your pocket after use and burn them at the next camp site or lunch site. Don't litter the trail with them. To those persons who cannot resist the temptation to nonchalantly toss paper tissues down along the trail after each use, we implore you to please stay with the handkerchief.

A bandana or very large handkerchief is frequently useful when worn as an item of clothing. When placed around the neck it will help keep out dust. The neck, particularly the back and sides, is very susceptible to sunburn. A bandana, worn as a neckerchief, will protect this sensitive area. It will also feel comfortable in a cold wind. To a degree, it provides protection from insects in the neck area.

UNDERCLOTHES

On a backpack trip, you can wear the same underclothes that you normally wear. Underclothes, as for other clothing, should be a bit loose rather than too tight. Many hikers prefer to go without an undershirt. An ordinary undershirt will usually become sweat soaked after a period of strenuous hiking. A fishnet type of undershirt, which will prevent this, is carried by most of the suppliers in Table 1. Some hikers prefer the fishnet style of drawers also. If you do not wear a fishnet type of undershirt, you will probably find that no undershirt is most satisfactory (better than wearing a conventional, tight weave undershirt). In such case you should wear an outer shirt made of thin, soft, cotton flannel or similar absorbent material.

PROTECTIVE CLOTHING

The mornings and evenings in the mountains and in northern wilderness areas can be very cool, even in the summer. At these times a fairly heavy jacket or sweater will feel very comfortable. Once the sun comes up, however, and you are hiking, you will warm up fast. A heavy jacket may weigh 2-1/2 to 4 pounds, and many times it will only be used for an hour or two in the evening and again in the early morning. It therefore becomes a matter of compromise as to how much weight you are willing to carry in your pack all day to provide snug comfort while exposed to several hours of low temperatures out of each day. Several layers of light outer clothing are preferable to a single heavy garment. They are more efficient because of the confined air space between the layers of clothing, and they are more adaptable because you can shed or add one layer at a time, as the temperature changes. If you move and work vigorously, it is surprising what little additional clothing you can get by on, even on a cool morning with temperatures down to freezing. If you are wearing a flannel shirt to hike in, an additional flannel shirt, and possibly a sleeveless wool sweater or Dacron (or down) vest, will be sufficient protection for temperatures down to freezing or slightly below. A down-filled vest or jacket, as for sleeping bags, will be the most efficient weight-wise. A good down vest which you purchase from a supplier will cost about $20.

"Do it yourself" kits, from which you can make a good down vest, are available and sell for considerably less.

In an emergency, an extra shirt, vest, or jacket can be worn in the sleeping bag at night if needed for warmth. This should not be done, however, if the article is dirty or damp (especially if damp). Determine the expected maximum and minimum temperature, humidity, and possibility of rain or snow for the area in which you will be backpacking. This is very important for proper planning of protective clothing. In the spring and fall, temperatures in the high mountains can change rapidly. In a damp climate you will need more clothing to keep you warm at a specific temperature than in a dry climate at the same temperature. If you are likely to be exposed to the wind, a light windbreaker type jacket is desirable.

DUPLICATE AND EXTRA CLOTHING

On trips lasting up to a week or ten days, the only duplicate clothing recommended is an extra set of socks (duplicates of whatever combination of socks you hike in). Some hikers may want more spare clothing, but the added weight and the nuisance of carrying around dirty laundry in your pack is seldom justified. You can rinse out underclothes or any other item of clothing in the evening and dry it overnight or by the campfire if you have a fire. You won't get them completely clean with cold stream water and a bar of soap, but it will help a little bit. Your shirt and trousers are going to get soiled with dirt, soot from the campfire, and many other things. However, it is not "dirty dirt" and it is surprising how you hardly notice it after a few days. It is recommended that you have a complete change of clothes, along with soap, towel, and wash basin, to leave in your vehicle at the roadhead, so you can clean up at the end of the trip before starting home. Otherwise, when you stop at a restaurant on the way home, you may get a "cool" reception.

Incidentally, when you dry articles of clothing near an open fire don't get them too close to the fire, and watch them almost continuously. Many hikers have "lost their shirt" (damp shirt) by attempting to dry it near the fire while going about other camp jobs. A slight, momentary shift in wind and you may be without that article of clothing for the rest of the trip.

A large group may find it desirable to carry (as common equipment) a wash basin or bucket of the folding canvas or plastic type while on the trail. This will facilitate personal bathing and washing of clothes, as desired. If much washing of clothes is anticipated you may want to carry a special soap for the purpose. Local stores carry a number of cold water soaps that will do a fairly good job of getting your clothes clean.

Following are some extra items of clothing to be considered:

1. Socks; duplicate of whatever socks you wear while hiking (six ounces).

2. Jacket, vest, extra shirt (or combination of these), for temperatures down to 25° F. (twenty ounces).

3. Optional: canvas (tennis) shoes, for crossing streams (twenty-four ounces).

4. Optional: raincoat or poncho; and possibly rain hat and rain pants (nine to twenty-two ounces).

5. Optional: pajamas (eleven ounces).

4

Food and Recipes

WATCH THE WEIGHT

There are a number of books available on camp cooking. It is a good idea to learn to cook a variety of foods using different types of fires and equipment. In this book it is assumed that the backpack trip you are about to take will be for the purpose of exploring, rock hunting, observing wild life, photography, fishing, or some similar objective and that you won't want to spend any more time than is necessary to prepare and cook your meals and still have good nourishing food to eat. Food and cooking equipment, more than anything else you will pack, will have a tendency to get out of hand by leaps and bounds, as far as weight and bulk are concerned. Yet it is certainly important that you eat well. Therefore, some skillful planning and preparation are needed in this area. That is why three parts of this book are devoted to this general subject.

DRIED AND DEHYDRATED FOODS

On a backpack trip the use of dried and dehydrated foods is important. Water is heavy, about one pound per pint. It should be added to the foods after you get to the camp site, rather than carried in with the food. Macaroni, spaghetti, rice, flour, oatmeal, etc., are dry foods by the nature of the product. Dried prunes, peaches, apricots, raisins, etc., are foods that have been dried to remove much of the water that is present in their natural form but not all

of it. Dehydrated fruits, soups, meats, etc., are foods that have been specially processed to remove substantially all of the water. A dried prune or apricot will be soft and "chewy." A dehydrated prune or apricot will be dry to the point of being brittle. The longer the trip the more important it is that meals be planned around dehydrated foods. A number 2 size can of peaches, for example, will weigh about one pound and will serve about four persons. If dehydrated peaches were used, about three or four ounces would serve four persons.

One process of drying and preserving foods without refrigeration is the freeze-dry method. Meat, eggs, vegetables, and fruits are now being preserved by this process. In general, foods preserved by the freeze-dry method are somewhat more expensive than conventional dehydrated foods. Some of the freeze-dried foods are quite tasty and are well worth the price. Others leave something to be desired.

TRY FOODS AT HOME

As with every product, there are good dehydrated foods and there are poor dehydrated foods. If you were to start experimenting with various dehydrated foods and brands of dehydrated foods, it would probably take a long while and you would run up quite a bill before you settled on a full line of foods that you liked. This book therefore suggests particular foods and brands for your guidance; the writer has tested these on the trail, and most backpackers

TABLE 6. SOME SOURCES OF SPECIAL FOODS FOR BACKPACKING

Supplier No.	Name	Address
1	Bernard Food Industries, Inc.	1208 E. San Antonio St. San Jose, California 95100
2	Recreational Equipment Co.	1525 11th Ave. 98122 Seattle, Washington 98101
3	Holubar	Box 7, Boulder, Colorado 80301
4	Trailwise	1615 University Ave. Berkeley, California 94703
5	Camp and Trail Outfitters	21 Park Place New York, New York 10007

find them to be satisfactory. There are quite a number of producers and suppliers of dehydrated foods and, if you wish to experiment a bit, order some of their foods and go ahead. Table 6 lists some sources of special foods for backpacking. Other suppliers are listed in Appendix B. One word of caution. You should not take any food on a backpack trip that you have not cooked at home, in your own kitchen, and proven to yourself that you like it. Then you can hit the trail with confidence that you are going to enjoy good food. Also, the experience of cooking the food at home will provide better assurance that you will cook it properly when you are on the trail and cooking under somewhat less than ideal conditions.

KEEP REQUIREMENTS SIMPLE

Cooking can be done with a Dutch oven, over a grill, with a reflector oven, etc. These all have a place in general outdoor cooking. However, in backpacking we don't want to take along a single item of cooking equipment or other gear that is not essential. The food recipes listed in this part are therefore chosen for light weight, for simplicity of preparation; they have been proven on the trail to appeal to most hikers' appetites. Every food recipe listed here can be suitably cooked in one of two basic utensils, either an open pan or a skillet. In general, the cooking periods listed are for altitudes of 6,000 to 8,000 feet. For a higher or lower altitude the cooking time will need to be adjusted accordingly.

MEAT

BACON. All bacon should be cooked by starting in a cold skillet and cooking over a medium fire. Do not grease the skillet. The fat on the bacon provides more than enough grease for cooking.

1. Store Bacon. One pound of store bacon will serve from three to five persons, depending upon how much other food you have with it. The bacon you buy in the store will have considerable fat on it. Unless this fat is saved and used for other cooking, it must be looked upon as excess weight in backpacking. Take a small can along, with a tight-fitting lid, to save the grease in. As the bacon cooks, pour off the excess grease into the can. About ten to twelve minutes of cooking is usually sufficient, depending upon how crisp you like it.

2. Canned Bacon. A convenient bacon for backpacking is Swift's canned bacon. It requires no refrigeration. It is precooked and only requires heating over a low fire for five to eight minutes. The can weighs seven ounces (gross) and it contains the equivalent of one pound of regular store bacon. The bacon is packed in a roll inside the can, with the layers separated by a heavy paper. The entire contents can be put into the skillet, including the paper. When the bacon starts to warm, the paper can be easily separated and thrown away. There is not much excess grease on this bacon but you should save what there is.

3. Bacon Bar. Some suppliers in Table 6 stock a bacon bar which is a concentrated prefried bacon. A three ounce bar is equivalent to about twelve to fourteen ounces of uncooked bacon. It can be eaten hot or cold.

4. Other Bacon. There are other canned bacons available, including Canadian bacon. Several suppliers listed in Table 6 carry a Canadian type of canned bacon. Several varieties of canned bacon are also available in some of the local stores.

TABLE 7. INFORMATION ON SOME FOODS FOR BACKPACKING

Item No.	Item	Brand	Weight (ounces)	No. of Servings	Supplier (see Table 6)
1	Bacon, canned	Swift	7	3 to 4	No. 2, 4
2	Bacon, bar	Wilson	3	2 to 3	No. 2, 3, 4
3	Beef, dried	Peacock	2	2 to 3	No. 2
4	Beef, dehyd. ground	Perma-Pak	1	1 or 2	No. 3
5	Beef, stick	Hickory Farms	(4 lbs.)	—	*
6	Beef, jerky	—	2	2 or 3	No. 2, 4
7	Egg, dehyd.	Durkee	1-1/4	2	**
8	Chow mein	Kamp-Pack	5-1/2	3 to 4	No. 1
9	Corn, freeze-dried	Co-Op	1	2 to 3	No. 2
10	Peas, freeze-dried	Co-Op	1	2 to 3	No. 2
11	Beans, string	Co-Op	1	2	No. 2
12	Beans, Boston style	Seidel	12	3 to 4	No. 2
13	Potatoes, sweet	Borden	3-1/4	2 to 3	local
14	Salad, dehyd. vegetable	Perma-Pak	1-1/2	3 to 4	No. 3
15	Salad, dehyd. potato	Kamp-Pack	4-1/2	3 to 4	No. 1
16	Applesauce	Perma-Pak	5-3/4	3 to 4	No. 3
17	Apples, vacuum-dried	Co-Op	2	2 to 3	No. 2
18	Peaches, freeze-dried	Co-Op	3/4	2 to 3	No. 2
19	Apricots, vacuum-dried	Co-Op	2	2 to 3	No. 2
20	Fruit mix, dehyd.	Seidel	3-1/2	3 to 4	No. 2
21	Pineapple Waikiki	Richmoor	5-3/4	4 to 5	No. 2
22	Prunes, vacuum-dried	Co-Op	2	2 to 3	No. 2
23	Pancake syrup	Kamp-Pack	8	3 to 4	No. 1
24	Pancake syrup	Seidel	9	3 to 4	No. 2
25	Trail Candy	Traubenzucker	2	8 pieces	No. 4
26	Trail Snack	"Energy"	3	2 to 3	No. 2
27	Cookie, enriched	Turblokken	8	6 pieces	No. 3
28	Chocolate, tropical	Hershey	1	1	No. 2
29	Pem fruit bar		1	1	No. 3
30	Lemonade mix	Wylers (with sugar)	7-1/2	3 to 4	local
31	Cocoa	Swiss Miss	1	1	No. 2
32	Wafer, whole wheat	Nabisco "Wheat Thins"	9-3/4	7 to 9	local
33	Wafer, whole wheat	Nabisco "Triscuit"	9-3/4	7 to 9	local
34	Ice cream, freeze-dried	Mountain House	2-1/2	3 to 4	No. 2
35	Cottage cheese, freeze-dried	Mountain House	2	3 to 4	No. 2
36	Lemon crystals	Lemon Queen	2-1/2	3 to 4	No. 5
37	Lime crystals	Lime Queen	2-1/2	3 to 4	No. 5
38	Pan coating oil	Vegalene***	4	—	No. 5

*Hickory Farms of Ohio, Western Division, P.O. Box 3306, Van Nuys, California 91401.

**Many brands of dehydrated eggs taste terrible. However, the Durkee brand is unusually good. If your local store doesn't carry Durkee brands, you might write to Durkee Famous Foods, 900 Union Commerce Bldg., Cleveland, Ohio 44101, and inquire as to a source in your area.

***Vegalene is used for coating all pans prior to cooking. It prevents food from sticking to pan and makes the dishwashing job much easier.

Note: The above foods and brands are those with which the author is familiar from personal experience and which he can recommend. This list represents a lot of "trial and error" testing of many dehydrated foods over a period of years. No aspect of backpacking is more important than having good, tasty foods. Yet, to find a full range of appetizing foods — meats, vegetables, salad, beverages, etc. — requires more time and expense than many backpackers can afford. With a few exceptions, this list is primarily concerned with foods for which no equivalent is available in local stores. There are probably other sources (suppliers) for many of the brands given.

SAUSAGE. Most local stores carry small cans of sausage links, with a gross weight of about ten ounces. The Libby brand is good. One can is usually sufficient for three persons for one meal (medium servings), with other food. Canned sausages which are packed in natural juices have better flavor than those packed in water. Dried sausage sticks, which do not require refrigeration, are available from some suppliers of trail foods and occasionally from local confectionery stores. About one ounce per person per meal is a sufficient ration.

SALAMI. This is available in most local stores. It will keep for several days if the weather is not too hot. Summer sausage is sometimes available from local stores and will keep better than salami.

FISH. On many backpack trips trout will be caught. They should be eaten soon after catching, preferably within several hours or less. There are special drying processes and other means of keeping fish without refrigeration, but they are not recommended for the usual backpack trip. Soon after catching, fish should be rough cleaned by removing the contents of the body cavity and bleeding the fish. Never soak cleaned fish in water. After cleaning, keep them dry until time to cook. Salt and pepper them lightly, inside and out, before cooking. Trout are very good without being floured before frying. However, if you must flour them a mixture of half flour and half cornmeal is good. Put the flour and fish in a large plastic bag together, using just enough of the flouring mixture for one meal. Shake the bag vigorously and the flouring job is done. The simplest method of cooking trout is to fry them. Bacon grease, cooking oil, peanut oil, or margarine (least satisfactory) can be used for frying. Have the grease medium hot before putting the fish in. Cook over a medium hot fire. During frying they may be basted with a mixture of melted butter and lemon juice, but this is not essential. About fifteen minutes of frying is sufficient for medium size fish.

Some cooks prefer to prepare trout of ten to twelve inches in length by cutting into the body cavity from alongside the backbone, rather than splitting the belly side. When this is done, the belly acts as a hinge and the thick back section is reduced to a better size for more uniform frying. Removing the bones before eating is a bit more difficult with this method, but the faster and more uniform frying improves the taste so much that it is well worth the effort. Trout which are thirteen or fourteen inches long or more, as well as many other fish of this size, should be prepared for the frying pan by filleting.

It is frequently difficult to maintain a firm grip on fish while you are cleaning them. Trout, especially, are hard to hold on to. One method that helps to hold the fish is to put salt on your fingers before handling them. However, if you have any small nicks in your fingers or hands, then getting salt in these cuts will probably send you into orbit. A better method is to carry a six inch square of wet sandpaper for this purpose. Hold the sandpaper in the palm of your hand, rough side up. Now lay the trout on the sandpaper, close your grip, and you have him.

If you are going to be cleaning a lot of fish at once, say for a large group, an old toothbrush is handy for cleaning out the "mud vein" (dorsal aorta) that lies along the inside of the backbone. Break up the "mud vein" with your knife to start; then it can be quickly removed with the toothbrush.

When fish are cleaned, it is frequently a problem to find something to put them in until you are ready to fry them. A spare pan is not always available, and if you use a pan it must be washed before it can be used for another purpose. A good solution to the problem is to make a small bag, about eight inches by fourteen inches in size, out of ordinary muslin or percale, Mark the bag plainly on the outside with the word "FISH," using a felt tip marker, before leaving home. After cleaning, the fish can be kept in this bag until you are ready to fry them. Rinse this bag out in the stream after each use, and dry on the clothesline. The wet sandpaper and the toothbrush (for fish cleaning) can be carried in this bag between meals. Fold the whole business into a small compact package, and carry it in a pint or quart size plastic bag, so that you will not have a fish smell on other items in your pack.

CHICKEN. Most local groceries carry small cans of boned chicken in a number of brands, such as Swanson, Richardson, etc. These are convenient to use as a meat base in a number of dishes, such as explained later in this part. Most of these small cans have a gross weight of about seven ounces and a net weight of about five ounces. Several of the suppliers in Table 6 carry dehydrated chicken which can be used and will have considerably less weight for the food value.

BEEF
1. Canned Hamburg. Small cans of hamburg, which usually contain five or six small patties, are available in some local stores. The Libby brand is good. Gross weight is about fourteen ounces (net weight twelve ounces). These can be heated and eaten separately, or used as a base for a main dish, like spaghetti and hamburg.

2. Dehydrated Ground Beef. A dehydrated ground beef will save weight, and some of the brands are very good. Follow the directions for cooking, which are usually very simple. One method is to put the meat in a skillet, barely cover with water and simmer about fifteen minutes, until the water is gone. Then add a small amount of butter to the skillet and fry very slowly for about five to eight minutes. Do not try to fry it to the point of crispness. It can also be added directly to soups or stews before cooking.

3. Beef Stick. A good beef product for trail usage is the "Beef Stick" manufactured and sold by the Hickory Farms of Toledo, Ohio. It is tasty when eaten cold. It can also be heated in a skillet, or cut into bite size pieces and added to soups or stews. This beef product will keep well without any refrigeration, even in warm weather.

BEEF JERKY. This is a dehydrated form of beef that will keep almost indefinitely without refrigeration. Most of the suppliers listed in Table 6 carry jerky. It can be cut into small pieces or ground and added to soups and stews. It can be soaked, then heated in a skillet, and eaten hot. It is also very good when eaten cold. It is relatively easy to make beef jerky, and it is recommended that you try it.

Top round steak, with very little or no fat, is recommended for making beef jerky. With a sharp knife cut the round steak into slices about 1/8 to 1/4 inch thick, about 1/2 to 3/4 inch wide (thickness of steak), and six to ten inches long. Using the blunt edge of a cup or similar tool, pound the strips as thin as possible, being careful not to tear them apart. Salt and pepper these strips quite heavily. Using a wire basket strainer like those used for making french fries, lower the strips into a pan of heavily salted, boiling water. Leave the strips in the water about fifteen seconds, just enough to blanch the meat, then take out and place on paper towels to drain.

Make a tube or cylinder out of cheesecloth, about three of four feet long and eight inches in diameter. You will also need a piece of stout clean cord about six feet long. Using a large needle and strong white cotton thread, pierce the cord near one end, then pierce a piece of jerky near one end, then pierce the cord again about one inch away from the first point, and so on. In this manner, "sew" the jerky to the cord. Now slip the cheesecloth cylinder over the sewed jerky and snap a rubber band or clothespin over each end of the cylinder to keep out flies.

Holding on to the two ends of the cord which

Beef jerky, drying on clothesline

protrude from the cheesecloth cylinder, carry the jerky outside and fasten the line of jerky between two tree limbs or to a clothesline (safest place) where cats and other animals cannot reach it. Select a place in the sunlight where there will be free circulation of air. If it rains, cover the jerky or take it inside. Leave it in the open for about five days, and you will have finished jerky. It will get stiff and brittle, and very dark, but it is good to eat and very nourishing. It will keep practically indefinitely. Store it in plastic bags, which in turn can be kept in a closed container such as a coffee can.

Sixteen ounces of fresh meat will provide about four ounces of jerky when the process is completed. A good way to eat jerky is to spread mustard on it and eat it cold. A "tangy" mustard, such as a horseradish mustard, is particularly good.

OTHER CANNED MEATS. Some other meats, which are suitable for short backpack trips, are available in canned form from local groceries. Some of these are Swift's "Prem," Hormel Chopped Beef, Spam, etc. Most of these only require to be cut into thin slices, placed in a skillet with a little shortening, and thoroughly heated. Gross weight of cans is usually about fourteen ounces (net weight twelve ounces).

EGGS

FRESH EGGS. Fresh eggs should usually not be kept more than one day without refrigeration. Even then, they should be kept as cool as possible. For an overnight camp they may be quite satisfactory. They must be carefully packed. They make a fine mess if they are broken in your pack. Aluminum egg carriers are available from several of the suppliers in Table 1. Another way to carry eggs is to use a small can with a tight-fitting lid, about the size of a baking powder can. Push a pint plastic bag down into the can as a "liner." Now break the eggs out of their shells and into the can. Close the bag and seal the top with a small rubber band. Then put the lid on the can and seal it with tape. As soon as you get to the camp, put the can in a stream or other cool place until ready to use. Do not try to keep fresh eggs for over a day unless you have a cool place to keep them.

DEHYDRATED EGGS. There is a wide difference in the taste of dehydrated eggs. Whatever brand you choose, you should by all means try it out thoroughly at home to be sure you are going to like it. One of the best tasting brands of dehydrated eggs that I have found is "Durkee," available in some local stores. It is also one of the least expensive brands.

Dehydrated eggs are very easy to fix. You simply mix with water into a paste (instructions are on the package) and add to a greased prewarmed skillet. Cook over a low fire for two or three minutes. Be careful not to overcook. When they are a nice golden brown, they are overcooked. Throw them out and start over. Stir the egg in the skillet almost continuously while it is cooking. One very good way to cook these eggs is to first crumble part of a bacon bar into a greased skillet and cook for several minutes over a low flame. Then add the scrambled egg mixture and continue to cook for about two minutes longer, stirring continuously. Remove from fire and add plenty of salt and pepper. Omelets made from dehydrated eggs frequently end up tough and "rubbery" (and tasteless). Most cooks prefer the scrambled version. A good addition to scrambled eggs is dehydrated onions, which can be put to soak the evening before (for breakfast), if desired.

Most freeze-dried dehydrated eggs are rather good. They are more expensive than ordinary dehydrated eggs, but some backpackers will consider them worthwhile.

CEREALS

OATMEAL. Many persons who wouldn't think of eating oatmeal for breakfast at home find it very much to their liking on a backpack trip. A number of brands of "minute" oats are available, such as "Mothers" oats. For each person you will need: 1/2 cup oats, 1/4 tsp. salt, and about one cup of water. You can start the oats in cold, warm, or boiling water. If creamy outmeal is desired, start it in boiling water. For a thicker, less creamy oatmeal, start it in cold water. Cook for a minimum of three to five minutes, even for one minute oats. At higher altitudes, ten minutes on the fire is not too much. Eat with sugar and milk or cream.

There are some instant oatmeals available, such as Quaker's, that are quite popular with some backpackers. Individual serving size packages are available, if desired. About 3/4 cup of boiling water is added to the individual serving, stirred, and the oatmeal is ready to eat.

OTHER COOKED CEREALS. You may prefer some other type of cooked cereal, such as "Wheatena." There are a number of such cereals. Most of them have a relatively short cooking time.

COLD CEREAL. Most of the cold cereals which are commonly eaten for breakfast at home are too bulky and too low in calories to be suitable for backpacking. Grape-Nuts is an exception, if you prefer cold cereal.

PANCAKES

A traditional camp food is pancakes with butter and syrup. A number of prepared pancake flours are available, such as Aunt Jemima brand, and they are very satisfactory. Add water or milk to the flour (not vice versa). Stir the mixture just enough to get the lumps out. A fork is a good stirring tool. Do not beat the batter. Hold back a little flour just in case you should get the batter too thin to start with. There is nothing worse than using up all of your flour in one grand start and then having the batter come out too thin.

Dip out three of four tablespoons of batter onto a hot greased skillet and cook over a medium hot fire. Turn only once, when bubbles have appeared over the top surface of the uncooked side. It is much easier to make one large pancake in an average size skillet than to make two or more small ones. Cut the large pancake into two or more pieces as soon as it is removed from the skillet and divide it among several persons who are eating so that each will have a hot piece. One large pancake will get partly cold just while it is being eaten.

A satisfactory pancake syrup can be made from brown sugar and water. Good prepared syrup mixtures are also available (see Table 7). In making syrup from brown sugar, use about one cup of sugar to 1/2 cup of water. Bring to a boil and stir until dissolved. Be very careful not to use too much water or the syrup will be too thin.

FRUIT

At least one meal each day should include fruit. If you plan to have fruit for breakfast, it is a good idea to cook it by simmering over the campfire in the evening. Dried fruits such as prunes, peaches, apricots, etc., are available. There are several types, as described in the following paragraphs.

ORDINARY DRIED FRUITS. Most grocery stores carry dried fruits. These have had much of the water removed, but not so much as to make them hard or brittle. Prunes usually come in a one pound box, apricots and peaches in a ten or twelve ounce box. Pitted prunes are available from suppliers of trail foods, and the pits do represent extra weight. However, on many backpack trips the weight will not be that critical. About 2-1/2 ounces of prunes per person per meal and two ounces of apricots or peaches per person per meal is the right amount. Put the fruit in a saucepan, cover with cold water, and simmer for twenty to thirty minutes. During the last five minutes on the fire, add two level teaspoons of sugar (or one saccharin tablet, 1/2 grain) for sweetening for each two ounces of fruit. These fruits are also good to munch on while on the trail, just as they come from the box.

VACUUM-DRIED FRUITS. The vacuum-dried fruits are available from most of the suppliers of trail foods. They have had most of the water removed, to the point where they are hard and brittle (before cooking). Removing this extra water saves weight, however. About one ounce per person per meal provides an ample serving. The vacuum-dried fruits are cooked in the same manner as ordinary dried fruits. Cover the fruit with cold water in a saucepan and simmer for fifteen to twenty minutes. Add sweetening during the last few minutes of cooking.

Vacuum-dried apple bits make a good side dish for lunch and dinner. Two ounces provide servings for two or three persons and can be cooked in five to seven minutes.

FREEZE-DRIED FRUITS. The freeze-dried foods are a relatively new product. Some of the freeze-dried fruits are quite tasty. They are very light, about one ounce (dried) providing medium size servings for three persons. Another advantage is that they are quickly and easily prepared. After removing from the package, soaking for about five minutes in cold water makes them ready to eat. No cooking is necessary. They also make a good snack while traveling along the trail. You can pop a piece of freeze-dried fruit into your mouth, suck on it until it softens, and it is quite good. The freeze-dried fruits (and other freeze-dried foods) are more expensive than the vacuum-dried fruits, but they have a place in many backpack food lists.

BEVERAGES

What you drink on a backpack trip, and especially how much you drink, is important. You will be exerting and perspiring and your body will lose a lot of fluid which needs to be replaced if you are to feel well. If you were to drink only water you would probably not take in as much liquid as if you have a few beverages. Therefore, some variety of beverages and a beverage with every meal is important. Alcoholic beverages have no place on a backpack trip.

COFFEE. The best coffee for backpack use is the instant or freeze-dried kind. No coffee pot is required (it would mean added weight) and instant coffee is light in weight compared to the regular kind. Two ounces of instant coffee will make about thirty cups. It can be made in either of two ways. One way is to simply bring water to boiling in a pan, pour the hot water into cups, add a rounded teaspoon of instant coffee to each cup, and stir. Another way is to put the desired number of cups (of water) into a pan, bring to a boil, and add the instant coffee directly to the boiling water in the pan. Let the water (with the coffee in it) boil for several minutes on the fire before removing and pouring into cups. Add cream substitute or sugar to taste.

TEA. The instant variety of tea is also recommended. Bring water to a boil in a pan and then pour into cups. Then add one level or rounded teaspoon of instant tea per cup (depending on the strength desired). Sweeten to taste. Never add tea to boiling water. The water must always be removed from the fire before adding the tea. Tea is very light in weight. One and one-half ounces will make thirty-five to forty cups. If you prefer to use tea bags rather than instant tea, you will find that two cups of tea can usually be made from one tea bag.

BOUILLON, INSTANT SOUPS. Bouillon is carried in most local food stores. The instant broth and instant soups carried by many of the suppliers of trail foods are much more flavorful and satisfying, however. Instant beef broth, chicken broth, pea soup and potato soup are common. Several good brands are conveniently packaged in individual size foil envelopes, providing for some variety at the same meal. All that is required is to add the contents of the package to a cup of freshly boiled hot water and stir. These soups and broths will have a place on most backpack food lists. While hikers are setting up camp or preparing other food items and waiting for them to cook, it is convenient and most satisfying to sip a cup of hot soup or broth. Bouillon may also be used to flavor rice and noodle dishes, giving a "gourmet" touch to meals in the woods.

HOT GELATIN. Most persons are surprised to find that they like hot gelatin for a drink. The Royal and Jell-O brands are good. These drinks are rich in protein and sugar, and the Royal brand also contains Vitamin C. About 3/4 ounce of gelatin powder is required for a one cup serving. Simply heat water to boiling point and dissolve the gelatin in the hot water. Drink it at the same temperature that you would drink hot tea or coffee. Any flavors are satisfactory, but orange and lemon flavors are particularly recommended as a hot trail drink.

COCOA. The instant variety of cocoa is recommended for its convenience. Place about three heaping teaspoons of cocoa in a cup, add hot water and stir. One of the most tasty cocoa products is the "Swiss Miss" instant cocoa. In your menu planning it should be noted that a serving of cocoa is relatively heavy, compared to tea or coffee. However, it does provide some nourishment (with the milk that is included in the instant products) whereas tea or coffee has no nourishment.

LEMONADE. Hikers will frequently develop a craving for something tart and sour while on a backpack trip. There will be times when you would "give your kingdom" for a dill pickle. It is not convenient or practical to carry dill pickles on a backpack trip. However, you will find that a lemon drink, strongly on the tart side, will satisfy your craving for something sour, as well as help make for a balanced diet.

Many persons, including the writer, prefer to use the pure lemon powder, without sugar or other additives, in making a lemon drink. For each cup of lemonade about one level teaspoon of lemon powder is required. A small amount of water is added at first and mixed thoroughly with the powder to make a paste. Then fill the cup with water, sweeten only very slightly and you will have a real tart drink. If you prefer the "ready to use" type of lemonade (with sugar already added), the Wyler brand is good. It is available in many local stores.

SOUPS

Most soups are an ideal backpack food. They are easily and quickly prepared and readily digested. They supplement beverages in replacing fluids lost from the body. Liptons, Knorr Swiss, Wylers and Campbells are some good dehydrated soup brands which are most commonly found in local stores. The directions will be found on the package and should be followed carefully, since they vary. For example, for some soups the contents of the package are added to hot water and for others are added to cold water.

VEGETABLE SALAD

Some of the dehydrated vegetable salads require boiling in hot water for a short period. Others only require soaking in cold water (such as the Perma-Pak brand), and this latter type is recommended, since most persons prefer their salads cool. One ounce of salad provides ample servings for three persons. Before you break camp in the morning you can put your salad to soak in a tight jar. When you stop for lunch (or supper) your salad is ready. Most salad dressings which are purchased in the store require refrigeration after they are once opened. A good salad dressing, which does not require any refrigeration, is made from the following ingredients. (It can be made at home and carried in a small plastic bottle.)

1/4 cup wine vinegar
1/8 cup salad oil
1/2 tsp. salt
1/4 tsp. black pepper
several cloves of garlic

Simply put the ingredients in the plastic bottle, shake well, and it is ready for use. If the garlic cloves are left in the bottle for a trip of several days or a week, it will gradually get stronger, but this spicy flavor tastes good in the out-of-doors, even to most persons who do not eat highly seasoned foods at home. The salad oil and the vinegar will quickly separate in the bottle, so shake well each time before using.

Another salad dressing, which does not require refrigeration, is made from the following:

1-1/2 tsp. lemon powder
6 tsp. water
1-1/2 tsp. sugar
3 tsp. Pream or other cream substitute
1/2 tsp. salt
6 or 8 shakes black pepper

Mix the above ingredients together, first making a paste of the lemon powder and water, making sure to get all the lumps out. Because of the nature of the ingredients, this salad dressing can easily be made up fresh at each meal where you use it.

POTATO SALAD

A potato salad in dry form (dehydrated potatoes) is now sold in many local food stores. One such brand is the Betty Crocker. A six ounce package is sufficient for three or four persons. The cooking time is about twenty to thirty minutes. Some of the suppliers of dehydrated foods also carry a potato salad.

BREAD

The bread which you normally buy in the store is not suitable for backpacking. It is bulky, if carried it usually ends up in crumbs, and it molds easily. It is therefore recommended that you use a bread substitute that does not have these undesirable properties. If you want to sacrifice some trip time that could be spent in other pursuits, you can of course bake bread or biscuits in camp. To bake consistently good camp bread or biscuits with an open fire usually requires the use of a reflector oven or similar device. A reflector oven will weigh about two to three pounds. In addition to the added weight that a reflector oven makes in the pack, there is some problem in keeping it clean enough to pack from place to place. This means extra time required during the dishwashing operation. Additional utensils are usually required for the mixing of ingredients and for the baking process in the oven. Assuming that all of the cooking in the oven turns out perfectly and that none of the "results" are thrown away (that would be rare), there is still a considerable investment in weight. For a lesser total weight you can probably provide an ample "bread" ration for each person by using canned bread and cakes, hard crackers, wafers, or other bread substitutes. The most food value per unit weight will result if you use a fortified biscuit, fruit cake, nut bread or similar product.

APPLESAUCE

A good side dish for many meals is provided with applesauce. There are several "instant" types of applesauce available. To make applesauce you simply mix the applesauce granules with cold water and let it stand for ten to fifteen minutes. No cooking is required. A number of suppliers also carry apple nuggets or diced apples, which require a short cooking time (usually about ten to fifteen minutes). Most persons find these cooked apples to be somewhat superior in taste to the instant applesauces.

POTATOES

Dehydrated potatoes are now a common item in most local food stores. In cooking, the potatoes are covered with salted water and boiled for about twenty to thirty minutes, or until soft.

Presoaking will decrease the cooking time. About four ounces of dehydrated potatoes are sufficient for three persons. A tasty addition to boiled potatoes is to add 1/2 cup of powdered milk (or equivalent cream substitute) and about three ounces of cheese during the last five minutes of cooking. Cut the cheese into thin slices and stir these and the powdered milk into the potatoes after most of the water has boiled off (or pour it off).

Dehydrated "instant" white potatoes are available in local food stores. In preparation of most of the instant potatoes, a measured amount of water is first brought to a boil. It is then removed from the fire and a measured amount of milk is added. (Dehydrated milk or cream substitute can be used to make the required milk.) The instant potato granules or flakes are then quickly added and stirred so as to obtain a uniform "mashed" potato. Instant sweet potatoes are also available. It is very important to carefully measure the amount of liquid used. Otherwise the potatoes will turn out too "soupy" or too "gummy."

CORN

Some local stores stock dehydrated corn. The John Cope brand is quite tasty. It is desirable that the corn be soaked all day, however, so that it will cook in about twenty to thirty minutes for the evening meal. Freeze-dried corn, available from some of the suppliers of trail foods, can be cooked in ten to twenty minutes, without presoaking. Corn makes a good side dish for a main meal, or it can be added to soups and stews. About 1/2 ounce of freeze-dried corn per person is ample.

PEAS, STRING BEANS

The freeze-dried peas and string beans, available from some of the suppliers in Table 6, are much more tasty than the ordinary dehydrated variety. About 1/2 ounce (before cooking) of freeze-dried peas or string beans is sufficient for one person, and they will usually cook in twenty to thirty minutes.

MAIN DISHES

Some meals, especially supper in the evening, are frequently planned around a main dish. A main dish should not be complicated to cook, and it should be filling. Unless you have fish or other meat with the meal, the main dish preferably should contain some meat or meat substitute. A few main dishes will be discussed in the following paragraphs.

SPAGHETTI AND HAMBURG

The following ingredients will provide a main dish sufficient for three persons:

7 oz. elbow spaghetti
1 pkg. spaghetti sauce mix
1 can cooked hamburg (about 10 oz.),
    or 2 oz. dehyd. ground beef

Put one quart of water in a saucepan, add 1/2 tsp. of salt, and bring to a boil. Then add the spaghetti and cook for about twenty minutes. While this is cooking, take the hamburg, chop into small bite size lumps, and heat thoroughly in a skillet. Do not fry it brown or crisp. If you use dehydrated ground beef, put it in a skillet, barely cover with water and simmer about fifteen minutes.

At the same time the above is cooking, have another person put the package of spaghetti sauce mix in a saucepan, add two cups of water, and bring to a boil. Then remove to low heat and simmer for fifteen to twenty minutes. Watch this mix very closely and stir frequently. The "Chef Boy-Ar-Dee" is a good spaghetti sauce.

When the spaghetti is cooked (taste it to see if it is soft), drain off the excess water, add the hamburg and the sauce mix, then mix the contents thoroughly and simmer five to ten minutes longer.

CHICKEN AND NOODLES

The following ingredients will provide a main dish for three persons:

5 oz. noodles (short pieces, break if necessary)
1 pkg. dehyd. chicken noodle soup (such as Wylers or Liptons)
1 — 7 oz. can cooked chicken, or 2 oz. dehyd. chicken

Put one quart of water in a saucepan, add 1/2 tsp. of salt, and bring to a boil. Add the noodles, cook seven to ten minutes, or until soft. Pour just enough water off the noodles so that about two cups of water still remain in the pan. Then add the package of chicken noodle soup and the can of chicken (or dehydrated) to the pot and cook about ten minutes longer.

MACARONI AND CHEESE

You will need the following, to serve three persons:

6 oz. elbow macaroni
4 oz. mild or sharp cheese, as preferred
some dehydrated milk or cream substitute

Place a little over one quart of water in a pan, add one teaspoon of salt, and bring to a boil. Add the macaroni and cook about fifteen to twenty minutes, or until soft. Now pour off practically all the water, leaving not more than 1/2 cup in the pan. Add several tablespoons of dehydrated milk or equivalent cream substitute. Cut the cheese into thin slices and add this. Stir the mixture thoroughly. Now place back on the fire, over low heat, for about five minutes, stirring frequently.

CHOW MEIN

Several of the suppliers of dehydrated foods carry a dehydrated form of chow mein. Most are satisfactory to use just as they are purchased. With a few additions, however, they can be made even better. The additions are indicated below. This will make a sufficient dish for three or four persons:

1 pkg. dehyd. chow mein, about 6 oz.
3 oz. dry chow mein noodles (available local stores)
1 — 7 oz. can chicken, or 2 oz. dehyd. chicken

Empty the contents of the package of chow mein into a pan containing 4-1/2 cups of warm water and soak for fifteen minutes. Then put the pan on the fire, bring the contents to a boil, and simmer for about ten minutes. Then add the chicken to the pan, mix thoroughly, and cook for five to ten minutes. When the mixture is finished cooking, remove from the fire and pour over the chow mein noodles, which have been divided up and placed on the individual plates. (Note: The chow mein noodles, purchased from a local store, usually come in a can. Repackage them in a plastic bag. They are a little bulky, but light.)

CHICKEN AND RICE

You will need the following ingredients to provide a main dish for three or four persons:

3 oz. Minute Rice
2 oz. peas (dehyd.)
2 oz. chicken (dehyd.)
3 oz. chicken rice soup (dehyd.)

Cook the peas separately, according to directions on the package. When the peas are about done (taste to see if soft), add the chicken, chicken rice soup mix, five cups of water and 1/2 teaspoon of salt. Bring the mixture to a boil and continue to cook over a medium fire for about ten to fifteen minutes. During the last five minutes of cooking, add the Minute Rice and stir frequently. (Dehydrated chicken noodle soup can be used in place of chicken rice soup.)

SPANISH RICE

Several brands of Spanish rice are available in many local stores which make a good main dish. One brand is Betty Crocker "Rice Milanese." A five ounce package makes sufficient servings for several persons. Another is the General Foods Minute Spanish Rice. Cooking time is about ten to fifteen minutes. Mushrooms, peas, diced chicken, meat bar, etc., can be added to these Spanish rice mixes to provide a complete meal.

HASH

The following ingredients will provide a main dish for three persons:

    4 oz. dehyd. potatoes
    2 oz. dehyd. onions
    3 oz. bacon bar

If the dehydrated potatoes are the kind consisting of small hard cubes, they should be soaked at least an hour, or even all day. The onions can be soaked with them, but this is not essential. (The dehydrated potatoes that are in the form of small thin slices need not be pre-soaked.) Put a quart of water in a saucepan, add 1/2 teaspoon of salt, and bring to a boil. Add potatoes and cook them for about fifteen minutes, or until they are soft (taste them). During this time, put the bacon bar in another pan, or on a dish, and shred it into small bits. Now put a heaping tablespoon (or equivalent) of margarine, bacon grease, or cooking oil in a skillet and heat it until it is very hot. Then ladle the potatoes and onions from the pan into the skillet, using a pancake turner so as to drain off the water in the process. Fry about half of the potatoes at once and they will fry faster. After they are in the skillet, add half of the shredded bacon bar to the potatoes and onions, mix thoroughly, and fry over a medium hot fire about ten minutes, stirring frequently.

Hash makes a good dish for breakfast. Soak the onions and potatoes (together) all night, and they will quickly fry to a finish in the morning. No boiling will be required. With other food for breakfast, the amount of ingredients recommended for three persons is as follows:

    2-1/2 oz. dehyd. potatoes
    1 oz. dehyd. onions
    3 oz. bacon bar

CHILI

Dehydrated chili beans are now found in many local stores. A good chili (sufficient for

three persons) is made as follows:

    5-1/2 oz. chili beans
    1/2 oz. onions
    2 oz. dehyd. beef
    1/4 oz. dehyd. tomatoes

The beans should be soaked from four to eight hours before cooking. After they have cooked about fifteen minutes, add the dehydrated beef, onions, and tomatoes. Continue cooking for another fifteen minutes or until tender. About 1/4 to 1/2 ounce of dehydrated bell peppers, available in local stores, can be added to give the chili a more spicy flavor, if desired.

DESSERTS

Your appetite for ordinary food will usually be sufficient that you won't need to pamper it with elaborate desserts. Most hikers do develop a yearning for some sweets, however, so it is a good idea to include some. Following are a few suggestions for desserts:

CANDY. In normal backpacking a lot of physical energy is expended. To sustain your energy at a high level, it is recommended that your protein intake be substantially increased over what you would eat at home, through use of such lightweight, nonperishable meats as beef jerky and hard dried sausages. Cheese, nuts, jello and eggs are also sources of protein and are recommended. Quick energy (but not long lasting) can be supplied by increasing your sugar intake. You can use bulk sugar, but a somewhat more pleasant way to increase your sugar is in the form of various candies. Even though you don't normally eat much candy at home, you will probably find it welcome and beneficial on a backpack trip. You will find candy in many lunch menus which follow in Part 5. When the cook rations out the candy at lunch time, slip it in your pocket. When you are on a steep climb in midafternoon, or simply beginning to feel "dragged out" after severe exertion, eat your candy then. It will give you a quick pick up.

Specially prepared, quick-acting candies are available from some of the suppliers listed in Table 6. For example, the Tex-Schmeltz Traubenzucker. Each two ounce package contains eight individually wrapped squares of lemon flavored, quickly absorbed, high energy candy. Other special candies, including high melting point chocolate such as Hershey's tropical chocolate, are also available from some of the suppliers listed. The M & M chocolate covered peanuts have a fairly high melting point. Peanut bars are also good. Both of these come in packages with a gross weight of about one ounce each, which is about right for one person (one

TABLE 8. MEASURING UNITS (APPROXIMATE) FOR FOODS USED IN BACKPACKING

Food		Volume		Weight (ounces)
Cocoa, instant		3 heaping tsp.		1
Coffee, instant		6 rounded tsp.		1/2
Cornmeal		1 cup		4
Flour		1 cup		4
Lemon powder		3 level tbs.		1
Macaroni, small elbow		1 cup		4
Margarine		1 cup		8
Noodles, fine, short		1 cup		3
Oatmeal		1 cup		3
Pepper		8 level tsp.		1
Pream (cream substitute)	(a)	3 rounded tbs.	(a)	1
	(b)	1 cup	(b)	4-1/2
Popcorn		1 cup		6
Raisins, store variety		1 cup		5
Rice, instant		1 cup		4
Salt	(a)	3 level tsp.	(a)	1
	(b)	2 level tbs.	(b)	2
	(c)	small cardboard shaker, 1-3/4" x 3-3/4"	(c)	4
Sugar, white	(a)	4 level tsp.	(a)	1
	(b)	1 cup	(b)	8
	(c)	2 tbs.	(c)	1-1/4
Sugar, brown		1-1/4 cup		8
Shortening, liquid	(a)	3 level tbs.	(a)	1
	(b)	1 cup	(b)	7
Tea, instant	(a)	11 rounded tbs.	(a)	1
	(b)	1-1/4 cup	(b)	1
Wheatena		1 cup		5
Hickory Beef Stick		2-5/8" x 5" cylinder		16

Note: One cup refers to one standard measuring cup. If you do not have a standard measuring cup, take a glass or other container, set it on a kitchen scale and fill with eight ounces of water. Draw a line on the container at the level of the liquid and you have approximately one standard cup.

3 level teaspoons (tsp.) = 1 level tablespoon (tbs.)
2 level tablespoons of water = 1 ounce
16 tablespoons of liquid = 1 cup

ration). Peanuts are also available in cellophane bags having a gross weight of about one ounce, or you can buy them in bulk and package your own. Glucose tablets are also good for quick energy.

A rather unusual candy product are the carob candies. Carob is a natural food which has a taste similar to chocolate. It is sometimes called "St. John's bread" because St. John was supposed to have survived on it in the wilderness.

For a hot day on the trail, sour hard candies can be very refreshing. It is best to get individually wrapped candies, whether for hot weather use or otherwise.

POPCORN. Around the campfire at night, popcorn is a real favorite. To cook the popcorn, take an aluminum saucepan and fasten an extension handle to it as described for the skillet in Part 6. You will need a piece of aluminum foil slightly larger than the pan opening (make it about ten inches square) for a lid. By repeated folding you can work this foil into a two inch square, and put it right in the bag with the popcorn when you pack the food. For several persons use about 2/3 cup of popcorn. Place the foil lid over the top of the pan, making slits where it meets the wire bail, and bend over at the edges. Add a rounded tablespoon of shortening to the pan and one or two grains of popcorn.

When those grains pop, lift the edge of the foil cover, dump in about 1/3 cup of popcorn (recommend popping in two batches), and bend the edge of the cover over again. Hold over a medium hot part of the fire, shaking frequently but gently, and you will have popcorn in four or five minutes. Don't leave it on the fire too long, and as soon as you remove it dump it quickly into another utensil (such as a skillet) or it will burn. Sprinkle it liberally with salt, and then get back so you don't get stepped on in the rush.

OTHER FOOD ITEMS REQUIRED

A few other food items and condiments are going to be required for your cooking. The basic items that are needed in the foregoing recipes will be briefly discussed.

SUGAR. If you use sugar in coffee or in other drinks, as well as on cereal and for cooking, it can add up to considerable weight for a week-long backpack trip. The sugar requirement can be cut down somewhat by using saccharin (or a similar sugar substitute) for some foods and drinks. Some hikers find it satisfactory to sweeten coffee, tea, lemonade, stewed fruit, etc. If you do not plan to use candy liberally in your backpack diet, however, it is recommended that you use sugar wherever sweetening is called for.

SHORTENING. Margarine can be used as shortening in most recipes. If you want a spread for bread or pancakes, margarine is usually acceptable. Butter will turn rancid much more quickly in hot weather than margarine. Margarine can also be used for frying, although it has a lower burning point than Crisco or a similar product. If you are frying fish regularly, much more shortening will be required than if you are

not. Analyze your menus to determine your requirements. Running out of shortening can be a real inconvenience. Several shortening products such as "Vegalene" and "Golden Clear" are packaged specifically for backpackers in convenient nonbreakable dispenser bottles. Coating the entire inside surface of a cooking pan with one of these products before cooking a food such as oatmeal, spaghetti, or chili will reduce the tendency of the food to stick to the pan.

MILK OR CREAM. Many brands of dehydrated milk and cream substitutes are available from local stores. The cream substitutes will weigh a bit less and are a little richer when used in recipes that call for milk.

CONDIMENTS. Don't take too many condiments. On many backpack trips, salt will be the only condiment, or possibly salt and pepper. Ketchup, mustard, fruit preserves, and various spices may be desired in some cases, but be prepared for a real mess if they are not packaged properly. Also, rummaging through a lot of small bags, or other small containers in which condiments are packaged, can be pretty exasperating when the cook is trying to find something he really needs. With all foods being grouped together in a few large bags it is far different from the situation at home when you are trying to find a certain food in a neatly arranged pantry.

SALT, PEPPER. Salt requirements are generally about 1/4 ounce per person per day. If you drink salt water instead of taking salt tablets, to replace salt lost in perspiration, this should be increased somewhat. The pepper requirement is roughly ten percent or one-tenth of the salt requirement.

5

Menus and Food Lists

GENERAL PLANNING

Whether you are to be on the trail for one day, one week, or more, you should have a written menu plan for every meal that you expect to eat. There is certainly no rigid rule that you must eat each and every meal in the exact order and amount as planned, but you should have a plan. With the menu plan you can then make up the food list, adding some extra food for an emergency. The amount of extra food will depend upon the length of trip, the distance from the roadhead, and your experience and skill in planning food lists. Some important factors to be considered in your planning are:

If the area you are going into does not have a sufficient wood supply for cooking and you must rely on a portable stove, then your meals will be different than if you have sufficient wood for cooking. Most of the wilderness and National Forest areas, as well as other areas that will be attractive to backpackers, will have wood. Camping above timberline is in a special category, from numerous standpoints, and is not intended to be covered by this book.

Whether you expect to supplement the plan with game or fish should be considered. Even if you expect to, you should still take enough food that you will have enough to eat in the event you do not get the game or fish you are after.

On trips into a wilderness area (and many other areas) you are completely on your own

after you leave the roadhead. There is no chance to pick up food along the way. On some trail routes, however, there may be an opportunity to add supplies along the way every few days, and this will affect your plan.

Weather may be a factor. If rain is to be expected, it may be desirable to include a few foods that can be eaten cold in the event you are caught in the rain at meal time.

The type of trip and daily routine has its effect. If you are to camp in the same spot after you reach a certain destination, the meals will be somewhat different than if you are hiking most of each day and making camp at a new spot each night. Some backpackers who hike most of each day prefer a hot breakfast and hot supper and a light, cold lunch at noon.

A FUNDAMENTAL RULE

Regardless of the type of backpack trip, however, a fundamental rule is to count the ounces and keep the pack light. When the sun is bearing down and the pack is starting to be felt at your shoulders, you will thank yourself for the extra time you took in planning and packing to enable you to keep your pack weight down. Insofar as possible, leave the cans at home. This does not mean you should not have a single can in your pack. Certain meats, especially, are best carried in canned form, since no refrigeration is available. It does mean that you should give very careful thought to each can you put in your pack and ask yourself if it is really necessary. On many backpack trips excess food is carried deep into a remote area, lugged around for a few days, and then packed out again. Carrying too much food is just as bad as too little. This is the result of poor planning, and it represents a lot of useful energy going to waste.

OTHER FACTORS INFLUENCING MENUS

Some other considerations that should go into your menu planning are:

1. Include in your menus only foods that you have had experience in cooking on previous trips or at home and which you have found that you liked. Also, the saying "If everything else fails, try reading the instructions" had best not be applied to cooking of foods on a backpack trip. If the cook wants to stay popular he had better know his recipes — but good — and follow them.

2. Leave out the food dishes that are complicated to prepare and those that take long cooking time. Try to take only foods that do not require more than thirty minutes of cooking time. If you must use a portable stove for cooking, concentrate on one-dish meals.

3. Foods should ordinarily not require special cooking equipment. Any cooking gear other than two open aluminum saucepans and a skillet is considered special. It is a good idea to know how to cook with a reflector oven, Dutch oven, broiler, griddle, etc., but they are not recommended for the usual backpack trip.

4. The menus listed in this part of this book are reasonably well balanced, as they should be. However, unless you are going to be on the trail for two weeks or more, don't worry too much about how the proteins, carbohydrates, etc., balance out. Assuming that you are on a good day-to-day diet before you start the trip, and that you will return to same when the trip is over, then a week or two of diet which is not perfectly balanced will not hurt you. You will probably feel better if you increase your protein intake over what you would normally eat at home. Sugar will provide quick energy, but proteins will provide more lasting energy and are needed for tissue and cell building. Proteins will "stick to the ribs." Some protein three times each day, and perhaps occasionally on the trail, is a good idea. One vitamin tablet per day, before breakfast, is recommended.

5. In general, three hot substantial meals each day are recommended. Lunch is the meal most likely to be skipped over lightly, and sometimes this is justified. However, the forty-five minutes to an hour which is needed to prepare and eat a good meal at lunch time, including some hot soup, will give you a good break from what you are doing, as well as needed nourishment. Lunch does not have to be a big meal, but fixing something substantial to eat will help avoid the physical "letdown" that frequently comes along about midafternoon. It will also eliminate the necessity for an extra big meal at supper, when you may be too tired to either fix it or to appreciate it after it is fixed. Further, your body does not digest food well when it is overfatigued.

6. Where unusually strenuous activity is required, such as a climb up a very steep trail for a considerable distance, it is best not to eat just prior to the climb, even though it occurs at meal time. Delay the meal (or any food) until the worst part of the climb is behind. After the strenuous climbing is accomplished, eat lightly on cold snacks before continuing the trip.

7. To some degree, your cooking gear influences your menus. For example, it is not too convenient to have fried fish and fried potatoes for dinner when you only have one skillet because excessive time would be required. Boiled potatoes, creamed potatoes, or potatoes with cheese would be a better choice to have with your fried fish, since they would be cooked in a pan.

8. Don't hesitate to repeat certain foods in day to day menus. If you are hungry, and the food is good, then the fact that you ate the same food dish two days ago (or even yesterday) won't be any problem. It is much better to do this than to start out with a large variety of foods that you are not familiar with. Also, it generally makes for easier packing if you hold to a reasonable variety.

9. The length of the backpack trip is a factor. On a trip of over three or four days you will want to use the most concentrated, lightweight foods, and many dehydrated foods. These are frequently more expensive than foods from the local store. On a short backpack trip you will be able to use many and perhaps all foods that are locally available.

10. In some groups, particularly large and formally organized groups, religious practices may influence the menu planning.

EXPERIMENTING WITH FOOD

If the cook likes to experiment with new food dishes, that is fine, but he should do his experimenting at home, not on the trail. Most hikers will not appreciate a cook who experiments with food that has been carried deep into a remote area on their backs, over many miles of rugged trails. Cooking any food dish for the first time is an experiment. Neither will hikers appreciate waiting an hour or more for more exotic dishes to cook when adequate, tasty and nourishing food can be cooked in half that time, with proper planning and selections of menus.

"FILLER UPPERS"

One of the important factors in keeping the food load light is to eat all, or substantially all, of the food that is cooked at any one meal. Food that is thrown out represents wasted energy of the hikers in carrying it. It isn't very convenient to pack a plateful of leftover spaghetti and beef and eat it at the next meal. In fact it just isn't feasible, from several standpoints, to try and save leftover cooked food from one meal to another while backpacking. The secret of eliminating the problem of leftover food lies first in proper selection of the amount and combinations of food, and in careful planning and weighing of food at home. Secondly, an important factor is to plan some "filler uppers" on many menus, particularly the lunch and supper menus. A "filler upper" is a food that is normally eaten cold and is conveniently packed and rationed out in one man portions. Candy, fortified biscuits, sausage sticks, beef jerky, peanuts, and cheese are examples of good "filler uppers." A wise cook will see that the soup, salad, main dish, and other foods that are cooked for lunch and supper (in particular) are well on the way to being finished up before he rations out the "filler upper" for that meal. Then if it turns out that some appetites are satisfied by the time the cooked foods are completely eaten, those persons can save their ration of "filler upper" until the next meal, or later in the day. A "filler upper" is not usually necessary for breakfast. Hikers will be fresh and rested and appetites keen at breakfast time, and a substantial meal will normally be assimilated with no difficulty.

BREAKFAST

The starting meal of the day should be a hearty one and should usually include the following:

FRUIT. Dried or dehydrated prunes, peaches, pears, or apricots.

HOT DRINK. Coffee, tea, or cocoa.

HOT CEREAL. Oatmeal, Wheatena, or a similar hot cereal. Pancakes, with butter and syrup, may be a suitable substitute in some instances, particularly on short backpack trips.

MEAT. Bacon or sausage is a good meat for breakfast. A good way to fix it is mixed with potatoes and onions for hash, or mixed with dehydrated eggs.

HASH. This may not appeal to you as a suitable dish for breakfast at home, but your viewpoint (and appetite) will change on a backpack trip.

EGGS. An important item on the breakfast menus of any backpack trip is eggs. They contain a lot of concentrated nourishment. On a trip of over a few days, alternating dehydrated eggs with hash works out well.

LUNCH

An occasional cold lunch may be satisfactory. Generally, however, a hot lunch along the following lines is recommended:

HOT OR COLD DRINK. On cool days, a cup or two of hot tea, coffee, or gelatin is good. On a warm day a pan of lemonade will hit the spot. If it is a bit on the sour side, so much the better. Orange or other fruit drinks may be substituted if you prefer, but will mean more weight in the pack.

HOT SOUP. The use of dehydrated soup in practically every hot lunch menu is recommended. It is easy to fix, nourishing, and readily digested. It will replace some of the liquid in your body that you have lost through perspiration.

SALAD. A vegetable salad, applesauce, or cooked apple nuggets goes good with lunch. It is refreshing, tasty, and helps make for a balanced diet. Instant sweet potatoes are quickly fixed and make a good alternate for salad, if you feel the need for something a bit more filling.

FISH OR MEAT. If you have caught fish in the morning, they should be eaten while they are fresh. They will be most tasty if they are eaten within two or three hours after they are caught. If you do not have fish, some sausage sticks, beef jerky, beef stick or cheese will supply some protein and help round out the meal. Salami can be used if the weather is not too hot (to cause spoilage).

DESSERT. If you feel you are still hungry, a ration of candy, peanuts, or raisins will probably fill the gap.

COLD LUNCH

There will be occasions when a cold lunch or other cold meal will be advisable. Foul weather may necessitate a cold meal. During a long and strenuous climb, a series of very light, cold snacks along the trail will be found better than a single, heavier meal. The following are some foods that are especially good for making up a cold meal or for cold snacks. As a substitute for a normal meal, a total of about six to eight ounces per person of the following foods will usually be found to be sufficient:

beef jerky
beef stick
dried beef (canned)
hard dried sausage
chicken (canned, boneless)
tuna fish (canned)
sardines
Cheddar cheese
Gouda cheese
fruit cake (canned)
hard cookies
Ry Krisp or Ry King
Triscuits
Turblokken
dehydrated milk
lemon powder
grapefruit crystals
orange crystals
peanuts, filberts, or cashews
peanut butter
jam
raisins
dried fruit
diced dates
lemon drops
Traubenzucker
tropical chocolate

SUPPER

Although this is usually the big meal of the day, don't try to eat too much if you are excessively tired. That is one reason why both breakfast and lunch are planned as substantial meals, to avoid the necessity for heavy eating at any single meal. It is also the reason why main dishes have been used which are easily prepared, yet filling and nourishing. There is no need to wear yourself out with a lot of complicated cooking at supper time.

HOT DRINK. While you are getting ready to start the rest of the supper, it is easy to heat water for tea, coffee, or a drink of hot gelatin. It will pick you up, and will again help to replace the water in your body that you lost during the day through perspiration. It is a good idea, while waiting for the water to boil, to drink a tall cup of cool water with 1/2 teaspoon of salt in it. Or, you can use salt tablets.

SOUP. A cup of soup will help to whet your appetite. If you don't feel very hungry, choose a thin soup, like onion soup or tomato soup.

MEAT. In many remote areas you will be able to catch some trout. If you caught some in the afternoon, this is the time to have them. If not, you will probably want some other meat, either small separate portions or mixed in with the main dish which follows.

MAIN DISH. A good main dish is a meal in itself. If you do not feel up to tackling a main dish, along with fish or other meat, try corn, peas, string beans or potatoes in its place.

AROUND THE CAMPFIRE

If you haven't worn yourself out during the day, so that you need to hit the sleeping bag soon after supper dishes are washed, you may want something more to eat or drink while sitting around the campfire. If you still feel thirsty, fix some tea to drink. Popcorn around the campfire usually goes over good and is easy to fix. It also has substantial food value and is good for you. When you plan to have popcorn around the campfire, the evening meal for that day should be a bit lighter than usual.

If you plan to have stewed fruit for breakfast, remember to put it on to cook while you are sitting around the campfire. If you plan hash for breakfast, put the potatoes and onions to soak in the evening. They can then be quickly cooked (by frying) in the morning.

OVERNIGHT HIKE

Now that we have discussed foods and menu planning, let's see what we can put together for an overnight hike requiring three meals to be cooked. The quantities given are for three persons, which is the minimum recommended for a trip into a remote area (for safety reasons). You can easily figure the food requirements for any other size group from the quantities given. Obviously, with a little ingenuity, there are many possible variations in these menus. The recipes for various food dishes are given in Part 4. Since an overnight hike will probably be your first experience in backpacking, these menus are planned around foods which are available in most local groceries. It is assumed that the trip will start after breakfast and that each hiker will take his own cold lunch.

TOTAL FOOD WEIGHT. All of the food adds up to a total of about ninety-six ounces, or about thirty-two ounces per person (eleven ounces per person per meal). This weight could

SUPPER

Item Number	Food	Requirement For Three Persons
1.	Tea	1/2 oz. (3 tea bags, makes 6 cups)
2.	Pea Soup	4 oz. (dehyd.)
3.	Spaghetti and hamburger	14 oz. hamburger (canned)
		7 oz. elbow spaghetti
		3 oz. spaghetti sauce
4.	Candy	3 oz.
		31-1/2 oz.

Note: Cook fruit for breakfast.

BREAKFAST

Item Number	Food	Requirement For Three Persons
5.	Coffee	1/2 oz. (6 tsp. instant makes 6 cups)
6.	Stewed apricots	6 oz. (dried, local store variety)
7.	Pancakes	10 oz. prepared pancake flour
	Syrup	6 oz. syrup mix or brown sugar
8.	Bacon	12 oz. (local store variety)
		34-1/2 oz.

LUNCH

Item Number	Food	Requirement For Three Persons
9.	Hot gelatin or cold fruit drink	3 oz.
10.	Salami or cheese	8 oz.
11.	Hard crackers or cookies	6 oz. (dehyd.)
12.	Vegetable beef soup	2-1/2 oz. (dehyd.)
13.	Candy	3 oz.
		22-1/2 oz.

OTHER FOOD ITEMS. In addition to the above foods, you will need the following, for preparing the food dishes listed:

Food	Amount	Needed for Item No.
sugar	3 oz.	1, 6
salt	1/3 oz.	3
margarine	3 oz.	7
cream substitute	1/2 oz.	5
	6-5/6 oz.	

be cut down by using dehydrated beef in item 3 (save about eleven ounces), vacuum dried apricots in item 6 (save about three ounces), and cooked canned bacon or bacon bar instead of store variety "fresh" bacon (save five to eight ounces). Pancakes are also a fairly heavy food item, compared for example, to dehydrated eggs or cooked cereal. This "fine" planning is not considered essential for an overnight trip where the food load is not a major item. However, on extended backpack trips it becomes very important.

THREE DAY BACKPACK TRIP

For a three day backpack trip the food weight will become a larger portion of the total pack load and more attention to the weight of the individual food items is necessary. However, some persons will not plan a three day trip sufficiently far in advance to allow time to obtain through mail order such special foods as dehydrated meat, vacuum or freeze dried fruits and vegetables, dehydrated eggs, etc. Therefore, the menus for this three day trip have again been planned around foods which are available in most local stores. If you want minimum weight in your pack, plan your trips far enough in advance that you will have time to mail order some of the foods. Or, simply keep an advance supply of such foods on hand, if you do sufficient backpacking. For minimum weight, select your menus even for short trips from those given for the week-long trip that follows the three day trip.

SUPPER *(First day)*

Item Number	Food	Requirement For Three Persons
1.	Tea	1/2 oz. (3 tea bags makes 6 cups)
2.	Vegetable soup	2-1/2 oz. (dehydrated)
3.	Potatoes and gravy	4 oz. instant mashed potatoes
		4 oz. dried beef (for gravy)
4.	Raisins or candy	6 oz.
		17 oz.

Note: Cook fruit for breakfast.

BREAKFAST *(Second day)*

5.	Coffee	1/2 oz. (instant; makes 6 cups)
6.	Stewed prunes	7-1/2 oz. (dried; local store variety)
7.	Oatmeal	4-1/2 oz.
8.	Bacon & eggs	12 oz. bacon (local store variety)
		7 oz. eggs (3 fresh eggs)
		31-1/2 oz.

LUNCH *(Second day)*

9.	Fruit drink (cold)	3 oz. (makes 1 qt.)
10.	Beef soup	2-1/2 oz. (dehydrated)
11.	Sweet potatoes	3-1/4 oz. (dehyd., instant)
12.	Salami or cheese	8 oz.
13.	Ry Krisp or Triscuits	6 oz.
		22-3/4 oz.

SUPPER *(Second day)*

14.	Hot gelatin	3 oz. (makes 3 cups)
15.	Onion soup	2 oz. (dehyd.)
16.	Chicken and noodles	5 oz. noodles
		3 oz. noodle soup (dehyd.)
		7 oz. can boned chicken
17.	Mixed nuts	3 oz.
		23 oz.

Note: Cook fruit; soak potatoes and onions for breakfast.

BREAKFAST *(Third day)*

18.	Coffee	1/2 oz. (instant. Makes 6 cups)
19.	Stewed apricots	6 oz. (dried, local store variety)
20.	Grapenuts	5 oz.
21.	Hash	2-1/2 oz. potatoes (dehyd.)
		1 oz. onions (dehyd.)
		10 oz. can pork sausages
		25 oz.

LUNCH *(Third day)*

22.	Fruit drink (cold)	3 oz. (makes 1 qt.)
23.	Tomato soup	2-1/2 oz. (dehyd.)
24.	Hard crackers or cookies	6 oz.
25.	Summer sausage or cheese	8 oz.
26.	Candy	3 oz.
		22-1/2 oz.

OTHER FOOD ITEMS. In addition to the foods given above, you will need the following, for preparing the food dishes listed:

Food	Amount	Needed for Item No.
sugar	9 oz.	1, 6, 7, 19, 20
salt	1-1/4 oz.	3, 7, 8, 16, 21
pepper	1/4 oz.	8, 11, 21
margarine	5 oz.	3, 11, 21
cream substitute	4 oz.	3, 5, 7, 18, 20
flour	1/2 oz.	3
	20 oz.	

TOTAL FOOD WEIGHT. All of the food adds up to a total of about 162 ounces. This amounts to about twenty-seven ounces per meal or about nine ounces per person per meal. Compare these menus with those for the overnight hike and note where the differences occur. Note the weight for the second meal, Breakfast (second day, and penalty in weight for carrying store bacon and fresh eggs (nineteen ounces) compared with the weight for a bacon bar and dehydrated eggs (six ounces).

ONE WEEK BACKPACK TRIP

For a one week backpack trip the food weight will become a very significant part of the total pack load, and some skillful planning is required to keep it from getting out of hand. Many of the foods listed will need to be mail ordered. In general you should allow a minimum of two weeks from the time you send in your order (preferably by air mail) until the order is received. We will again assume that the trip starts in the morning (after breakfast) and that the first lunch will be a cold bag lunch, each hiker providing his own. On the trail a hot lunch is recommended in most instances. However, two cold lunches are included in these menus, to illustrate suitable foods and quantities for those occasions where a cold lunch is desired.

SUPPER (First day)

Item Number	Food	Requirement For Three Persons
1.	Tea	1/4 oz. (instant makes 6 cups)
2.	Onion soup	2 oz. (dehyd. for 3 cups)
3.	Spaghetti & Beef	7 oz. elbow spaghetti
		3 oz. dehyd. ground beef
		2-1/2 oz. spaghetti sauce
4.	Ry Krisp or Triscuits	3 oz.
5.	Candy or raisins	3 oz.
		20-3/4 oz.

Note: Cook fruit for breakfast.

BREAKFAST (Second day)

6.	Coffee	1/2 oz. (instant makes 6 cups)
7.	Stewed apricots	3 oz. (vacuum dried)
8.	Oatmeal	4-1/2 oz.
9.	Eggs and bacon	3 oz. dehyd. eggs
		3 oz. bacon bar (mixed with eggs)
		14 oz.

LUNCH (Second day)

10.	Lemonade	1 oz. lemon powder (6 cups)
11.	Chicken noodle soup	2-1/2 oz. (dehyd.)
12.	Cooked apple nuggets	3 oz. (vacuum dried)
13.	Dried beef or sausage	6 oz.
14.	Ry Krisp or Triscuits	3 oz.
15.	Candy	3 oz.
		18-1/2 oz.

Note: Soak salad for supper.

SUPPER (Second day)

16.	Hot gelatin	3	oz. (makes 3 cups)
17.	Tomato soup	4	oz. (dehyd.)
18.	Macaroni and cheese	7	oz. macaroni
		4	oz. cheese
19.	Vegetable salad	1	oz. salad (dehyd.)
		1	oz. salad dressing
20.	Peanuts or other nuts	3	oz.
		23	oz.

Note: Soak potatoes and onions, cook fruit for breakfast.

BREAKFAST (Third day)

21.	Coffee	1/2	oz. (instant, makes 6 cups)
22.	Stewed peaches	3	oz. (vacuum dried)
23.	Wheatena	4	oz.
24.	Hash	2-1/2	oz. potatoes (dehyd.)
		1	oz. onions (dehyd.)
		3	oz. bacon bar
		14	oz.

Note: Soak chili beans for supper.

LUNCH (Third day)

25.	Gouda cheese	4	oz.
26.	Beef stick	5	oz.
27.	Ry Krisp or Triscuits	5	oz.
28.	Candy	3	oz.
29.	Raisins	3	oz.
		20	oz.

SUPPER (Third day)

30.	Tea	1/4	oz. (instant makes 6 cups)
31.	Pea soup	4	oz. (dehyd.)
32.	Chili	5-1/2	oz. dehyd. chili beans
		1/2	oz. dehyd. onions
		2	oz. dehyd. beef
		1/4	oz. dehyd. tomatoes
33.	Ry Krisp or Triscuits	4	oz.
34.	Mixed nuts	3	oz.
		19-1/2	oz.

AROUND THE CAMPFIRE (Third day)

35.	Popcorn	4	oz.

Note: Cook prunes for breakfast.

BREAKFAST (Fourth day)

36.	Coffee	1/2	oz. (instant, makes 6 cups)
37.	Stewed prunes	3	oz. (vacuum dried)
38.	Oatmeal	4-1/2	oz.
39.	Eggs and bacon	3	oz. dehyd. eggs
		3	oz. bacon bar (mixed with eggs)
		14	oz.

LUNCH (Fourth day)

40.	Lemonade	1	oz. lemon powder (6 cups)
41.	Vegetable beef soup	3	oz.
42.	Beef jerky or sausage sticks	3	oz.
43.	Sweet potatoes	5	oz. (dehyd., instant)
44.	Candy or raisins	6	oz.
		18	oz.

SUPPER (Fourth day)

45.	Hot gelatin	3	oz. (makes 3 cups)
46.	Potato soup	3	oz. dehyd.
47.	Chow mein	5	oz. dehyd. chow mein
		3	oz. dry chow mein noodles
		3	oz. dehyd. chicken
48.	Ry Krisp or Triscuits	3	oz.
		20	oz.

Note: Soak potatoes and onions, cook fruit for breakfast.

BREAKFAST (Fifth day)

49.	Coffee	1/2	oz. (instant, makes 6 cups)
50.	Apricots	3	oz. (vacuum dried)
51.	Wheatena	4	oz.
52.	Hash	2-1/2	oz. potatoes (dehyd.)
		1	oz. onions (dehyd.)
		3	oz. bacon bar
		14	oz.

LUNCH (Fifth day)

53.	Lemonade	1	oz. lemon powder (6 cups)
54.	Vegetable soup	4	oz. (dehyd.)
55.	Cooked apple nuggets	3	oz. (vacuum dried)
56.	Ry Krisp or Triscuits	4	oz.
57.	Candy	6	oz.
		18	oz.

SUPPER (Fifth day)

58.	Tea	1/4	oz. (for 6 cups)
59.	Tomato soup	4	oz.
60.	Potatoes with cheese	4	oz. potatoes (dehyd.)
		3	oz. cheese
61.	String beans	1-1/2	oz. (freeze dried)
		1	oz. sour cream sauce
62.	Beef stick	3	oz.
		16-3/4	oz.

AROUND THE CAMPFIRE (Fifth day)

63.	Popcorn	4	oz.

Note: Cook fruit for breakfast.

BREAKFAST (Sixth day)

64.	Coffee	1/2	oz. (instant, for 6 cups)
65.	Stewed peaches	3	oz.
66.	Oatmeal	4-1/2	oz.
67.	Eggs and bacon	3	oz. dehyd. eggs
		3	oz. bacon bar (mixed with eggs)
		14	oz.

LUNCH (Sixth day)

68.	Lemonade	1	oz. lemon powder (for 6 cups)
69.	Pea soup	4	oz. (dehyd.)
70.	Hot potato salad	6	oz.
71.	Gouda cheese	3	oz.
72.	Candy	3	oz.
		17	oz.

Note: Soak salad for supper.

SUPPER (Sixth day)

73.	Tea	1/4 oz. (for 6 cups)
74.	Vegetable beef soup	4 oz.
75.	Rice Milanese	5 oz. (rice, flavoring, etc.)
		2 oz. dehyd. beef (added to rice)
76.	Vegetable salad	1 oz. salad (dehyd.)
		1 oz. salad dressing
77.	Mixed nuts	6 oz.
		19-1/4 oz.

Note: Soak potatoes and onions, cook fruit for breakfast.

BREAKFAST (Seventh day)

78.	Coffee	1/2 oz. (instant, for 6 cups)
79.	Stewed prunes	3 oz. (dehyd.)
80.	Wheatena	4 oz.
81	Hash	2-1/2 oz. potatoes (dehyd.)
		1 oz. onions (dehyd.)
		3 oz. bacon bar
		14 oz.

LUNCH (Seventh day)

82.	Lemonade	1 oz. lemon powder (for 6 cups)
83.	Mixed fruit	1 oz. freeze dried
84.	Turblokken	7 oz.
85.	Beef jerky	3 oz.
86.	Candy	3 oz.
		15 oz.

OTHER FOOD ITEMS. In addition to the foregoing foods, you will need the following items, in preparing those foods:

Food	Amount	Needed for Item No.
sugar	28 oz.	1, 7, 8, 10, 12, 22, 23, 30, 37, 38, 40, 50, 51, 53, 55, 58, 65, 66, 68, 73, 79, 80, 82, 83
salt	4-1/2 oz.	3, 8, 9, 18, 19, 23, 24, 35, 38, 39, 43, 46, 51, 52, 60, 61, 63, 66, 67, 70, 75, 80, 81
shortening (including at least 8 oz. margarine)	14 oz.	4, 9, 14, 24, 27, 33, 35, 39, 43, 48, 52, 56, 63, 67, 81
cream substitute	9 oz.	6, 8, 18, 21, 23, 36, 38, 49, 51, 60, 64, 66, 78, 80
pepper	1/2 oz.	9, 19, 24, 39, 52, 67, 76, 81
mustard	4 oz.	13, 26, 42, 62, 85
	60 oz.	

TOTAL FOOD WEIGHT. All of the food adds up to a total of 378 ounces. There are eighteen meals and two campfire snacks. This amounts to an average of twenty-one ounces per meal, or about seven ounces per meal per person. Compare these menus with those for the overnight hike and for the three day hike and note where the differences occur. These meals provide generous portions and in a large group there will be some food wasted. Experienced backpackers, who have learned to plan food menus and cook without waste, will be able to cut quantities on some items so as to reduce the overall food weight by about ten to fifteen percent. This particularly applies to small groups of experienced adult backpackers. In general, the larger the group and the more teenagers in the group (if any), the more wasted food. Fish have been omitted from these menus. However, on many trips into wilderness areas, and other remote regions, trout would be caught and this would make some further reduction in the food weight.

FOOD LIST

The total food list and total weight of the separate food items is easily arrived at. Simply go through the menus, writing down the name and weight of the food the first time it occurs on the menu, and adding the necessary weight for each repetition of the item.

6

Cooking

PLANNING

One of the most important jobs to be done on any backpack trip is the cooking. Choose your cook carefully. He should not only be interested in outdoor cooking (on the trail) but he should have had significant experience in cooking dehydrated and other trail foods on actual backpack trips. Prior to the trip the cook will be responsible for preparing the menu, getting the food and cooking gear together, assuring that it is properly packed, and distributing an equal load to each hiker. He should call on the other hikers for help in these preparations, but it is important that some one individual, a leader, have the overall supervision of the job. The cook should know how to properly prepare every item of food on the menu. He should have note cards, or a small notebook, showing each menu and the recipe for each food item on the menu (so that there will be no guessing on amount of food, ingredients, seasoning, cooking time, etc.).

For a trip of over a few days in length much of the food will be dehydrated and some will probably need to be obtained by mail order. It is desirable that this order be sent approximately one month prior to the takeoff date. Allowing two weeks until mail order foods are received, an additional two weeks is then available for packing; this is none too long when the packing is done in your spare time. An alternative is to keep a supply of certain dehydrated foods (those not available from local stores) on hand at all times.

PACKING FOOD

Most of the individual foods carried on a backpack trip are suitable for packing in bags and should be so packed. Some of the plastic bags (pint and quart size) sold for home use in packing foods for deep freezers are suitable for this purpose. Many are too light in weight and will not stand up under trail usage. Some of the suppliers listed in Appendix A carry plastic (polyethylene) bags for this purpose. A common weight is two mills, which means the plastic material is .002 inches in thickness. Depending upon the size of the party, the pint size bags will do for many of the food items. When the food is used the bag is burned in the fire. Macaroni, flour, sugar, dried fruit, coffee, and all other dry foods should be packaged in these bags. Dehydrated food that comes in heavy paper and foil bags, and any food in boxes, should be repacked into these lighter bags. Double bags, one inside the other, should be used for fine particle foods like flour and sugar.

Small rubber bands can be used for closing the bags at the top, after they are filled with food. These are not as readily installed and removed, however, as a wire "twister" type of closure. The wire "twister" closures with paper cover, that are furnished with the plastic bags sold in most local stores, are generally unsatisfactory for trail usage. The paper cover is not sufficient protection for the wire. Some of the wire ends will poke into adjacent bags, puncture them, and you then have spilled food (and a mess). A good solution is to use ordinary tobacco pipe cleaners, cut in half. After cutting in half with pliers, the ends of the pipe cleaner should be doubled back and crimped with pliers so that no sharp ends protrude to puncture other bags. These pieces of pipe cleaner, or "twisters," are simply twisted around the top of the bag after putting in the food.

It is particularly recommended that such "twisters" be used on bags which hold sugar, tea, coffee, dehydrated milk, and other food items wherein the bag is opened and closed repeatedly during the trip. For those bags that hold one meal portions of such foods as macaroni, spaghetti, noodles, etc., and the bags are destroyed the first time they are used, a rubber band closure is usually suitable.

OTHER CONTAINERS. For packaging of certain foods, you may want some durable plastic or light weight metal containers. Such containers should be kept to a minimum. The writer has made many trips where only one such container, a lightweight aluminum can for margarine, was taken. Some of the suppliers listed in Appendix A carry suitable containers. Glass containers should not be carried on a backpack trip. They are not needed, and they are not suitable. They are too heavy and they are subject to breakage. If you want to take some food that comes packaged in a glass container, you should repackage it. If for some unusual reason a glass container is carried on a backpack trip, it should be carried home again after the contents are used. Glass containers cannot be satisfactorily disposed of. For all practical purposes they are nondestructible. Wherever you leave them they will be there for the next 100 years. Under certain circumstances sunlight shining through glass may start a forest fire.

Experienced backpackers will be on the look-out throughout the year for various plastic and lightweight metal containers that will serve their needs when it comes time to go backpacking. A baking powder can may make a suitable container for margarine or fresh eggs. A large plastic pill bottle, with screw top lid, is suitable for carrying lemon powder.

Shortening, store bacon, sausage sticks, and other foods that tend to be greasy should be packaged with particular care. Don't depend on the thin cellophane wrapper on store bacon to provide adequate protection in backpacking. Repackage the bacon in a heavy plastic bag, tightly sealed. The plastic or metal container in which shortening is carried should, in turn, be carried inside a heavy plastic bag also. In warm weather the outside of the container will become greasy and soil other articles if not properly protected.

WEIGH OR MEASURE FOOD

All foods should be weighed with a scale reading in ounces or measured (by "standard" cups) before placing in the individual plastic bags. An ordinary kitchen scale, which measures in ounces, is good for this purpose. Do not guess at the amounts. This can be disastrous.

A postage scale, calibrated in 1/2 ounce increments (up to two pounds), is particularly useful for weighing food items. When on the trail a small spring scale can be used for weighing equal loads of food, cooking gear, and other common equipment for distribution to hikers at the start of each day.

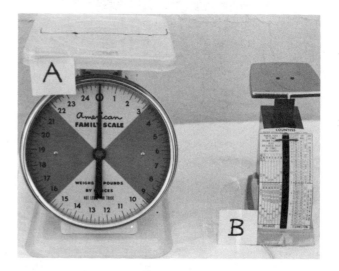

WEIGHING SCALES. The kitchen scale (A) will weigh quantities up to 25 pounds, in one ounce increments. It is useful for weighing large food items and some items of equipment. The postage scale (B) will weigh items up to two pounds, in fractional ounce increments. It is particularly useful for weighing small quantities of food and small equipment items.

LABEL THE FOOD BAGS

Label all bags before putting the food into them. The ink markers with a felt tip, commonly sold in drug and variety stores, are good for this purpose. You can write directly on the bag. It is desirable to mark each bag with the name of the food and the weight. For those bags that are used repeatedly during a trip, like bags for sugar, tea, coffee, milk substitute, etc., an ink marking on a polyethlene bag will gradually wear and become faint. Protect the marking by an overlay of transparent tape, or use gummed white paper labels for those bags.

FINAL FOOD PACKING

For final packing of the individual bags it is recommended that large, heavy plastic (polyethylene) bags be used. Bags measuring approximately eight by four by twenty inches, with a material thickness of two or three mills, are most suitable for this purpose.

There are several approaches to packing food so you can find the particular foods for a given meal when you want them. Rummaging through all of the food bags looking for one or two food items can be quite exasperating and time consuming. You can package foods so that all meats, cheese, shortening, etc., are grouped together in a large bag; products such as macaroni, noodles, soups, etc., in another; sugar, salt, tea, coffee in another, and so forth. You can put all foods for a given day in one bag, with three bags within that bag being labelled "Breakfast," "Lunch," and "Supper."

However, the recommended method is for all foods for breakfast to be together in one large bag(s); lunch foods in another bag; supper foods in a third bag; and a last bag to be labelled "EXTRA." The "EXTRA" bag will contain sugar, salt, candy, tea, coffee, shortening and similar food items that are either common to many meals or planned as surplus. This latter method has been found most satisfactory on most backpack trips.

It is important that only one person, the cook, be responsible for packaging the foods into the various large bags and for repacking them after each meal. Unless this is done you will have a situation like a housewife trying to get a meal with some other person rearranging the contents of the cupboard each time just before she starts.

Try to put the foods into the proper bag for the meal for which they will be used but, in order to make the weight of the bags balance out evenly (for distribution to the hikers), it may be necessary to put a food used for supper into the breakfast bag, etc., when you first start the trip. As you use the food from the bags you will soon be able to pack all of them in the right bag.

Pint size plastic food bags, suitable for packaging of many of the individual foods, weigh about one ounce for each ten bags. Plastic bags, suitable for holding a quantity of the pint (or quart) size bags, bacon bars, and other food items, weigh about one-half ounce each (nine inches by twenty inches size). Use only plastic bags which are absolutely new.

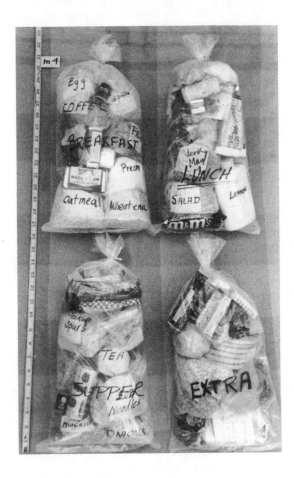

FOOD READY FOR TRAIL. Four plastic bags, each 8" X 4" X 19" X .002", weighing a total of 365 ounces, contain all the food for three adults for a week-long backpack trip.

COOKING UTENSILS

KEEP THEM SIMPLE. The recipes listed in Part 4 were chosen not only for light weight of the foods required and simplicity of preparation, but also because they require a minimum of cooking gear. All of the menus for the meals given in Part 5 can be prepared with the following cooking utensils. The capacity and number of utensils is ample for a group of three or four hikers. For a larger group, simply use the same type of cooking pans but of greater capacity, and a skillet of greater diameter, or more units. These are the cooking utensils required:

1. Two aluminum cooking pans, capacity two quarts each. No lid required. In cooking over an open wood fire, most foods need to be watched almost continuously and stirred very frequently. If you had a lid it would probably be off the pan as much as on.

2. Teflon skillet, about ten inches in diameter.

3. Plastic jar (pint or quart size) for soaking dehydrated foods. Not required if you do not

plan to soak food (in your pack) while hiking.
    4. Two tablespoons, aluminum.
    5. Small wood or plastic turner.
    6. Can opener.
    7. Pan gripping tool (optional).
The weight of the above cooking utensils is about twenty-nine ounces. Now let's discuss them a bit.

COOKING PANS. These can be bought in most department and variety stores for about one dollar each. A two quart size is recommended for a group of three or four persons. They should be adapted to hanging from a pole (dingle stick) by drilling three small holes (about 1/16 inch diameter) at equal points on the circumference of the rim, just below the top edge. Through these holes run three flexible wires and twist together at the top to form a bail. When pans are suspended from a pole by a three wire bail (using light gauge, easily bent wire) they are much more stable than when using a conventional bail (one heavy wire), running from one side of the pan to the opposite side. Cut off the handles of the pans so that only about a two inch stub remains (for gripping with needle nose pliers) and they will be lighter. After the pots are well blackened on the outside by the cooking fire they will do the job better. Cooking pots should be packed in a pan bag, as discussed later, to keep them from blackening up other equipment in your pack.

Cutting off the handles of the pans also serves a purpose for a safety standpoint. If there is no handle you are not likely to grab the pan with your hand and possibly get a good burn in the process if it has been on or near the fire.

In packing the cooking pans, simply push the wire bails down into the pan. Unless you put a very sharp kink in the wire (bending it back on itself) it can be repeatedly bent and it will not break. Replace the bails at the start of each backpack trip and carry about two feet of spare stove wire with which to replace a bail during a trip if it becomes necessary.

SKILLET. There are a wide variety of shapes, sizes and weights of teflon-coated skillets available in local stores and many are not expensive. With some searching you can find a ten inch diameter teflon skillet, weighing about twelve ounces, that will be suitable for backpacking. Your skillet is a most important item of equipment. A teflon skillet is recommended over aluminum or plain steel because it will fry your food more evenly with less shortening and the result will be more tasty. Aluminum skillets may be used but the food will burn quite easily and much more shortening will be required. There are certain precautions that should be observed in using a teflon skillet. The cook will want to instruct the hikers, who are helping with the cooking operation, rather carefully in regard to the following precautions:

    1. Although the instructions for many teflon skillets say it is not necessary to use shortening after the skillet is once "broken in," it is recommended in cooking over an open fire that you use a small amount of shortening each time. Coat the entire inside surface with shortening, right up to the rim of the skillet. Put a small spoonful of additional shortening in the bottom.
    2. Don't thrust a cold teflon skillet into a hot flame and hold it there. Heat it up somewhat gradually.
    3. Use only a wood or plastic turner for handling food in the skillet, never a metal utensil. A metal turner will mar the inside teflon surface and the skillet will soon become burnt and useless.
    4. A teflon skillet can usually be satisfactorily cleaned by simply rinsing in cold water. Warm water or warm soapy water may be used if necessary.
    5. Never use a metal cleaning pad or pot scratcher in cleaning a teflon skillet. Use only a rag or a plastic scrub pad.
    6. In packing the skillet be sure that metal objects are not next to it which may rub the inside surface and mar it. A separate lightweight bag is recommended as a cover.

SOAKING JAR. If you want to be soaking dehydrated food while you are hiking, then a leak-proof, unbreakable plastic jar is recommended. If you are staying at the same camp after you reach a certain destination then such a jar may not be essential. You can have dehydrated food soaking in camp by placing it in a strong plastic bag and hanging it from a tree limb. It can also be put to soak in an open pan. (Better hang this from a limb also if you leave camp so that animals cannot get into it.)

TABLESPOONS. These are needed for measuring and stirring food while cooking and for serving. Aluminum tablespoons are lighter than steel. The difference will not be important on a short backpack trip but on a long trip it will be.

PLASTIC OR WOOD TURNER. This is needed in frying, and a wood or plastic turner must be used with a teflon skillet.

CAN OPENER. The "GI" baby can opener, listed by several suppliers in Table 1, will save weight (weighs about 1/4 ounce), and it will do the job. It just takes a little longer than most can openers. It is so small that it can easily become lost. Tie it to the handle of the turner (drill a hole if there is none there) with stout cord or a rawhide thong so you will know where to find it.

PAN GRIPPING TOOL. If you have a pair of needle nose pliers these will serve very adequately to handle the pans mentioned and they will also be useful for other camp and trail jobs. Grip the pans by the stub of the handle or at the top of the wire bail. There are also a number of aluminum pan gripping tools available which grip the pan edge, some of which have a unit weight of about one ounce.

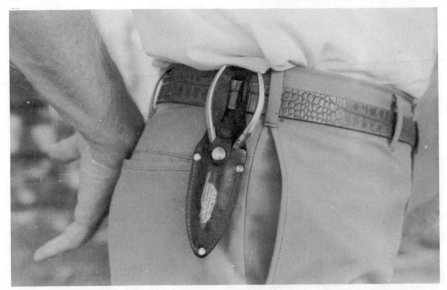

A pair of small needle-nose pliers is probably the most useful of all camp tools. You cannot grab a pan, or the bail on a pan with your bare hand after it has been on the fire. I use needle-nose pliers continually while working around an open fire.

CARRYING BAG. All cooking utensils should be carried in a bag which you can easily make at home out of ordinary muslin or percale. This will keep the utensils together and will keep the soot on the pans from getting onto other items in your pack. Make the bag of generous size with a tie string at the top. You should use new material so the bag will be strong. Don't try to use a paper or plastic bag for this purpose. The bag will split open and the inside of your good pack bag will get coated with soot from the pans. The inside of the carrying bag will be thoroughly blackened during each trip and should be washed at home before the next trip. Plates, cups, and materials for dish washing can be carried in another cloth bag.

EATING UTENSILS

PLATES. Aluminum plates are recommended although some persons may prefer plastic. The

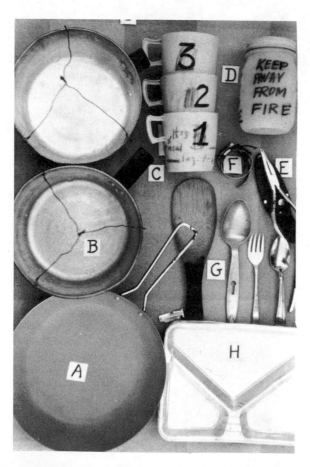

COOKING AND EATING UTENSILS. The following utensils are ample for three persons: (A) skillet, (B) two pans, (C) cups, (D) food soaking jar, (E) needle-nose pliers, (F) hose clamps, for skillet extension handle, (G) silverware, (H) plates. Total weight of these cooking and eating utensils (including three plates, cups, forks, spoons) is forty-eight ounces.

three compartment rectangular aluminum plates, about seven inches by nine inches, in which some "TV" dinners are packaged, are lightweight (about 7/8 ounce) and satisfactory. They should be in new condition. If used with reasonable care they will last for a week or two of backpacking. Do not use them to fan the fire because flexing the plates back and forth will cause them to crack and come apart at the seams. These plates can be bought from some retail suppliers.

CUPS. Plastic cups are good. They will take considerable rough treatment, are light in weight, and can be used for either hot or cold liquids. Such cups are available in many local stores. One such cup weighs 1-1/3 ounce, holds about 1-1/2 "standard" cups, stacks easily, and costs about thirty cents. Numbering the cups on the outside with a felt tip ink marker will help each hiker to know which cup is his when he sets it down some place during a meal. Cereals such as oatmeal, stewed fruit, and soups are most conveniently and efficiently eaten from cups, rather than plates.

SILVERWARE. Each person needs one spoon and one fork for eating, preferably of aluminum. Most foods can be eaten without difficulty with just the spoon. For the foods that require use of a knife while eating, you can use your pocket knife. Do not carry the common silverware knives that you use on the table at home. They are much too heavy and they are not needed in backpacking. If you must carry a separate knife for eating use a small plastic knife such as those sold with picnic supplies in local stores. The silverware can be carried in a small light-weight cloth bag measuring about five inches by eleven inches with a drawstring at the top.

USING COOKING UTENSILS

EXTENSION HANDLES. Even a small wood cooking fire can be uncomfortably hot when you are continuously close to it while cooking. Since a skillet will usually be held while it is being used it is a good idea to use an extension handle with it. Find a piece of stout wood about 1-1/2 inches in diameter and cut it (if you have a saw) or break it to a length of about twenty-four to thirty inches. Place one end alongside the skillet handle. Wrap the two handles together at several places with tape or wire. You can also use two automobile radiator hose clamps instead of tape or wire and get a more positive fastening. Use the type of radiator hose clamps that have a screw thread adjustment. For special purpose cooking (like for popcorn) an extension handle can also be used with the cooking pans in the same manner, placing the hose clamps very close together on the stub of the pan handle. The handle of a spoon or fork will usually fit the screw head for adjusting the hose clamps. If not, a little modification of the end of the handle with a file (before leaving home) will make it fit.

When a skillet is being held while cooking, the least tiring way is to find a log or stone on which to rest the extension handle (at the end nearest the skillet).

One of the problems of backpacking is to find some lightweight devices for holding or suspending pots, pans and skillets over an open fire while cooking. Shown here are some recommended devices and methods.

Two automobile radiator hose clamps, used as shown here, will hold the skillet securely to the extension handle.

An extension handle for your skillet, five or six feet long, supported on a rock will keep the cook from getting uncomfortably hot during the relatively short period that is required for most frying.

DINGLE STICK. This is a good method for suspending pans over an open fire and is quickly rigged. Note the three wire flexible bails on the pans; this is more spill-proof than a single heavy wire bail.

THE DINGLE STICK. There are numerous ways of suspending pans over the fire while cooking. They can be set on two parallel stones or suspended from a tripod or ridge pole (supported by forked stakes). Another way, which can usually be quickly rigged and will not be likely to dump the cooking pots into the fire, is the dingle stick.

The dingle stick is a pole, preferably green wood, about eight to ten feet long, three to four inches in diameter at the base, and one or two inches in diameter at the tip.

The dingle stick is rigged so that the large end is on the ground (away from the fire) and the other end is suspended about eighteen to twenty inches above the ground, over the fire. Laying the dingle stick over a rock or short log, at about its midpoint, will elevate the tip end. The base end is weighted with several rocks to hold it in place.

If you use a three wire flexible bail on your cooking pans, as discussed earlier, they can be easily suspended on a dingle stick so that they will not tip. If you keep your fire at the right size for a cooking fire there will be no danger of burning the dingle stick.

A GRATE. For a short backpack trip, or for a fairly large group where the additional weight is justified, the use of a wire grate with folding legs may be desirable. Many grates are too heavy to be suitable for backpacking. (Why don't "they" make a grate to last one or two seasons instead of five?) A wire tray from a stove oven may be suitable. It has the disadvantage of being somewhat unstable unless you can find about four good size rocks for "legs," of roughly equal height, flat on the top and "tip proof" (not an easy job — try it sometime!).

Grates with folding legs are available. They provide a surface area of about ten by fifteen inches and have a total weight of about one pound. Some backpackers may consider these satisfactory. Grates with folding legs should be examined carefully before buying. The type and strength of attachment of the legs to the grate top frequently leaves something to be desired. Many are designed so that there is a "bump" in the grate surface at each point where a leg is attached. This effectively reduces the usable surface area. If a flush mounting is used an additional cooking utensil can be set on the grate as contrasted to the same size grate that does not have the legs flush mounted.

As with cooking utensils, a grate (if you use one) will become thoroughly covered with soot after each use. You will need a sturdy cloth bag in which to carry it between meal stops.

Dishwashing is frequently a chore, especially

A backpacker's grill is another method of supporting pans over an open fire.

The backpacker's grill in use. It will get very black and must be carried in a substantial cloth cover, in being packed from place to place.

the job of washing out the cooking pan(s). Remains of oatmeal, macaroni, stew or whatever else you cooked in the pan will cling stubbornly to the sides and bottom. However, this problem can be essentially eliminated. Carry a small bottle of cooking oil and about a square foot or two of ordinary paper towels. Before you start to cook use a very small piece of paper towel soaked in cooking oil to thoroughly coat the entire inside surface of each cooking pan. Several special products are also available for this purpose. One goes under the name of "Vegalene." After thoroughly coating the inside of your pans with the oil, add water and go ahead with your cooking process in the normal manner. When it is dishwashing time you will find that pans "prepared" in this manner clean very easily.

THE COOKING FIRE

Wood for your fire can frequently be picked up off the ground if there have been no recent rains. Large limbs lying on the ground will usually have some branches protruding up in the air that will not be damp in case the wood on the ground is damp. Dead branches can also be broken off the lower limbs of trees (squaw wood). If there have been recent rains you may need to look under cliff overhangs, under large trees lying on the ground or in similar protected places in order to find a dry wood supply for starting your fire. Once a good fire is going you can dry out fairly wet wood by laying it very near or on the fire, then removing it (for later use) before it starts to burn.

Have a good wood supply before you start to cook. Nothing is worse than having the fire die down when you are halfway through with your cooking and then having to stop everything and go look for more wood.

If you are building your fire near a stream, try to pick out a spot of sand or dirt in the stream bed, free from small rocks, or a large flat solid stone area on which to build your fire. When a fire is laid on shale, porous rock, or wet stones some of the stones may explode and cause injury.

If your fire is to be built away from a stream, take every precaution to build the fire on sand, dirt, or solid rock. It should be away from brush, dead grass, and overhanging tree limbs. Never build the fire against a log or tree stump or between two parallel logs. Such a fire is next to impossible to put out, if you are to be absolutely sure that it is out. It may require considerable time, if you are away from a stream, to find a suitable place for a fire and to exercise the necessary precautions so that there is no fire hazard. If you are not willing to take that time, or if such a place just isn't available, then eat cold food for that meal.

Many times you can start your fire simply by gathering twigs, pine needles, etc., holding a country match under a few until they ignite, and then adding larger twigs and sticks. Frequently, however, the match will go out just when the twigs are about to get started to burn. That is where fire starting aids are useful. Fire cubes, fire starting jelly, or a candle will save time and are considered worthwhile by most backpackers. Have your supply of small dry twigs handy. A good handful of these should be about the diameter of a wood pencil and some of them only half as big. Using two short, parallel sticks about one inch in diameter as a platform, lay a few "pencil size" sticks on top. Use these as a base for fire starting cubes or jelly. Light the fire aid and then very slowly add additional twigs,

FIRE STARTING AIDS

one at a time, placed very carefully on the flame until the fire is started. In using a candle, simply hold the lighted candle under the platform until the material is burning well, then withdraw it for future use.

If you expect rain a thin plastic sheet about six or eight feet square can be a big help. Gather some dry twigs and small sticks in the evening, put under this sheet, and weight the corners with rocks. Then if it rains you will have some dry wood to start the fire in the morning.

For a group of three or four persons cooking together at least one person's job should be to help the cook with the food that is cooking and to feed the fire so that it burns steadily. A small wood fire will burn down quickly if not constantly attended to. Feed the fire one or two sticks (about one to three inches in diameter) at a time. Do not build it up into a big fire. It will waste wood and it will be uncomfortable to cook with. When using a dingle stick build your fire "long" rather than "round."

As soon as your fire is going well you are ready to cook. Cooking over coals may be a bit more romantic (and necessary for some cooking), but heat is heat and it doesn't matter to food inside a utensil whether the heat is coming from coals or an open flame. You are going to waste a lot of time and have some very hungry people getting restless for food if you wait for coals. It is important that you have a controlled flame, however. Don't have it blazing all around the pans one minute and almost going out ten minutes later.

If you should use any canned foods during the meal, or have other unburnable refuse, take time to dispose of it properly. When you travel the well-used trails of our National Forests and Parks it is recommended that you carry out all materials that cannot be burned. In the case of tin cans, wash the can clean of all food particles when you wash dishes. Then smash it flat with your foot, put it in a cloth carrying bag, and back into your pack sack for carrying home.

In very remote (and no other) regions it may be permissible to bury cans. In that event you should throw the emptied can into the fire while the fire is burning well. Before leaving the site remove any cans from the fire place, smash them flat with your foot, and either bury them or place them under a substantial rock well away from the site. They will soon rust away. In contrast, cans that have not had the protective coating burned off will require a long while before they rust away. Food odor and food particles will also remain on unburned cans. If there are bears in the area they will dig up such cans every time, no matter how deeply buried, and make a general mess.

When you are finished cooking put the fire out with water, dirt or sand, and take every precaution to see that it is completely out. More than one wood fire that was supposed to be out has blazed up again after the campers had left it, especially with the aid of a little wind. This is one way of starting a forest fire. If you carry water in one of your cooking pans for putting out the fire, use a minimum of three full pans to put out a small cooking fire. When you are sure it is out make one more trip to the stream. Poke around in the ashes with a stick (or your hand) to be sure they are all well doused with water. Never leave a cooking fire or any other fire unattended in the woods, even for short periods. When you go to bed at night put the fire out just as completely as though you were leaving the area. Any party that "had" to keep a fire going all night for warmth should best keep the story to themselves. This is simply admitting that they were not properly prepared. It is a very poor practice.

A COOKING STOVE

In most of our forests and wilderness areas sufficient wood will be found for cooking, particularly in "off the beaten path" areas that will be attractive to backpackers. If there is any doubt, however, you will probably want to include a small cooking stove in your equipment. Some of the small stoves are quite "temperamental." Make certain you are thoroughly acquainted with any stove that you take on a backpack trip. In the case of a gasoline stove it is best to include a spare generator and necessary wrench for installation. Extra gasoline should be carried only in tight metal containers specifically designed for the purpose. Only one person should carry the stove and extra gasoline in his pack for the entire trip. That person

PRIMUS STOVE. In some areas wood may be scarce or expected weather may preclude the use of wood cooking fire. The Primus is a light weight, reliable stove.

SVEA STOVE. The Svea stove is also a favorite among many backpackers who must depend upon a stove for cooking. A set of nesting pans is available as part of the stove "kit." This is a reliable, lightweight stove, and is relatively "tip proof".

should not carry any food items. Food is easily contaminated by gasoline fumes and odor when they are carried together.

Keep the extra gasoline supply well back from the burning stove while cooking. The burning stove should never be set near an open fire or other intense heat. It may explode! This can happen when pine needles or other material near the stove accidentally catch fire, so keep the stove away from any such material. Plan your cooking operation so that it is not necessary to refill a stove while it is hot. A gasoline stove should be watched just as closely as a wood cooking fire. If the stove goes out it should be relit at once.

DISHWASHING

Heat water for dishwashing in the two cooking pans. As soon as a pan is emptied during a meal rough clean it with natural materials (grass, sand, etc.) which are at hand. Unless you have burned the food in the pan this will not take too long. Then fill the pan with water, put it back on the fire, and finish your meal while the water is heating.

Use bar soap in washing dishes and put it directly into one of the pans of hot water (take it out in several minutes or you will have too many suds). Each hiker should rough clean his own eating utensils before they are washed with soap and hot water. Use a sponge in washing the dishes. As each plate, cup, or spoon is washed, one person should rinse it in a pan of clean, very hot water (that has been boiled for a few minutes), holding on to it with needle nose pliers or a similar tool. Use a cup to dip the hot water and pour over it. Then drop it directly into the carrying bag (cups or plates) or the silverware bag. The use of dishcloths and dishtowels is not recommended. They are not needed, drying them is a problem, and after a few meals they will look like you washed the family car with them.

A teflon-coated skillet is usually easily cleaned in either cold or warm water without soap. An aluminum or steel skillet may require special effort in getting it clean. Cold washing won't help much. Instead, put a small amount of water in the skillet and have one person hold it over the fire until the water is hot. It will heat quickly. Then go to work on it with a pot scratcher and soap.

After all dishes are washed, rinse out the cooking pans that were used for dishwashing. Don't try to scour the cooking fire soot off the outside of the pans. It is beneficial. Take a quick pass over the outside, however, to remove any loose dirt or soot. When the job is finished squeeze out the sponge, rinse out the pot scratcher, and drop them into the pan bag. With coordination and cooperation the dishwashing can usually be done in ten minutes.

RESPONSIBILITY

It is again emphasized that the food, and all matters pertaining to menus, food packaging, and cooking should be the responsibility of one person, the cook. This is one of the most important functions connected with any backpack trip, and it cannot be emphasized too strongly. If you divide the responsibility, or change it from meal to meal or day to day, you will probably have less than satisfactory results. This does not mean that the cook should not get the advice of others on certain matters pertaining to food. He should consult others, especially in planning the menus before leaving home. However, all final decisions pertaining to food, especially after you are on the trail, should be the responsibility of the cook. With various people getting into the food and being responsible for the cooking, you are going to run out of certain food items before you had planned to. You will probably also end up with too much or too little of certain foods at some meals, as well as some foods that are either underdone or overcooked. The cook should know or have a record of the recipe of every item of food on the menu. He should give overall supervision to the preparation of every food item at every meal, even though others are preparing it or helping in the preparation. While others are washing dishes, the cook will be repacking the food, getting it ready for the trail again, putting some foods to soak for the next meal, and making up equal food and cooking gear loads for distribution to each backpacker. The cook has an important job. Give him your full support, and it will pay off in the long run with better food, better dispositions, and a more enjoyable trip in general.

WEIGHT SUMMARY

The following table summarizes the items required for cooking, eating, dishwashing, and related activities (requirement is for party of three, one week trip):

TABLE 9. EQUIPMENT REQUIRED FOR MEALS

Item	Weight in Ounces
COOKING UTENSILS	
Two aluminum cooking pans, 2 quart capacity, 5-1/2 ounces each	11
Teflon skillet, 10 inch diameter	12
Food soaking jar	4
PLATES, CUPS	
Three each: plates and cups	7
OTHER ITEMS REQUIRED	
Can opener, turner, 3 forks, 3 spoons, 2 tablespoons, 2 hose clamps	11
Soap, pot scratcher, sponge, plastic sheet (about 2 feet square)	5
Food packing bags, small containers	8
	58
OPTIONAL	
Pan gripping tool, aluminum	1 to 3

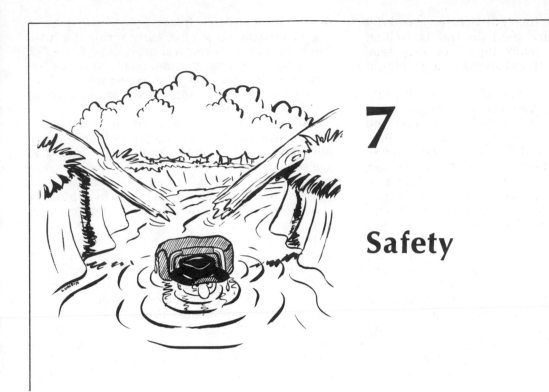

7

Safety

SAFETY VERSUS FIRST AID

You should by all means know your first aid well before you attempt a full-scale backpack trip. You should also carry a good first aid kit and a snake bite kit. The subject of first aid is very well covered in a number of readily available books. Therefore, there will be no lengthy discussion of first aid in this book. One point should be emphasized. It is far better to practice safety on the trail, and in camp, than to have to use your first aid.

CAUSES OF ACCIDENTS

It takes some know-how to plan a backpack trip and a daily routine that will take you safely from place to place in a wilderness or other remote area. Assuming that you have this know-how, or that the leader of the group does, then the two main contributing causes of accidents on the trail are: (a) traveling too fast, and (b) allowing yourself to get too tired.

GETTING IN A HURRY. If your trip is properly planned, there should be no need for getting in a hurry. You should not plan to make more than ten to fourteen miles per day in mountainous areas where you can use reasonably good trails. If you are going to be rock hunting, fishing, or engaging in some other activity during the day besides hiking, this distance must be scaled way down. You should stay near the trail, or stick to suitable terrain

with which someone in the party is familiar. Then you should avoid such mishaps as running out of water, coming up against blind cliffs or precipices and having to retrace your steps, or falling and breaking a leg by trying to hike through terrain that you should not have attempted.

However, it is possible that you took these precautions, and you may still have an accident because you got in a hurry. Let's assume you have a stream to cross. You could take off your shoes and wade across at a certain point, but you don't want to take that much time. Instead you decide to use a tree which happens to bridge the stream near where you want to cross. It is not a very good bridge and it is dangerously high above the water, but you decide to risk it. On the way over one hiker's pack throws him off balance and he goes into the river, breaking a leg in the process. This accident was caused because you got in a hurry (and failed to use good judgment).

GETTING TOO TIRED. Don't see how many miles you can cover on a backpack trip. It should not be an endurance contest. It is always better to underestimate your ability to cover miles than to overestimate. It is extremely difficult to judge distances and traveling time in mountainous terrain from a map. Where you must do this, multiply scaled distances by a factor of two or three and you will probably be about right. However, there are still some unknown factors. Unless some member of the party has been on the trail before, you don't know for certain how good the trail is. Neither do you know how many times you may temporarily lose the trail and spend time to pick it up again.

Five or six hours of hiking (with a full pack) for the first day or two will be enough unless you are a seasoned hiker. Seldom should you plan to hike more than eight hours per day. When you get too tired you are a safety hazard to yourself and others. You will stumble and you may fall where ordinarily you would not. Your reactions are slower. You can easily hurt yourself doing simple camp jobs or other things that usually would not be dangerous at all. For example, the writer once witnessed a very tired hiker breaking wood by laying sticks on a log and stomping on them with his foot. One of the pieces flew up at an odd angle and caught the person just above the eye, making a bad cut, which bled profusely. Had this person not been "dog tired" he would probably have easily dodged the flying stick. If you push yourself to the point of exhaustion you are inviting trouble. Why not settle for fewer miles, a more leisurely pace, and enjoy yourself?

When you get too tired your judgment and thinking are also impaired. You may find yourself doing things — or planning to do things — that ordinarily you would not do. Extreme fatigue acts in much the same way as a drug.

WEATHER CHANGES

A very important contributing factor to accidents and tragedies in the wilderness is weather. For example, after a few weeks of early balmy spring weather a party of hikers takes to the mountains. The days are bright, the weather is warm. Wild flowers have started to appear. Temperatures at night may be barely freezing. Off goes the party of hikers, wearing normal summer hiking clothes, light jackets, etc., and carrying corresponding equipment. But . . . after they are on the trail a few hours, or perhaps a day or two, a storm front may move in suddenly. Within several hours time, temperatures may plunge to far below freezing. Heavy snowfall causes the party to lose its way. Panic sets in. The matches which the party has are hastily used up in trying to start a fire under adverse conditions. Within a matter of a few hours the party is hopelessly lost. One or more members may perish. As this is being written (Spring, 1971) three such accidents have occurred in the state of New Mexico within the past few weeks. This type of tragedy is fairly frequent in the spring of the year. It also happens to parties of hunters in the fall, with a fair degree of regularity. It sometimes happens

to day hikers (often hiking solo), who take to the mountains on a nice, early spring day with the intention of taking a short hike of just a few hours and returning the same day. Never underestimate the fury of the wilderness and its harshness on the unprepared, under adverse weather conditions.

Unseasonably warm weather can cause snow runoff at a much more rapid rate than normal. Mountain streams which were easily waded at the same time the year before are now a foot or more higher. Don't take lightly the tremendous force of ten or twelve added inches in depth of a fast moving mountain stream. It can cost you your life.

So — be prepared for sudden changes in weather when you enter the mountains, particularly in the spring or fall of the year, when sudden deep snowfalls can make trails impassable and easily lost to hikers. At these seasons temperatures can change fifty degrees within a few hours time. Have the necessary clothing and equipment for such an eventuality. Don't depend upon matches alone for starting a fire under such conditions. When you are in a semipanicked state of mind you are not going to want to whittle sticks of wood into shavings or "fuzz sticks" or take the necessary time to gather good fire starting materials, as you would in a normal situation. Have a long burning, hot flame plumber's candle, fire starting jelly, or a similar material in your fire starting kit. Remember, it is one thing to sit in your easy chair at home and half-heartedly plan what you would do in such an emergency situation in the woods. It is quite another thing to be in the woods, trying to cope with that situation, unprepared, and with "time running out."

For those who hike into the mountains, make it a routine that you carry a pack, even for a short duration hike. The pack should contain added clothing, fire starting materials, first aid kit, drinking water, a few items of emergency food, knife, etc. Follow this practice whenever you go out, if only for a day, regardless of how brightly the sun may be shining or how warm the day when you start out. If you have come from some distance away for your hiking or backpacking adventure, make inquiry in advance of weather conditions in general and possible very recent changes in weather. Don't hesitate to cancel or alter your plans if weather conditions warrant. That dollar you saved by not making a last minute long distance phone call to inquire about the weather may look pretty small later on.

Backpackers who venture forth in the early spring or late fall or who go into the very high mountains at any season, should study the table below and note the effect that wind has on the effective temperature. If you have ever ridden in the back end of a pickup truck at thirty miles an hour on a cold morning, you will realize how important it is to consider not only the tempera- ture but the temperature-wind combination. It is also recommended that you obtain the booklet "Hypothermia; Killer of the Unprepared" (See "Other Literature," page A-26).

TABLE 10. WIND CHILL FACTOR

When the temperature/wind speed factor falls in the area shaded below, frostbite, especially of the face, is a serious hazard.

When Thermometer Reads	When the wind blows at the m.p.h. below, it reduces Temperature to								
	Calm	5	10	15	20	25	30	35	40
+50	50	48	40	36	32	30	28	27	26
+40	40	37	28	22	18	16	13	11	11
+30	30	27	16	9	4	0	-2	-4	-6
+20	20	16	4	-5	-10	-15	-18	-20	-21
+10	10	6	-9	-18	-25	-29	-33	-35	-37
0	0	-5	-21	-36	-39	-44	-48	-49	-53
-10	-10	-15	-33	-45	-53	-59	-63	-67	-69
-20	-20	-26	-46	-58	-67	-74	-79	-82	-85
-30	-30	-36	-58	-72	-82	-88	-94	-98	-100
-30	-40	-47	-70	-88	-96	-104	-109	-113	-116
-50	-50	-57	-85	-99	-110	-118	-125	-129	-132
-60	-60	-68	-95	-112	-124	-133	-140	-145	-148

To measure speed of wind without instruments: When CALM (smoke rises vertically); 1-12 m.p.h. (just feel wind on face, leaves in motion); 13-24 (raises dust or loose paper, snow drifts, branches move); 25-30 (large branches move, wires whistle); 30-40 (whole trees in motion, hard to walk against).

For the properly clothed, there is little danger down to -20° but caution should be used with regard to all exposed flesh. At below -20°, take no unnecessary chances.

(Courtesy of Sport House, Concord, Massachusetts.)

SOLO TRAVEL

Backpacking by yourself in remote areas is not recommended. If you should break a leg, or get sick, you have a serious situation, which could cost you your life. Having a companion will provide a very significant added margin of safety. If one person gets sick or injured the other person can take care of him or go for help. A minimum of three persons is actually recommended. One person can then stay with the sick or injured hiker while the other goes for help. Another good reason for having a companion or two is that pack loads will be lighter because of the sharing of cooking utensils, general camp equipment, and other common gear. Additionally, for most of us (even though we may shun large hiking groups) a companion or two to share our "adventures" makes a backpack trip more enjoyable. Regardless of the size of party, it is important to let someone know when and where you are going and your itinerary, just in case you do not return when you are supposed to. A ranch or farm near the roadhead or a

Forest Service office in the nearest town are good places to leave such information. Further, a relative or close friend back home should by all means have this information. They should also have the license number and general description of the vehicle in which you will be traveling to the takeoff point. If an emergency back home requires that someone get in touch with you while you are traveling on the highway, this information will be of utmost importance to state police or others who are attempting to find you.

Forest Service personnel and other professional outdoorsmen sometimes go into remote areas alone. It is part of their job. However, not only are they usually expert woodsmen, but their headquarters knows where they are and will soon be looking for them if they do not show up or check in according to a prearranged plan. Further, such persons usually travel by horseback and having a well-trained horse provides an added margin of safety.

On some of the well-known, regularly maintained and frequently traveled trail systems, such as some sections of the Appalachian Trail, a few hikers will be found traveling alone. If it is a section of the trail that is known to be frequently traveled the risk in traveling alone is certainly not as great as in solo travel in some of the wilderness areas or other remote regions. However, it should be recognized that there is risk involved in any solo travel away from "civilization." Important factors to consider are your experience, your knowledge of the area and trails, and the time of year and probable weather. Each year many hundreds of dollars are spent in locating lost hikers, and the searchers are subjected to additional risk and possible accident in doing so.

The Sportsman smoke signal, made by the Superior Signal Co. of Spotswood, N.J., provides a dense cloud of smoke instantaneously. It may be a worthwhile item to some backpackers. It is often very difficult to produce a dense cloud of smoke for signalling purposes from materials at hand.

HATCHETS, SHEATH KNIVES

A hatchet is a useful and important item of camp equipment. So is an axe. You should know how to use them safely, pack them properly, and keep them sharp. They are not required items of equipment on most backpack trips, however. Wood can usually be had by simply picking it up off the ground or by breaking dead limbs off the lower branches of trees. A jack saw will usually do the few, really necessary jobs that a hatchet would ordinarily be used for on a backpack trip. A satisfactory jack saw weighs as little as four ounces and an average hatchet about twenty-eight ounces; that is a pretty good reason in itself for leaving the hatchet at home. A sheath knife may be taken, but a good pocketknife will do the essential jobs that a sheath knife would be used for. Also, in reference to sheath knives, it is usually a good idea to keep your belt free of equipment on a backpack trip. Most of the better pack frames employ a waist strap, and a waist strap cannot be properly used when there is equipment on your trouser belt. Hatchets and sheath knives are a common source of accidents in camping. They represent a hazard when used by persons who have not had good instruction and experience in their use. Firearms are in the same category.

RAIN STORMS

A little wetting on a warm day won't hurt you, but don't try to continue hiking in a bad storm. Seek the best shelter you can find, make yourself comfortable and wait it out. If there is a hard rain, put up a plastic sheet or a tarp on a ridge line, and keep yourself and your equipment dry. If your pack is not waterproof or you are not sure whether it is, by all means take extra precautions to keep it and its contents dry. If your pack gets thoroughly soaked it will be so heavy you can hardly lift it, let alone carry it. Besides, if everything in it is wet or damp you will have a mess. Under a tarp, stretched as a fly, you may even be able to build a small fire, providing you had time to gather a few sticks of dry wood. Build the fire at one edge of the tarp, downwind, or the smoke will be as bad as the rain. If your tarp is a plastic sheet, keep the fire very small and at the edge of the tarp, or it will "evaporate."

LIGHTNING

In many mountainous regions sudden electrical storms are very common at certain seasons of the year. Your chances of being struck by lightning are small, but it does pay to have some basic knowledge of how to protect yourself. In an electrical storm you should observe the following precautions:

MOUNTAIN PEAKS. Stay off mountain peaks, expecially those which are relatively sharp and prominent. At a good distance downhill from the peak, say several hundred yards, you should be quite safe. A mountain with a broad ridge or rounded top is less dangerous than those with sharp, prominent peaks. In any case, in event of an electrical storm, get off the top of the mountain as fast as possible.

CLIFFS, CAVES. The overhang of a cliff should be avoided. It is a very risky place to be in an electrical storm. If you are under the overhang, a bolt of lightning coming down the cliff is likely to jump across the edge of the overhang and pass through your body. Likewise, do not seek shelter in a small, shallow cave. It is better to get wet (and stay alive). Only fairly large caves are safe. If you do seek shelter in a cave, or under a very large overhang, do not stand but sit. Stay back from the cave entrance and avoid the walls of the cave. A sitting position near the center is best.

CREVICES. Avoid a crack or crevice that leads up the slope of a hill or mountain. These may be a good attractor of lightning, especially if filled with damp earth or if there is a trickle of water flowing.

PROMINENT OBJECTS. Lightning may be attracted to a prominent object on the landscape, such as isolated or very tall trees, buildings, large boulders, etc. If you yourself are the most prominent object on the landscape, you should sit or lie down. You can also move into the general area of some other more prominent object, but keep a distance away from it equal to about twice its height. Don't get directly under it.

SIT OR LIE. Wherever you seek shelter, it is best to sit or lie on the ground during an electrical storm. Pick out a dry spot if possible and insulate yourself from the ground with clothing, pack frame, loose rocks, etc. A fully inflated air mattress is a good insulator.

INSECTS

Except in unusual circumstances, insects are simply a nuisance, rather than a threat to safety. Like other wild things, they are generally harmless if left alone. At certain times of the year, in some areas, insects such as mosquitoes or flies may be so thick as to require the use of a head net that fits over a broad brimmed hat and ties around the neck. Long sleeved shirts and trousers are also important. Use reasonable precautions and you will probably avoid being bitten by spiders, scorpions, and the few other insects which do represent some degree of hazard. Before you put your shoes on in the morning, shake them hard to get rid of any insects that might have crawled inside during the night. Or, you can carry a very lightweight plastic bag and put your shoes in this at night. Do not pick up loose rocks on the ground without first turning them over with your foot. There may be a scorpion underneath, and you could get a bite on the hand. Don't thrust your hands into thick vegetation, cracks in rocks, holes in stumps, or other places where you cannot see well. In other words, use reasonable precautions and insects should present no problem to your safety.

Ticks are found in many sections of the United States, most often in wooded areas. Their prevalence in a given area often varies from year to year. An area having few ticks one year may have many the next time you visit there. Ticks vary in size from about one-fourth to one-half inch in length. They are usually dark brown in color and always have eight legs. They attach themselves to the skin and bite by probing their entire heads into the flesh. If they have not started to probe they can be brushed off easily (but carefully). Once they have fastened themselves, special measures are necessary. Light a match, blow it out and apply the hot end to the exposed part of the tick. He will back out. Or, cover the entire tick with grease or oil.

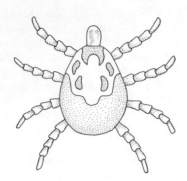

TICK (enlarged). Many varieties of ticks are found in the United States. All have the same general shape and eight legs. A well-fed female tick will be about one-half inch long, others much smaller. Examine your skin and clothing frequently when in a tick area.

When in tick country hikers should frequently inspect one another during the day for possible ticks that may be on outer clothing or on exposed skin areas, such as head, neck, chest and back of legs, where another person can see the area better than yourself. In tick country take time to shake clothing out frequently. Inspect underclothing occasionally. Look carefully for ticks around your waist, on the skin under your belt. Certain serious diseases are spread by ticks, in addition to the painful bite that they may inflict. Only a very small percent of ticks carry such diseases, however.

POISONOUS PLANTS

Poison ivy, as well as poison oak and poison sumac, is a widespread plant that everyone should learn to recognize. If you have recognized a poisonous plant and know that you have touched it, immediately wash the affected part with water and soap. Chances are that a rash or blisters will not develop. If you are particularly allergic to poisonous plants, you should carry a lotion, such as calamine lotion, which you have found to be effective in treatment.

On a well planned backpack trip it should not be necessary to eat wild plants to supplement the food which you carry. About 1/3 ounce of prepared dehydrated salad provides a generous serving for one person and there are some tasty dehydrated salads available. The energy spent in carrying several ounces of dehydrated salad in your pack will probably be far less than the energy required to search for, find, and clean some wild growing salad substitute at meal time. There is always the possibility of wrong identification of wild plants, unless you are an expert, and this can lead to severe illness — or worse.

Water hemlock grows along many mountain streams and is very poisonous. Other common poisonous plants are wild cherry, oak, elderberry, and black locust.

SNAKES

Some persons have a very morbid fear of snakes. To avoid going into the mountains or desert because of that fear is very foolish, but not to have some knowledge of snakes and to take a few reasonable precautions is equally foolish. Rattlesnakes are the most widely distributed of all our poisonous snakes. You may hike hundreds of miles without seeing a rattlesnake. Then, probably when you least expect it, there is one in your path. Rattlesnakes are found over most of the United States. They do not travel much in the daytime as they do their hunting for food mostly at night. In hot weather they will never be very far from shade. Unless you step on a rattlesnake or get very close to it, he will move out of your way if you give him a chance. Following are a few precautions you should take when traveling in country where there may be rattlesnakes.

Wear long sleeved shirts and trousers. A rattlesnake may penetrate these when he strikes, but they offer significant additional protection, compared to bare skin.

When bushes are in or near your path, walk several feet out around them, rather than brushing up against them. Then, if there is a rattlesnake coiled there, it won't matter. Otherwise he may strike. Stay out of dense grass, brush, and foliage, insofar as possible.

In climbing either up or down hillsides, do not put your hands or feet down in places where you cannot fully see whether they are clear. Putting your hand over the edge of a blind cliff is asking for trouble.

If a stone or log is in your path, just assume that there is a rattlesnake coiled on the blind side and act accordingly. If you cannot see over the object, step up on it, then down, or go around.

Carry a snake bite suction kit in rattlesnake country. Also carry a sharp single edge razor blade, to shave the hair from the surface of the skin so that you can get good suction. In using a suction type kit, wet the rim of the rubber suction cup with your tongue, to further aid in proper suction. A tube of ethyl chloride (a compound used for spot freezing of the skin surface) provides additional treatment if you have had expert instruction in its use. The same applies to an antivenin kit. If you carry ethyl chloride be sure to get the metal tube type of container with the small valve at the top rather

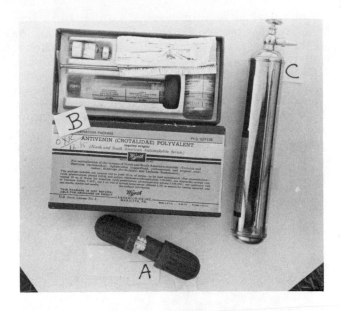

ANTIVENIN KIT (A), ETHYL CHLORIDE (B), AND CUTTER SUCTION KIT (C). These are good items to have when traveling in a remote area where rattlesnakes are prevalent. The same antivenin is also effective for water moccasin and copperhead snake bite.

than the glass bottle type of container. Make no mistake about it, antivenin kits and ethyl chloride are dangerous materials to "fool" with.

If the trail goes along cliffs, walk several feet out from the face of the cliff. Then if a rattlesnake is coiled on a ledge of the cliff, you will probably avoid being bitten. A bite on the face, or on the trunk of the body, is much more serious than on an arm or leg.

It may be of some comfort to know that most persons in good health (except very young or very old) would recover from the average rattlesnake bite even if it were not treated, but don't count on it. Know the first aid treatment for snake bite and use it if the occasion arises, which it probably never will. If you are interested in statistics, in the United States about 3,400 persons are bitten each year by poisonous snakes. Of this number about sixty persons die. It is believed that intense fear on the part of the victim is an important factor in most of these deaths.

ANIMALS

There are no animals in our wilderness areas that will cause you any harm if you leave them alone and do not get too close to them. They will normally go out of their way to avoid you. Never try to corner or capture a wild animal. This applies to everything from a chipmunk to a deer or bear. Particularly avoid getting close to young deer fawns or bear cubs. The mother will usually be close by and may give you a hard time. When in camp keep food stored out of reach of animals, preferably in bags suspended by ropes from trees or on a very high clothesline. Keep food out of tents and away from where you sleep. Most animals have a keen sense of smell, and they will sometimes enter a camp area in search of food. Food stored in your tent may encourage the animals to come in. On rare occasions a bear or other animal may enter a tent during the night, even though there are persons sleeping there, if you have food stored in the tent with you. A candy bar in your pocket is food, and the smell is readily picked up by some wild animals.

The most dangerous wild animals are not the completely wild ones, but rather those that are partially tame. Normally wild animals are more afraid of you than you are of them. The bears in some of our National Parks are examples of partly tame wild animals. In some areas of the Parks, the bears become so accustomed to people that they are no longer afraid of them. In fact, they may become quite agressive about coming into camp, stealing food or begging for it, and getting into mischief. As long as you leave these animals completely alone, and keep food and other attractions out of their reach, there is normally nothing to fear from them. When you start feeding them by hand, teasing them, and so forth, it is a different story. You may end up without a hand, or worse! Observe all wild animals from a respectful distance and do nothing more than observe. If you want a close-up photograph use a telescopic lens.

As you hike along a mountain trail, if you see many good sized rocks that have been freshly turned over, a bear has probably been along that trail recently. A bear will often do this in looking for beetles, grubs, ants, and other insect "tidbits." Most bears have a keen sense of smell but poor eyesight. You may see a bear coming toward you before he sees you. If you do, just "ease away" and go around. Don't run. If you run a bear or other animal is more likely to chase after you.

A particular danger when traveling in bear country is to come upon a bear unexpectedly, at close range. Their reaction when surprised is generally unpredictable. If you are traveling where thick vegetation, brush, or terrain may lead to a surprise encounter with a bear, carry a whistle or bell. (Loud conversation or other noise will help, if you don't have these.) Blow on the whistle frequently when you are in or near thick brush. The bell can be fastened to your pack where it will provide a continuous sound as you hike. Bears hearing the noise will take off in the opposite direction.

If you make camp for the night near a stream, don't set up camp right at the edge of the stream. Bears will often follow along a stream during the night. Stay back from the stream a good fifty feet or more. Do your cooking and keep all food stored a good distance from tents or sleeping bags. To put a sleeping bag down in the area of your cooking fire where food odors persist and bits of food are scattered about is inviting possible disaster. That is just where a bear will go if he enters camp. If you use a previously used camp site you should normally do your cooking, if by open fire, where a fire was previously built. If you should observe any dirt in the camp area that is freshly turned over, garbage may have been buried there, and a bear was probably digging for it. Keep your tent or sleeping bag away from such places. The bear will probably be back.

PREDATOR TRAPS

A possible source of danger, particularly to backwoods travelers in the Western States, is predator traps. These take a variety of forms, which normally are of no consequence if you are reasonably alert, but they are not to be fooled with. The U.S. Fish and Wildlife Service is one branch of the government that engages in predator control. An example of one predator device is the cyanide gun. A cyanide gun takes a special cartridge and discharges a load of cyanide. It is sometimes used in controlling coyotes in an over populated area. The gun mechanism is usually buried below the surface of the ground except for one small projecting part. This is the "business end" which is baited with food or a scent attractive to coyotes. When a coyote finds the bait and tugs at it he gets a shot of cyanide in the mouth, which results in quick death. Poison meat and poison grain are sometimes used in predator control also, but a hiker should have no occasion to expose himself to these hazards.

Still other devices used in animal control are game traps. These generally take the form of a small cage, which is baited so as to cause the door of the cage to close when the animal tugs at the bait. Bears are frequently live-trapped by such devices in order to transfer them to another locality.

There are rather strict procedures pertaining to the use of devices such as those mentioned. One of the procedures is to place conspicuous signs at all places where these controls are employed, warning persons that such a device is close by and not to tamper with it. Obviously, such warnings should be rigidly observed. As

you travel in remote areas, if you should come across any piece of mechanical equipment or other man-made item, leave it strictly alone. Blasting caps are an example of such equipment, frequently found in remote areas. They have turned more than one hiking and camping trip into a tragedy. If you should discover a blasting cap, don't touch it! Note its location carefully, and report it to the nearest Forest Service Office.

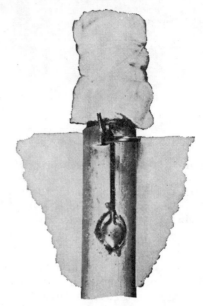

COYOTE GUN. This is the "business end" of a coyote gun, with a "wad" of scented bait projecting a few inches above ground. (The remainder of the gun is buried.) A coyote, tugging on the bait, discharges the gun and gets a shot of cyanide (and sure death). If you come across such a device leave it alone. (Photo furnished by courtesy of Fish and Wildlife Service.)

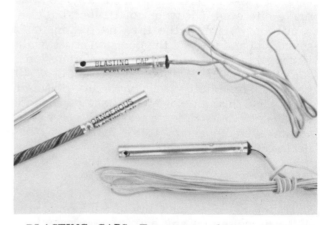

BLASTING CAPS. Two types of caps are shown. Those with wires are electric caps. Such caps are often found in an area where there has been construction work or mining. They are very dangerous. If found, leave them alone and report their location to the nearest authorities.

WATER SUPPLY

It is very important to keep in mind when planning your day-to-day route the location of all sources of water. If potable water sources are more than four or five hours apart, you should seriously consider another route or make very certain that you have ample water for every member of the party, plus some to spare. In determining whether a spring or other water source is safe for drinking, observe the plants and aquatic life in and about the spring. The water may be crystal clear but, if it is completely free of small aquatic insects and other life, it is highly suspect. The water in many mountain streams and from most springs in the mountains will be safe to drink without treatment of any kind, but not always. If there is any doubt, boil it or treat it with halazone or other water purification tablets. When you wash dishes throw the dirty dish water on the ground away from the campsite, not into the stream. Unless publicly approved, swimming and bathing in mountain lakes and streams should only be done in very remote areas, never in generally frequented areas. In many of the high mountain lakes swimming can be quite dangerous.

WATCH YOUR STEP

When hiking on a wilderness trail, don't walk along with your "head in the clouds." Watch your step! Few wilderness trails are level like city sidewalks. There will be holes, loose stones, tree roots, and other things in the trail over which you may stumble and fall. When you stumble, it is much more difficult to recover your balance with a full pack (or if you are tired) than it is without a pack. Stepping at an odd angle on a loose stone may give you a wrenched ankle, which will be very unpleasant to say the least. It can even mean the end of the trip.

Keep your eye on the trail. This doesn't mean you can't glance up once in a while as you hike along, but govern the length of your glances according to the difficulty of the trail. If it is really rugged, you had best watch where you "pick 'em up and set 'em down." If you like to admire the scenery under such circumstances (and who doesn't?), stop frequently on your feet for a few seconds in order to do so.

Remember when hiking through rugged country or through brush that your pack projects beyond your body outline and that places where your body may squeeze through, or just slip by, may not allow your pack to do so. When you are going along at a good clip and your pack suddenly catches on a tree limb or other projection, it can be a rude awakening, and it can mean a spill. If you are crossing a "bridge" provided by a fallen tree and your pack catches on a limb, it can tumble you off the tree and into the creek or whatever else is below.

In going up a short steep slope that has loose rock on it, go up one hiker at a time. Those standing below should be out of the way where they will not be struck by rocks dislodged by the person making his way up.

In crossing swift mountain streams, rig a hand line across the stream and use it, even though the stream may be only a foot or so deep. If you are using a waist belt on your pack, unbuckle the belt in crossing such places. You should also loosen up your shoulder straps at bad crossings so that you can slip out of your pack quickly if the need occurs. In crossing swift streams, keep sideways with the current. Walk at a quartering downstream angle. A walking staff may prove useful in steadying yourself but should not take the place of a hand line in swift water. In some places, you may want to rig a "trolley" and move your packs over separately. Your footing in a swift stream will usually be more secure without your pack. Use tennis shoes or a similar type of shoe to protect your feet when wading, rather than attempting to wade with bare feet or in your hiking shoes.

CAVES, MINE SHAFTS

Unless the trip is specifically planned to include the exploration of caves (under expert guidance), they should be avoided. Special equipment and clothing is required in the science of cave exploration (speleology). Abandoned mine shafts will be found in some remote areas. Avoid them like you would avoid the plague.

YOUR GENERAL WELL-BEING

Although not exactly in the category of accident prevention, there are certain things you can do on a backpack trip that will benefit your general well-being and thus help you to get more enjoyment out of the trip. Here are a few of them:

DRINK WATER FREELY. You will frequently be so engrossed in what you are doing that you will actually forget or neglect to drink enough water. You will probably be perspiring considerably, and your body will lose water as well as salt. Make a point of taking a drink of water at least once each hour. If you are perspiring freely or have been exerting strenuously, it is a good idea to take a bit of salt with it, or take a salt tablet one to three times a day. The extra salt is very important.

AVOID OVER-FATIGUE. Don't push yourself to exhaustion. Especially go slow for the first day or two until you see how much you can take. Get at least eight hours of sleep each night, and preferably nine or ten.

In addition to inadequate sleep, fatigue can also be caused by concern and worry. If you have never carried a thirty-five pound pack for twelve miles through the mountains on a hot day, you will have some apprehension the first time you try it. While you are on the trail, this apprehension is going to increase the fatigue that you would normally experience from such physical effort. After the hike is accomplished, this apprehension is going to give way to a sense of elation because of your accomplishment, and some of your fatigue will disappear. It is not unusual for beginning backpackers to become so fatigued during the last few miles of hiking into a remote area that they can "hardly take another step." Upon reaching camp they are so elated that they then want to go for another hike around the area. The cure for fatigue due to apprehension is practice. When you are confident of your ability and you keep your efforts within the bounds of that ability, this kind of mental fatigue is no problem.

If you have been so unfortunate as to acquire a blister or sprained ankle, concentrating on the pain will cause fatigue in a hurry. If you have properly treated the blister or other problem, take your mind off it. Think about a recent pleasant activity or a contemplated one, but don't allow yourself the luxury of concentrating on the pain or other negative thoughts. Your mind and your attitude have a real and important bearing on how well you feel and how fatigued you become. Carry on a conversation, hum a tune, or joke with one another to avoid monotony. The miles and the hours will pass much faster and at the same time be more enjoyable.

KEEP REGULAR. Your daily routine will be changed quite a bit from your normal habits when you go on a backpack trip. Individuals who have very regular bowel habits at home may find themselves having difficulty on a backpack trip. Two to four milk of magnesia tablets, taken daily, will provide a mild and harmless laxative and keep you "regular." These are usually mint flavored and easy to take. More stubborn cases may require the use of glycerin suppositories, and a few of these may prove useful. They are also harmless.

A SUNTAN. No matter how great the temptation, do not try to acquire a suntan on a backpack trip. Most of the hikers who do so end up wishing they hadn't. You will get plenty of sun without purposely exposing yourself. Even though they wear a hat, long-sleeved shirt, etc., most persons need the help of a protective cream or lotion on their hands and face to keep the skin from getting too dry and uncomfortable. The back of the neck is particularly susceptible to sunburn. Your pack may offer some protection, depending upon how high it is and the angle of the sun. A broad-brimmed hat will help. A bandana worn as a neckerchief is good. Don't overlook the backs of your hands when applying sun protective cream. It's a susceptible spot. If your nose gets dry and "crusty" inside, put a bit of cream on a paper tissue, and coat the inside of your nose with it.

YOUR FEET. Take care of your feet. They must get you where you are going and bring you back again. Carry some moleskin patches in your pocket. At the first sign (don't wait for a rest stop, meal stop, or until camp at night) of a tender spot on your foot or toe, stop and put a moleskin patch over it. In this way you will probably avoid a blister. If you do not have moleskin, put plain adhesive tape over the tender spot (not a Band-Aid) and leave it there. When you have a chance during the day, wash your feet. Use clean socks and change them daily even if they do not appear very dirty. If your feet sweat considerably, you will want to change your socks more often. In this case, have a pair of extra socks handy and change them as necessary. Hang the sweat-soaked socks on the outside of your pack, so that they will dry as you hike along. The use of a good foot powder may also be desirable.

EATING. Eat several substantial meals each day rather than one or two lighter meals and a heavy meal. Eat plenty of proteins and fruits. Never eat heavily or even normally just before you are about to undertake a hard climb or other strenuous physical activity. Before starting a really hard climb, eat very lightly, if at all. For example, eat several pieces of jerky. At intermediate points during the climb eat some dried fruit or candy if you feel the need for it. When the climb is finished then eat a bit more — to hold you until time for the next regular meal. In general you will probably eat quite a bit more on a backpack trip than you would at home. However, being on a backpack trip should not be reason for stuffing yourself with food. You will feel better and enjoy the trip more if you keep this in mind. Never eat large quantities of food in an attempt to combat fatigue. For true physical fatigue you need rest and a moderate quantity of food, if any, preferably eaten after the rest.

DISHWASHING. One of the most common illnesses in backpacking is dysentery. This is usually picked up from unclean dishes or from soap left on dishes during the dishwashing operation. Prevention is not difficult. You may rough-clean your dirty dishes with sand, snow, grass or other natural materials. Regardless of how clean they may appear, however, this should always be followed by washing all dishes and cooking utensils thoroughly in hot soapy water, followed by a good rinsing in very hot water that has been boiled for a few minutes. An important camp rule is that each person drinks only from his own canteen and that eating utensils are never shared.

KEEP CLEAN. Don't be too fussy about your clothes. They are going to get dirty, but good. However, good body cleanliness can still be maintained. In warm weather plan to bathe fully every day. With a few changes of water, plus some skill and dexterity, you can take a full-fledged bath from a one pound coffee can. Or, you may prefer to carry a canvas or plastic wash basin for the purpose. Water for bathing can be heated in cooking utensils over the campfire, and the shadows of the night will provide the necessary privacy. Getting back to clothes again, don't be too fussy about their appearance, but a few reasonable precautions will help a bit. Don't wipe your hands on your trousers after cleaning the fish. Don't sit in the dirt when you can find a clean rock or log to sit on. When your hands get black from the cooking pans, wash them instead of wiping them on your clothes.

Remember that the temperature of the body is greatly affected by the temperature of the extremeties (head, arms, legs). Therefore, bathing your face, hands, and arms frequently on a hot day will help you to keep cool and feel better, as well as to keep clean. That piece of thin toweling in your hip pocket will come in handy when you want to sponge off. Or, in the dry climate of some of our western states, you may prefer to remain wet and let the air do the drying. If you have an opportunity during the day, wash off your feet and legs also.

FIRST AID

You may make trip after trip into the wilderness and never need to use any first aid beyond putting a Band-Aid on a cut finger. The nature of first aid, however, requires that the supplies and techniques be available for use at a moment's notice. There are a number of good books on first aid and this book therefore does not go into the techniques of first aid. It is desired, however, to stress two things: (1) practice safety, so that you will avoid the need for first aid, and (2) know your first aid well and have the essential first aid supplies and knowledge at your fingertips, ready for action if and when an emergency occurs. How long has it been since you thoroughly reviewed a first aid book? Are you sure you know the difference between sunstroke and heat exhaustion? The symptoms and treatment are very different. Heat exhaustion, in varying degrees, is quite common. Do you know your first aid well enough that you will not panic when the need occurs to really put it to good test? Giving an injured or sick person the wrong first aid treatment is frequently worse than if you gave them no treatment at all. Look over the contents of your first aid kit and review the techniques!

Aftermath of a forest fire. These photos were taken soon after a fire had ravished many acres of good forest land, not far from the author's home. Within one to three years time insects will move in and will "finish off" the charred trees that remain standing. Please put out your fires!

8

On The Trail

THE DAILY ROUTINE

It is best to start the day soon after dawn. You can hike more miles with much less effort in the cool of the morning than in the afternoon. If you have breakfast at 6 A.M., you should stop for lunch at 11 A.M. There is often a tendency to "keep pushing" and lunch sometimes ends up at one or two o'clock in the afternoon. This puts the whole day off schedule and you will probably find yourself getting very tired and maybe "headachy" by midafternoon. Starting lunch at about eleven o'clock, you will be ready to hit the trail again by about twelve o'clock. Another four hours of hiking and you should be ready to make camp by 4 or 4:30 P.M. When you get tired on the trail, or winded, don't sit down to rest. Instead, stop often on your feet. You will travel much further than if you stop less often but for longer periods. Also, you will probably stiffen up if you sit or lie down. Don't try to make an endurance contest out of your hiking. Give consideration to the slower and inexperienced members of your group. On the other hand those members should properly prepare themselves for the trip, insofar as possible, by taking some preconditioning hikes before the trip and checking out their pack and gear. Get plenty of sleep. At home you may get by easily with eight hours of sleep. On a backpack trip you will probably find that ten hours of sleep more nearly fills the bill.

SETTING THE PACE

Hike with some spring in your step, and with toes pointed forward rather than outward. Walk with a determined pace, not hurried, but as though you were going someplace. Never run, trot, or even walk extremely fast with a pack on your back. Keep hands out of pockets and don't carry gear in your hands. Normally if there is gear left over that you have to carry in your hands, you are not properly packed. Although your pack will interfere somewhat, swing your arms a bit rather than letting them hang like dead weights. Don't saunter or stroll. Too slow a pace is just as tiring as too fast. Anyone who has ever led a slow-moving, stubborn, one-speed pack animal along a wilderness trail knows how tiring an unnaturally slow pace can be.

If you are climbing a very steep trail, use a slow but steady pace and stop often on your feet for fifteen or twenty seconds, rather than pushing yourself to the point of "giving out" and then stopping for a longer period. If you feel a bit light-headed, prop one foot up on a rock or log (with your arm resting on your thigh) when you stop for a breather, and lean over (keeping your pack on) so that your head is about at the level of your hips. If you are exerting hard over a period of time, drink some salt water or take a salt tablet, even though you are not visibly sweating a great deal. (In the dry climate of some of our western states you can be perspiring heavily and hardly notice it.) If the weather is hot, stop for a "breather" in the shade. If it is cool, stop in the sun.

Do not cut across switchbacks. They are there for a reason. The switchback represents the easiest, energy-conserving route up (or down) the slope. Further, cutting across switchbacks leads to erosion.

Take every precaution to avoid sweating when the weather is cool. On a cool morning you may start hiking while wearing an extra shirt, sweater, or other heavy clothing. In your desire to keep moving down the trail, you may forget or neglect to stop and remove unneeded outer layers of clothing when you warm up. This is a serious mistake. Heavy exertion can take the place of a lot of clothing insofar as keeping you warm is concerned. It is far better to be a bit cool when you are exerting than to be perspiring. On a cool day, if you allow your shirt to become wet with perspiration your body is going to cool down rapidly as soon as you stop or slow down in your exertion. Wet clothing quickly loses its insulating value. Also, the evaporation of the water from your perspiration-soaked shirt or jacket will cool your body too suddenly. This is why several layers of clothing are better in cool weather than a single heavy layer. You have a better range of adjustment to suit the outside temperature.

When on the trail, hikers should walk in single file and should not follow one another too closely. A distance of twenty-five to fifty feet between hikers is usually about right but in open terrain it can be greater. It is very annoying to have a hiker follow so closely that each time you stop or change pace a bit he has to do likewise to keep from running over you. On the other hand, hikers should keep together as a group, unless they specifically plan to break up into more than one group. The leader should not need to make frequent checks to determine where certain members are. Stragglers should be eliminated at home before the trip starts, not on the trail.

For groups of more than several persons, the leader should appoint experienced and responsible "assistant leaders" to help in maintaining the right pace while on the trail. These "assistant leaders" will be spaced evenly along the line of hikers. By their experience they will know when the pace should be slowed or speeded up and when to take "breathers." By visual contact hikers will in turn know when to change their pace. In most of the short stops that hikers will make during the day, of a few seconds to one or two minutes in duration, they will be stopping in their individual places, not as a group. If too many stops are made as a group, an "accordion

effect" results. When the leader stops it takes from a few seconds to several minutes for the nearest and furthest away hiker, in turn, to catch up. By the time those furthest away have caught up (or before) the leader is ready to move on again. This can be pretty exasperating, particularly to those furthest from the leader. One of the reasons you came on this trip was to "get away from it all," including crowds of people (remember?). Your backpack trip will give you more of a feeling of a wilderness adventure as an individual if your trail pace and stops are patterned along the lines described.

A factor that will sometimes govern the distance between hikers is dust. If there is much dirt in the trail it will often become ground to a powderlike consistency. This is particularly true of trails that are heavily traveled and those frequented by animal pack trains. Each hiker will stir up his own little dust cloud in hiking along such a trail. Walking in one another's dust is not only unpleasant but it is actually harmful to your lungs and to your health in general. Therefore it is recommended that on dusty trails the distance between hikers be such that walking in dust clouds is not necessary.

Animal pack trains may be encountered on some of the main trails of our National Forests and Parks. These animals and their handlers have the right of way over foot travelers. When you see such a pack train approaching, step well off the trail (on the outside edge) and stand quietly while they pass. Any sudden movements you make can readily cause some animals to shy and give their handlers real trouble. Practice courtesy.

TRAIL STOPS

If you make stops along the trail during which you remove your pack (whether they are rest stops, lunch stops, or whatever else), keep your equipment together. Don't set your pack one place, lean your fishing rod against a tree another place, and put your camera or canteen on a rock in still another place. It is recommended, in such temporary stops, that you set your pack on the ground and that camera, binoculars, canteen, or anything else that is not in the pack be set on the ground beside it. In this way you will probably avoid such problems as getting two or three miles down the trail and suddenly remembering that you left your camera hanging from a convenient limb on a nearby tree at the last rest stop. In stopping for lunch, set your pack and gear back far enough from the work area (where you are getting lunch) that other hikers do not have to stumble over it and possibly step on some piece of gear in the process. Such stepped-on (and possibly broken) gear is usually considered to be the responsibility of the hiker who left it there, not the person who stepped on it. It is best to lean your pack against a tree trunk, bush, or rock, away from the work area, and put any other items of equipment right beside it. Fishing rods not fastened to the pack should be propped against the pack or something else so that they are off the ground. More than one backpack trip has been seriously affected and bruised feelings have resulted from leaving fishing rods lying on the ground and having them stepped on. The same general idea applies in camp also. Stow your gear in one place, insofar as possible, and keep it away from the general work area where others are working and walking about.

It is much more tiring to stand still with a full pack on your back than to walk with it. If a trail stop is to be more than three or four minutes long, it is best to remove your pack. Getting out of your pack and getting it back on again is a maneuver that calls for some skillful manipulation and gymnastics, but it is not difficult once you get the "hang" of it. In removing your pack, bend far forward so that the full weight of the pack is resting on the middle of your back and it is loose at the shoulders. Now remove one arm from its shoulder strap. Then "roll" the pack off the other arm with a swinging motion, lowering it to the ground, while steadying it with the free arm. Putting the pack back on is just the reverse. Lay the pack on the ground with the back panel facing upward. Lift the pack with a hand on each shoulder strap, momentarily balance the pack on your left knee as you roll it onto your back, slipping the left arm under its shoulder strap in the process. Keep your body bent far forward, make like a contortionist, and work your free right arm into the other shoulder strap. While still bent forward, grab the lower ends of your pack with your hands and push upwards, then let the pack settle back down onto your shoulders, straighten up your body, and you are in business. Some hikers prefer to help one another in and out of their packs, but most experienced backpackers prefer to do the operation by themselves even though it is a bit more difficult without help. With a good rock or tree trunk to lean your pack against, you can also wriggle in and out of it from a sitting position. In getting up from a sitting position with a full pack, first turn your body so that you are in a kneeling position on the ground. Then push up from the ground with your arms and your legs.

There are no rest rooms along backwoods trails. Toilet stops should be selected according to the terrain and privacy afforded by natural cover. For a mixed group, one sex can go to the left of the trail while another goes to the right. If the terrain will not accommodate this arrangement, men can go forward on the trail for a suitable distance while women remain behind for an agreed period of time. All human refuse should be thoroughly covered, without exception, making use of "cat holes" where possible. If there is a mixed group, designate two separate toilet areas at each meal stop and campsite also. These areas should be in essentially opposite directions. Make sure all members know where each toilet area is. Making this clear will be far less embarrassing than the possible consequences if you don't make it clear.

STAY ORIENTED

To be oriented means to know where you are. Unless you have been over a trail before and know it well, you probably cannot stay oriented without a map. Before you start out on a new trail, especially one in a remote area, make every reasonable effort to find and talk to some person who is familiar with that trail. Ask them about check points and prominent landmarks that will help you to stay on the trail. Inquire about those places where you are likely to miss a turn and lose the trail.

From the time you leave the roadhead, follow your progress on the map. A stream crossing, a swamp, a spring, and a mountain peak in the distance (that will provide a compass bearing) are all good check points that will appear on a topographic map and help you to stay oriented. A fallen tree across the trail, an abandoned cabin, a prominent rock formation, and so forth, are possible check points that you should ask others about because they won't appear on a map.

Keep in mind where the trail is going. The purpose of a trail is to get from one point to another. It will usually be the shortest route, consistent with the terrain. Most trails in the West, as well as some other regions, are laid out to accommodate horses and pack animals. If you find yourself scrambling among boulders, confronted by very many logs in the trail, going through thick brush, or using your hands to negotiate a steep slope, then you are probably on a deer trail and off your chosen trail. Trails having very many of the obstacles mentioned would not normally be used for horse travel.

Most frequently the trail that you will be following will have been blazed by the Forest Service. Depending on the wilderness, national forest, or other area you may be in, and the frequency of usage of the trail, its general condition may be very good, fair, or "pretty rough." A main trail will usually have small, neat signs at the takeoff from the roadhead showing the trail name or number and the distance to the major objectives. Along the trail, at points of intersection with other trails, there will frequently be additional signs showing where those trails go and the distance, as well as the remaining distance of your trail to its objective. Blazes on trees, usually about shoulder height off the ground, will give you reassurance as you hike along that you are on the trail. Where the trail cuts into the mountainside, the outside edge will frequently be reinforced with logs or stones to prevent erosion. On steep slopes, more stones or log formations will often be laid across the trail for the same purpose. Such trails are usually very easy to follow. Except for reading the signs along the trail and an occasional reference to your map, no significant effort is required to stay on the right trail.

If you believe that all trails in our national park or wilderness system are as described above, prepare yourself for a rude awakening. It isn't so. On most government trails there will still be the sign at the roadhead, but that may be the last one you will see for a good while if you are in a remote area. Availability of manpower for maintaining the trail and infrequency of usage simply make it impractical to accomplish any more maintenance than perhaps the occasional removal of a large tree that falls across the trail and makes it impassable for horses. The blazes may be very old and faint or obscured from sight by growing limbs.

Deer paths that intersect with your desired trail may be more used than the trail itself and can easily lead hikers to follow them and get off the main trail. The trail that appears as a good solid line on the map you are holding in your hand may be faint indeed, in actuality, and overgrown with weeds and brush. The writer well remembers one trail turn-off that has been marked for many years by a rusted horseshoe and a more rusted condensed milk can, hanging by a rope from a low bush (no other marking).

Is all of this bad? Not by a long shot. Few of us that have frequented such areas would want it any other way. We do not particularly look forward to "progress" and improvements dictated by advancement of "civilization" into such areas. This will call for replacement of such markings by small neat signs and "brushing up" the trail, and the area will then be frequented by more people.

This is simply mentioned so that you won't take too much for granted in your pretrip planning when you study that nice, pretty map, with its very distinct lines marking the trails. What may appear as a very easy problem in path finding when the map is spread out on your living room table at home may be much more of a problem when you are out there in the mountains with the sun boiling down, perhaps a bit fatigued, and trying to figure out "where the heck the trail went to."

As you progress along the trail, keep a mental or written record of important check points that you pass and the time of day that you pass them. Fix in your mind the approximate time that you should arrive at the next check point. When you arrive at a check point, make sure that it is the particular check point that you think it is. (There may be lots of stream crossings, more than one spring, and more than one fallen tree in the area where you are looking for such a check point.)

Keep a mental note of your general direction of travel. The trail will continue in a given general direction as shown on the map except where it is necessary to temporarily deviate to avoid difficult or impassable terrain. These deviations may not be apparent on a map and at times they may amount to a complete change in general direction. In some unusual situations it is possible to get so turned around that you may start back down the trail in the direction you just came from. In foggy or stormy weather, where there is no sun to aid you in determining general directions, it is a good idea to take a look at your compass occasionally. In using a compass be sure that the close proximity of a pocket knife or similar metallic object is not affecting its reading. Simple as it may seem, make very sure you know which end of the needle points north (before you get in a situation where you must know).

Your trail may top out on a windswept, rocky ridge where there are no trees to be blazed. You may assume that it goes on down the other side of the ridge, but when you look there you don't find it. The heat of the noonday sun, fatigue, and your anxiety to keep going ahead may impair your judgment. You finally pick up a trail on the other side of the ridge and follow it. However, you may have picked up a deer trail and after a while you decide it's the wrong one. Backtrack! Don't go cross country, even for a short distance, in the hope of picking up the right trail. Chances are that going cross country will require more time and energy than back tracking. There is a good chance that you may cross your desired trail at a place where it is a bit obscure, not recognize it, and keep right on going. You may soon become thoroughly lost.

Your trail may lead down into a dry arroyo. You assume that it crosses the arroyo and continues on up the other side. However, when you look for the trail on the other side it is not there. In all probability the trail has gone right up the middle of the arroyo (or down) in order to pick up a better section of terrain for climbing out. There may not be any trees lining the arroyo which are suitable for blazing, hence the trail is not marked there (and right when you most needed that marking). Water rushing down the arroyo after an occasional rain has obliterated any sign of the path on the ground. These little problems add to the difficulty (and pleasure) of backpacking. They are most apt to occur in remote areas, off the beaten path. That ten dollars per day and food that the ranch boy wanted for guiding your party may start to look rather insignificant about this time. Before you go into remote areas be sure that your technique, your knowledge of the area, and your general preparedness are a match for the job at hand.

LEAVING THE TRAIL

There will be some occasions during backpack trips when you will want to temporarily leave the trail you are following. This may be for the purpose of exploring a particular area, rock hunting, fishing, or some similar objective. If it is just a short side trip you may not need to mark your path in order to find your way back to the main trail again. For a longer distance, possibly an overnight hike to a particular point of interest, it may be desirable to take some special precautions.

Do not blaze trees in order to mark your trail. This is prohibited in many areas. When you leave a main trail and want to mark your path, there are a number of ways of doing so without blazing trees; these will take much less energy than tree blazing and be just as effective for temporary marking. First there is the matter of simply making mental notes of your position, prominent features in the terrain, and following your progress on a map or sketch of the area. Stop and look backward occasionally. It is surprising how different the same area can look when viewed from various angles. If you come to a particular spot where you think you may have trouble staying on the trail on the way out, make a note of it on a three by five inch card or in a small notebook, take a compass reading on the back trail and prominent objects, and record them.

If you want to mark the trail in some stretches, you can use a grease pencil to make a small marking on rocks. It will deteriorate in a few weeks and you have not marred the landscape. You can also use eight or ten inch lengths of crepe paper and tie them to tree limbs and bushes with a single overhand knot. They too

This trail marker is made by Sport House, Box 103, Concord, Mass. It is unusual in that it is made of a gelatinous material. It completely disappears with the first rain. (No litter!).

will deteriorate in a few weeks, and in much less time if there is rain. A somewhat more permanent marking, but one which will also deteriorate in several months, is to use ten inch lengths (about one inch wide) of lightweight cloth, such as parachute cloth. Put a number on each strip of cloth with a felt tip marker before leaving home. When you mark the trail with it, enter a description of the back trail in your notebook, identifying the note with the number on the cloth strip. There are a number of good books available on use of map, and compass and it is recommended that you read one or more of them before going on a wilderness trip. The purpose of marking a trail, as suggested, is to find your way back along the same route. You can therefore pick up the cloth or paper markers on the way out. You may miss a few, but they will deteriorate.

Occasionally during a backpack trip it may be desirable for trip members to be temporarily separated. This may occur during a period of fishing, rock hunting, wild life observation, and so forth. It is recommended in such case that all persons travel with one or more companions, rather than alone. Sometimes it happens that you don't know whether a group or certain individuals are ahead on the trail or behind. This can cause some anxiety, as well as wasted effort in locating them. For example, some persons by prearrangement may be traveling parallel to the trail but 100 yards or more to one side. This sometimes happens when fishermen are fishing a section of mountain stream that parallels a trail. Engrossed in what they are doing, they fail to notice whether certain companions have moved on ahead. They finally make their way back to the trail, but they don't know whether to hurry and catch up or sit down and wait.

This problem can be solved in several ways. If it is a small group, persons traveling along the trail can use a stick and make a distinctive mark (such as an "X," "—," or "O") where there is soft dirt in the trail, doing so each several hundred yards or more. Other companions coming along the trail will see that mark and will know that the person or group assigned that particular mark is somewhere ahead on the trail. Distinctive colors of crepe paper, tied on tree limbs or bushes, or small cards bearing initials or a name (and hour) and impaled or tied to twigs, can be used in the same manner. The last person(s) coming down the trail can pick up the pieces of paper or cards and burn them at the next camp site.

MAPS AND TRAIL INFORMATION

On most backpack trips you should provide yourself with some maps of the area, as well as sketches and notes that you make yourself. Depending upon the area that you choose for your backpacking adventure, the following are sources of maps that will usually be found helpful.

U.S. FOREST SERVICE. The U.S. Forest Service has maps of the National Forests and Wilderness Areas, which are available to the public free of charge. These may be obtained by writing to the Supervisor of the National Forest for the forest or wilderness that you are interested in. A list of the national forest and wilderness areas is given in Appendix E. The Forest Service maps generally show trails, streams, springs, prominent mountains, fences, and buildings (if any). They do not have contour lines.

The Forest Service maps generally show trails, streams, springs, prominent mountains, fences, and buildings (if any). They do not have contour lines.

If you have some questions concerning the area you plan to pack into, write to the nearest Forest Service office. The writer has always found members of the Forest Service to be very helpful in furnishing information on forest and stream conditions, trails, and in supplying similar data important to the planning of a backpack trip.

U.S. GEOLOGICAL SURVEY. The maps published by the U.S. Geological Survey will be found very helpful in most backpacking. These maps show all of the important natural features, as well as trails, roads, and isolated buildings. Elevations are shown by contour lines and this is an important feature when traveling in rugged terrain. The quadrangle maps are most commonly used by backpackers. An index of the maps (free), as well as the maps themselves (costing about fifty cents each), is available from the U.S. Geological Survey. (See Appendix F for address.)

TRAIL ORGANIZATIONS. Detailed maps and information on the Pacific Crest Trail are available from the Sierra Club. Information on the Appalachian Trail is available from The Appalachian Trail Conference. Helpful information on the Long Trail, which winds along the Green Mountains in Vermont, can be obtained from the Green Mountain Club. (See Appendix F for addresses.)

OTHER SOURCES. The Chamber of Commerce of a city in the general vicinity of the area of interest will frequently be able to furnish some maps and information which will be of value. Large cities often have local hiking clubs, and the City Chamber of Commerce can furnish names and addresses of these clubs, if you are interested. Some states have a State Chamber of Commerce, usually located in the capitol city.

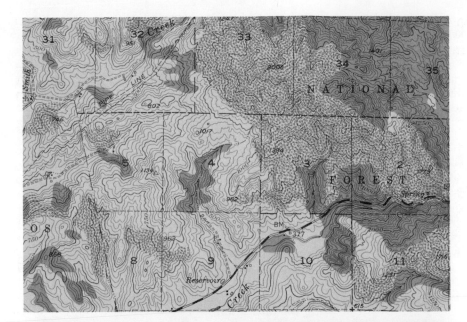

This is a section of a U.S. Geo-logical Survey map. This is the type of map most frequently carried by backpackers.

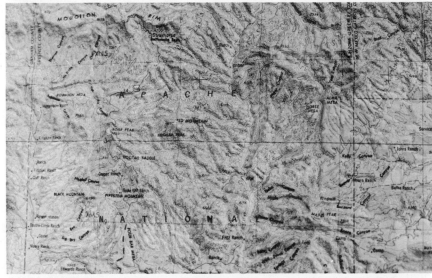

This is a plastic relief map. These maps are not suitable for carry-ing in the field. They are very useful in getting a "bird's-eye view" of the area you are pack-ing into and studying it over before the trip. These maps are available from the Army Map Service, Fort Sam Houston, Texas.

This is a close-up view of a small section of the map shown above. A framed map of this type, of your favorite backpacking area, makes a nice wall decoration for your den or study.

Practically all states have a state fish and game department, or its equivalent, which can furnish information that will frequently be helpful in your planning. Some of the suppliers listed in Appendix A have maps and books available giving detailed information on areas of particular interest to mountaineers and backpackers.

CARE OF MAPS

To protect your maps from moisture, dirt, and wear, it is recommended that you use transparent plastic which is available for this purpose in sheet form. You can get this from some of the suppliers listed in Appendix A and frequently at local stationery stores. When the paper backing is removed from one side of the transparent plastic, an adhesive surface is exposed onto which your map or map section is placed to accomplish a bond.

On many backpack trips you will only be concerned with a small area of the map, rather than the entire map. Don't carry a thirty inch by thirty inch map when you are interested only in a small part of the area shown on the map. Cut out the section of interest with a razor blade. (Reinsert it after the trip, using transparent tape.) When it is necessary to carry a large map, it should be folded with an accordion style fold. With the map face up, draw an imaginary horizontal line from west to east, dividing the map into two equal halves. Now fold the map along this horizontal line, back surface to back surface, with the printed side of the map on the outside. Next starting at the northwest corner of the map, fold it accordion style, into sections about four inches wide. When the folding is completed the northeast corner of the map will be on the outside. With this type of fold, you can read your map in the field without unfolding the entire map.

9

In Camp

GIVE YOURSELF TIME

As you hike along your trail, you will probably see many "picture book" campsites. Quite frequently, however, you may not find such a campsite when you need it most (when it's time to make camp). Once you have agreed on a time to make camp, you should usually take the first acceptable campsite that you reach within a half hour after that time, unless you are familiar with the area and know absolutely that a better campsite is only a short distance away. If you do this, you will probably avoid such problems as being caught in the darkness on the trail, still faced with finding a campsite, making camp, cooking your supper, and washing dishes. It takes the "fun" out of these activities if you have to do them after dark. It is also hard on flashlight batteries and dispositions. If you are traveling in the vicinity of a stream in late afternoon, don't leave that stream and go chugging off up the mountainside unless you know that there will be a water supply when it's time to camp. Better to camp early and have some leisure time than to be caught in an unfamiliar area, away from any water supply, and having to make a dry camp. Give yourself time to properly prepare your chosen campsite for the night, and to cook your evening meal. This usually means making camp a minimum of two hours before darkness.

CHOOSING A CAMPSITE

Many of the conditions pertaining to selection of a camp in general camping also apply to campsites for backpacking. However, some deserve special emphasis. Two prime requirements of a good campsite in backpacking are wood and water. (If you do your cooking on a portable stove, and carry a fuel supply, then wood is no problem.)

In planning your trip, the length of travel each day should be gauged so that you will have a stream or spring available as a water supply when it comes time to make camp. It is far better to underestimate how far you will travel in a day than to overestimate. It is possible to make a "dry camp" away from any water supply, but this should be avoided if possible.

You do not need to cook and eat in the immediate area of your campsite, however. For example, the general area chosen for camp may be along a stream that offers no nearby level places for beds. However, there may be a good level knoll several hundred yards above (higher than) the stream. You can lay out the sleeping bags and other gear on the knoll and take a five-minute hike down to the stream at mealtime.

When you first enter a prospective camp area, don't set up camp immediately. Spend a few minutes walking around and looking it over.

Hikers are frequently in too much of a hurry to set up camp. Then when it is about set up they discover one or more features that make them wish they had chosen another spot. Some other factors to be considered in selecting a campsite, in addition to wood and water, are:

On some backpack trips you will be packing into a base camp and then working out from there each day, returning to the same camp at night. In setting up such a base camp, give some consideration to locating it near prominent features in the terrain that will help you find it when returning at the end of a day's activities. For example, in a dense forest where the view is limited and many areas look pretty much alike, finding your way back to camp can turn out to be quite a chore. On returning to camp in a dense woods you may pass within a hundred yards of it, never see it, and pass right on by. (You now have a problem.) Try to set up such a base camp near a prominent tree, an unusual rock formation, the fork of a river or some other irregular feature in the terrain that will be of assistance in locating it.

Avoid a low, swampy area for a campsite, and stay away from thickets or dense undergrowth, particularly during insect season. An exposed area, on fairly high ground, where you get the benefit of any breeze, is a much better choice.

The natural inclination of a group when entering a clearing that they have chosen for a campsite is to select the biggest tree in the area and drop their duffle there. Soon after they will be laying out their beds in the same spot and otherwise preparing the camp for the night. The dead wood that you find lying on a forest floor comes largely from live trees, and it has to come off the tree sometime. It might come loose during the night while you are under it. Avoid picking out the biggest tree in the area and making your bed under it. (It may also attract lightning.) If you are camping where there are trees, pick out medium size trees and look them over carefully for dead limbs before you decide to make your bed there.

Hikers have been known to make their beds right in the middle of ant colonies. Look the ground over, as well as looking for nearby dead trees or dead limbs.

Pick out a spot that looks like it would drain well in the event of rain. Do not ditch your site, however, unless you are certain it is going to rain. If in doubt keep the ditching instrument (sharp rock, stick, etc.) handy but don't dig the ditch. Ditching mars the ground and leads to erosion. If you find it necessary to ditch, fill it in again before leaving the campsite.

Near the bottom of a rock slide is a poor place to camp. The rocks may slide some more.

Directly under a high cliff or near the bottom of a very steep slope is a poor place to camp. Animals moving about, or changes in weather, may dislodge stones or boulders and send them down into your camp area.

You should try and select an area that is generally level, and in particular has enough fairly level places of "sleeping bag size" to accommodate the number of persons in the party. However, no area will be absolutely level. A few inches in elevation where you choose to sleep may mean the difference between whether you stay dry in the event of rain or whether water runs into your sleeping bag area. Observe which way water is likely to flow over the ground in case of a hard rain. The nature of the ground surface is also an important consideration. Rain will not soak into hard packed, bare ground as it will into a forest floor or ground that has a covering of pine needles, grass, etc. Bare ground also means more difficulty in keeping your bedding and other gear clean. Spread out the individual sleeping sites, rather than cloistering them too close together. Again, one reason you probably had for making this trip was to get away from crowds. Most people like some privacy. This applies on a backpack trip as well as at home.

SETTING UP CAMP

One of the first things to do in making camp is to put up one or more short rope lines, as high as you can reach. Towels and any wet clothing should be hung on the line. Large bags containing food can also be hung from a short rope line or from limbs of trees. Keep all food off the ground except during meal preparation. Food left within reach of animals is inviting them to a treat, and they may accept the invitation. You can put rope, jack saw, sharpening stone, toilet tissue, soap and other common equipment in large plastic bags and hang these from a rope line also for ready accessibility by all members. Or, they can be put in some other designated place.

Individual members will soon be looking for suitable spots for their sleeping bags, and other personal gear will usually be stowed near their chosen spot for sleeping. Your pack should be suspended off the ground from a tree limb by a single short, stout cord, tied to the horizontal frame member where the top end of the shoulder straps meet. Do not leave packs on or near the ground. Some "irresponsible" porcupine or deer may feast on pack straps or other sweat-soaked equipment for the salt that is in them. If there is any doubt about your pack bag being waterproof, you should have a waterproof cover for it. Large heavyweight polyethylene bags, about fifteen by eighteen by thirty-two inches, sold by some of the suppliers listed in Appendix A, make a fairly good pack cover in camp. Unless your sleeping bag is inside a tent, it should also be kept off the ground until you are ready to make it up for the night.

You can stow your clothes in your pack or under your sleeping bag to keep them dry. Don't stow your clothes in these places, however, unless they are absolutely dry. A more desirable way of stowing clothes is to make a clothes hanger from a stick of wood, about one inch in diameter and sixteen inches long, and put your clothing on this. Using a stout cord about two feet long, tie a small loop at the center of the cord, then tie the ends of the cord to the ends of the stick. With another piece of cord, tied to the loop at the center of the first cord, suspend this "hanger" from a tree limb. Drape your shirt and trousers on the hanger and pin socks and other small items of clothing to it. If you suspect rain, better place a plastic bag over the whole business, bottom side up. Punch a small hole in the bag through which to thread the rope that suspends the hanger from the tree limb. Reinforce the edges of this hole with tape. Do not close the bag at the bottom.

MAKING YOUR BED

If the spot you select for your bed is not absolutely level (the usual case) you will be most comfortable if you put the head end of your sleeping bag at the higher end. Go over the ground carefully (on your hands and knees), and remove pine cones, rocks, and sharp twigs before putting down your air mattress or ground pad. Spend a good five minutes in doing this — more if the spot is not fairly smooth — and it will pay off. When your sleeping bag is on the ground and not in use keep it rolled up, at least loosely, with the head end in the middle of the roll. This will keep ants and other insects out of the bag.

If a poncho or rain fly of some kind is stretched over your sleeping bag, make sure that the outer edges of any ground cloth you may be using are well within the area covered by the rain fly. Otherwise, any rain running off the fly will fall on the exposed edge of the ground cloth, be unable to soak into the ground, and will run under your sleeping bag. You will become much wetter than if you used no ground cloth at all. If you use a ground cloth, mark one side of it (using a felt tip marker) with the word "UP" in large letters before leaving home. When you use the ground cloth, lay it on the ground so that the side marked "UP" is always the top side and the opposite side is next to the ground.

The ground side will collect dirt over a period of usage, and there is no point in having this dirt next to your good sleeping bag. In using a clear plastic ground cloth, in particular, it is not always obvious which side was next to the ground the last time it was used.

In putting up a plastic tarp or rain fly, use round or smooth rocks to anchor the sides. Sharp-cornered rocks will cause the plastic to tear where it contacts the corners of the rock, especially if there is a little wind. A one-foot length of 1/8 inch diameter shock cord, inserted in the ridge line, will provide "give" and help avoid tearing the plastic. Use plenty of rocks, very roughly the size of an indoor baseball, and anchor the sides securely so that they will not flap during the night. A little breeze can make a loose tarp flap loudly, and it sounds even louder when you are trying to sleep. You can also tie down corners or edges of a plastic tarp with heavy cord and small, smooth stones about an inch in diameter. Push the stone into the plastic and tie your cord around the bulge in the plastic on the opposite side.

Remember that it is the confined air in your sleeping bag that keeps you warm. Fluff it up well before going to bed. A feature of a goose down sleeping bag is that it has good resiliency. It will compress into a small bundle when pressure is applied and will spring back into a large volume when the pressure is released. It will therefore compress under your body while you sleep.

If you wake up cold at night, reach your arms outside of your sleeping bag and fluff up the sides and top with your hands. Now roll over, moving the sleeping bag with your body, so that the fluffed-up side is next to the ground and the compressed side is skyward. You are now lying on your stomach and you will need to roll over on your back carefully, without turning the sleeping bag with you. Do this and then fluff up the sides and top again with your hands and you are in business. By this time the sleeping bag hood is probably not where you want it so you may need to do a little more twisting and organizing. However, the sleeping bag has now been fluffed up on all sides, and you should sleep warmer for a while. If you have a liner in your sleeping bag there is not much point in trying this trick unless the liner is made of very smooth material and also firmly anchored to the inside of the sleeping bag at several points with tie tapes because it will get hopelessly twisted. If you are brave enough you can of course step out into the night air and fluff up your sleeping bag the "easy" way.

Walk around the area before dark and note the location of any large stones or logs that you may walk into or trip over after dark. Dead limbs or twigs at eye level are dangerous. Break them off or hang white rags, a towel, or paper on them, to avoid injury after dark. This precaution applies to the area around your sleeping site as well as to the camp in general.

BEFORE YOU GO TO SLEEP

Before you retire for the night, make sure you have certain items within reach of your sleeping bag. You may want your flashlight during the night. Once you have it you should be able to find other items within reach without too much groping around. After a hard day of hiking, regardless of how much water you drank during the day or in the early evening, it is not uncommon to wake up thirsty during the night. Have your canteen handy (within reach), with water in it. Just before going to sleep it may be a good idea to take one or two aspirins. You may not have a headache, but you will probably have a few muscles that are a bit tired and achy. A couple of aspirins will help you relax, ease those aches, and get a good night's sleep. If you are not under an insect screen, then have your insect lotion within reach in case you have to "do battle" during the night. Do you have the habit of thinking about the next day's activities just before falling asleep? Several three by five inch note cards and a pencil stub within reach will be useful for jotting down certain reminders for the next day.

If the weather is at freezing or below, it is best to put your flashlight (and canteen) inside your sleeping bag. It shortens the life of batteries if they are exposed to freezing temperatures.

THE FIREPLACE

If you are in an area that has sufficient wood for cooking, you will want a place to build a fire. Choose your fireplace carefully. It should preferably be in the open, away from overhanging limbs, dense brush, or grass that may start a forest fire. If there are leaves, pine needles or other burnable materials on the ground, clear away a large circle of all such material (down to the bare earth) before building your fire. A campsite that has previously been used by campers probably will already have a place that was used for a fire. Don't build your fire in a new spot unless there is an extremely good reason for doing so. Each new fireplace mars the ground surface.

The danger of forest fires is an ever-present problem in many wilderness and forest areas. No matter how great the temptation and the convenience, you should not make a fire on a forest floor that is covered with pine needles or other inflammable materials. If you are near a stream, walk down to the stream bed to do your cooking and eating. If you cook and eat in the stream bed, within a few feet of the water's edge, there will probably be little danger of spreading the fire. There will be plenty of water handy to douse the fire when you are through. A forest fire is a fearsome and terrible thing. Never take a chance with fire!

Where it is safe and possible to build a fire in the camp area, the fireplace will usually be the center of camp activity. Hikers will frequently be found at the fireplace, whether to cook, to eat, to talk, or to just sit and stare at the fire. The campfire for the evening will usually be in the same spot, but built up to somewhat larger proportions than the cooking fire. Because of the heavy traffic at the fireplace, the soil around it will frequently become ground to a fine dust from the passage of many feet. It is therefore recommended that you plan your camp layout so that the place for the cooking and campfire is at one end or one corner of the camp rather than near the geometric center. This will cut down on unnecessary "by-traffic" of persons who are simply going from one point in the camp to another.

Open containers of food, butter, etc., may have dirt kicked into them if they are set on the ground or on low stones around the cooking fire. Bags of food may be stepped on and split open. It is therefore recommended that your "work table" for meal preparation be removed from the immediate vicinity of the cooking fire. Choose a spot about fifteen or twenty feet away from the cooking fire; it should be grassy, covered with pine needles, provide a flat rock, or an otherwise nondusty area. Your "work table" is simply a small square of medium-heavy plastic spread on the ground at this spot. This is the place to lay out eating utensils, silverware, food, and condiments for that particular meal. It will usually be a cleaner and better spot to wash the dishes also, rather than in the immediate area of the fireplace.

The cook needs still another work space. He needs a small clean area, away from foot traffic, where he can sort through food bags and equipment after the meal is over, while others are washing dishes. Find a small, clean spot about twenty to thirty feet in some other direction. Here the cook will have the room and the necessary solitude to concentrate on what he is doing as he sorts through food bags, finding the right bags for the particular meal, getting the individual bags back into the larger carrying bags, and so forth. Here he will make up equitable loads for each hiker to carry, or following the supper meal will put the food into suitable duffle bags for hoisting off the ground, using a rope thrown over a tree limb. He will check off the food that has been used for the meal just completed and plan for the next meal, putting the proper foods to soak, making sure other needed foods are where he can find them, and so forth.

When fire starting conditions are difficult (like just after a hard rain) take more than the usual amount of time to gather a good supply of dry timber before you try to start a fire. Damp hikers are frequently somewhat impatient to get a fire started, and this impatience may lead to more delay in the long run. An inadequate supply of dry twigs, etc. will be quickly used up, perhaps before larger pieces of wood start burning. Then you must take time and go look for more fire starting material, and the time spent in gathering the supply for the first attempt has been wasted. Possible sources of good fire starting materials on a rainy day are the underside of down timber which is partially propped off the ground by limbs, the overhang of a cliff, the underside of a pile of driftwood near a stream, hollow tree trunks, and on the ground under trees having dense foliage. Dead limbs on live trees (squaw wood) and limbs on down timber which are projecting in the air will be drier than wood lying on the ground. Don't overlook used paper tissue, candy wrappers, etc. which you may have in your pocket. Pine needles are excellent fire starters, and where they form a thick carpet on the forest floor some dry needles can usually be found, even after a good rain.

When you go to bed at night the fire should be thoroughly extinguished, dousing it with water. Be just as careful to assure that it is completely out as you would if you were leaving the area. There should be no need for having a fire going at night. However, if for some reason you do keep a fire going at night you should take turns watching it. An unattended fire is potentially very dangerous. It is unsafe if you are asleep, even though you are only a few feet away.

LOSING GEAR

It is easy to mislay eating utensils, jack saws, knives, and other small items of camp gear and leave them behind when you leave camp. There are several things which can be done which will minimize the possibility of losing such items. First, do not set such items down in out-of-the-way places. Immediately after using such equipment as saws and knives, put them in an assigned place. Very small items, like a can opener, can be tied to a larger piece of equipment. Secondly, small items such as silverware can have the handles or other surfaces coated with a bright colored, nonlead paint, which is nonpoisonous and will make it easy to locate. A small piece of bright colored rag can also be tied to the item. Thirdly, spend the last five minutes before leaving camp in walking around the area and making a last check to see that some item of equipment has not been left behind. Specific individuals should be in charge of specific items of all common equipment. Those individuals should have a check list and should use it to check off all items for which they are responsible before the group leaves each lunch site and campsite and moves on down the trail.

CAMP SPIRIT

A proper camp spirit has a lot to do with making the trip an enjoyable experience for everyone concerned. When you take to the woods on a backpack trip it is seldom that everything works out exactly as it was planned at home. There are always some unknowns. If you knew precisely what experiences and problems you were going to have, what the weather would be, and so forth, it would no longer be an adventure. Each individual should be mentally and physically prepared to make the most of the situations that are encountered, whether they are good or bad. You will probably plan your next backpack trip by "including out" those hikers that display "camp spirit" along the following lines:

1. They did not check out their hiking boots; nor did they take the time to make a few conditioning hikes before the trip. After a few hours on the trail they start to complain of sore feet, an uncomfortable pack, and so forth.

2. They did not check out their equipment before leaving home. They have trouble with some of their gear and frequently ask to borrow some items (not "common equipment") from other hikers.

3. They "surprise" the other hikers by hauling out a transistor radio the first night in camp, and play it long and loud, even though it was specifically agreed that such equipment would be left at home.

4. They always manage to stay in their sleeping bag until someone else gets up in the morning and has the fire going. When breakfast is about half cooked they straggle out and finish dressing by the fire.

5. They take needless risks that are a threat to their individual safety and to the trip in general.

6. When meals are being prepared, they

always manage to have some item of personal equipment that needs attention at that particular time, or they may simply wander off and go fishing or exploring.

7. They frequently hold up the group from starting their next activity, as planned and agreed to by the majority.

8. They are chronic complainers about the weather, the trail, the food, the fishing, or a dozen other things.

9. They brag about their equipment. If some hiker is getting along with blankets from his bed at home it isn't necessary to call his attention to the luxury of a goose down sleeping bag. A single glance on his part at a good sleeping bag will do the job very nicely. If he wants details he will probably ask for them.

10. They raid the food supply. They may also take more than their share of a certain food without first asking others if they have had all they want. (The cook is in charge of the food supply, and he is responsible for seeing that everyone gets enough to eat. Getting into the food supply without the cook's permission is strictly against the rules.)

On a backpack trip you will be with your companions for twelve to fourteen hours each day. This is more hours per day than you usually spend with members of your immediate family. All personalities have certain idiosyncrasies (except you and me). Sooner or later one of your companions is going to say something or do something that you do not like. To avoid spoiling a good trip, hold your temper. Take a walk, bite your fingernails, or go kick a big boulder, but don't "spout off." Make an extra effort to get along with other members of the group and to be considerate. Give someone else the first cup of coffee, the first plate of food, the first drink at the spring, the first cast at a trout pool, and show other kindnesses. It will pay big dividends in the long run and assure maximum enjoyment from the trip for the time and effort you have invested. The rule "Do a good turn daily" is a good plan to follow.

When the trail is long and hard, the weather foul, and the food burned (how bad can things get?), dispositions have a way of getting "on edge." Thorough planning and preparation at home and setting reasonable schedules on the trail will do much to counteract this. Be kind to one another. Punctuality, helpfulness, and cheerfulness all have an important place in backpacking. If you are to meet with individuals or a group at a certain place on the trail at a specified time, be a few minutes early rather than a few minutes late. When the time for meals is established, all members should report promptly to the scene of action. Everyone should help with the operation from the time cooking is started until the last dish is washed and packed. Be considerate of the group's welfare. That piece of cheese that someone decides to snitch from the food supply for a private snack may be just what the cook was planning on to flavor a pot of macaroni at the next meal. The old sleeping bag feels mighty snug on a frosty morning, but someone has to get up, start the fire, and put the coffee on. Why not you this morning?

DON'T LITTER

The wilderness and national forest areas are yours. Take care of them as you would any other prized possession. Be thoughtful of those who will come after you. Don't leave a trail of debris as you travel through the wilderness. Police your campsites carefully before you leave them. In well-traveled areas, all nonburnable refuse should be packed out. In very remote areas it may be permissible to bury refuse or place it under large rocks, well off the trail and away from the campsite.

When on the trail, hikers should not throw candy and gum wrappers, bits of string, foil, tape, and other litter along the trail. Such material should be put in the pocket and burned at the next camp. (Foil will usually burn if the fire is hot and the foil is unfolded into a single layer, not crumpled. If it doesn't burn, pack it out please.) For those backwoods travelers who leave a trail of cans, bottles, cast-off clothing and equipment, carved initials on logs and tree trunks, and so forth, there really isn't much to be said — that's printable. They are the types who apparently throw trash and debris into their own backyards at home — if they don't find the walk into the yard too tiring.

We will probably never have any more wilderness areas than we have right now, and we could have less. Take an interest in wilderness legislation and in other legislation that seeks to preserve a part of the natural beauty of this country for the generations to come. Don't take too much for granted. If you are in doubt as to how to proceed, Appendix G is a partial list of some well-known organizations that are fighting the battle to ensure that your children and mine will have clean air to breathe, clean rivers, and wilderness and forest areas for wholesome recreation. These organizations need your support. Please give it to them! As a starter, why not write to your congressman and ask him to take action toward preventing mining in wilderness areas. (It is now permitted.)

10

Preparing for a Backpack Trip

SETTING A DATE

One of the first things that needs to be done in planning for a backpack trip is to set a date for the trip. This may seem like a simple thing, but it does require some thought. For a full-scale backpack trip, the date should be set at least a month in advance, and preferably somewhat longer. In using dehydrated foods, some of them will probably be ordered through the mail and about three weeks should be allowed for delivery from the time you send in your order. It is desirable to package the food at least a week in advance because there are usually some unexpected matters that come up during the last week before a trip, and you will want to get as much of the routine preparation out of the way as possible.

Trying to get three or more persons to agree on a date for a trip can be quite a job in itself. At the same time you should reach agreement on an alternative date, in the event that you have unexpected bad weather move in just prior to the takeoff date, someone gets sick, or there is some other emergency. With the planning and preparation that is required for such a trip, when someone backs out for reasons of "personal convenience" just a few days before takeoff, this is usually reason for "exclusion from the club" as far as future trips are concerned. At the minimum, it means repackaging of practically every food item, which is no small job. If only three persons were going, and someone backs out, it possibly means cancellation of the trip. In some very remote areas a group of three is considered a minimum from a safety standpoint.

When you set a date, every member of the group should work conscientiously toward that date. At the same time you need to condition your thinking to the fact that if a real emergency occurs or definite bad weather moves in, you will delay the trip to the alternative date. There are types of persons who, after setting a date and telling their friends, neighbors and others about the proposed trip, feel that it almost amounts to a bad mark on their reputation if they do not take off as planned, regardless of what comes up in the meantime. That is why agreement on such matters and on an alternative date is important.

Do as much of your trip preparations as far in advance of the trip date as possible. Nothing is more frustrating than working right up to the time of takeoff in repairing or locating equipment or doing numerous other jobs that could have been done weeks in advance. You will enjoy the trip much more if you can spend the week or two prior to takeoff in making daily conditioning hikes and so forth without being bothered by a lot of last minute details.

BE PREPARED

If possible, store the equipment that you use in backpacking in a special place. Since it all goes in or on your pack, it doesn't take up much room. A few medium size cardboard boxes will usually hold all of it. The time to make repairs or changes in your equipment is as soon as possible after a trip. Don't wait until just before another trip to get it in order. If something needs repair, repair it; if it needs sharpening, sharpen it. If you plan to try out a new piece of equipment or a new food, do so well in advance of another trip. In other words, "Be prepared." Following are some suggestions as to just a few jobs in this category that should be done weeks before the next trip rather than at the last minute:

1. Immediately after each trip thoroughly air and sun your sleeping gear and any items of clothing which are not washed. Store sleeping bags in a fluffed condition, rather than rolling them tight. The ideal way is to suspend them vertically from a hanger and not roll them at all.

2. Soon after each trip wash pan bags, silverware bags, any cloth food bags, etc. Replace any worn drawstrings or tie strings on such bags. Thoroughly wash all cooking and eating equipment. Replace soap, pot scratchers, sponges, and so forth. Replace wire bails on cooking pots with new wire. Store this gear in large plastic bags to keep it clean.

3. Repair or replace any equipment or clothing that is torn or broken. Lubricate zippers on packs and clothing. A soft lead pencil or a candle will work well, or there are special zipper lubricants available.

4. Make some notes as to what you intend to do differently on your next backpack trip. Admit your mistakes, and plan how you are going to correct them.

5. Go over your check list after every trip. You will probably want to make a few changes. Keep your check list and notes from trip to trip.

6. Sharpen knives, fish hooks, and so forth.

7. Clean hiking boots and the lugs on the boots. Use a waterproofing material, after cleaning, if the need is indicated.

8. Try out a new trail food. The place to first try it out is at home.

9. Review your first aid technique. Check over the contents of your first aid kit. Replace aspirin, moleskin, etc. Check the rubber suction cups on snake bite kits. After several years the rubber frequently becomes hard and brittle, and the suction cup may be worthless for the purpose intended, even though it has never been used.

10. Check over fishing equipment, rock hunting equipment, cameras, and other special gear.

11. Replace "old" matches in match containers. Matches that are more than six to nine months old do not work as well as "fresh" matches. Only wood stick or "kitchen" matches are recommended.

SELECTING NEW EQUIPMENT

From time to time some of your equipment will need to be replaced. With most gear there must always be some compromise between weight and ruggedness. A cast iron skillet will last a lifetime, but that doesn't make it a good piece of backpacking gear. You will enjoy carrying a lightweight teflon or aluminum skillet much more, and it will serve the purpose, even though it needs to be replaced periodically. You may buy a pair of hiking boots that will last five years or more, and with each step you take you may have to pay for that durability by lifting an extra pound of weight. A lighter boot may need to be replaced each one or two seasons but that is of no consequence if you have enjoyed many miles of extra comfort in hiking as a result of less durability. If you are buying a fishing rod for backpacking, buy one with a detachable handle and with sections nearly equal in length. Avoid heavy, over-designed equipment and clothing. This particularly applies to war surplus items.

When you order equipment from catalogues, be sure to note the difference between weight of the item and its shipping weight. If in doubt, write to the supplier and ask for a clarification of weight before placing a positive order. When ordering hiking boots, ask what the weight of the shoe is in your size. The catalogue weight given for some of the hiking boots can be quite misleading.

ORGANIZING

Would you like to participate in a backpack trip that is a comedy of confusion, frustration, wasted effort and hurt feelings? It's very simple. Just take any group of reasonably well-qualified hikers and backpackers, and "assume" that because of their experience you don't need to do any significant amount of planning or have any definite organization in preparing for the trip you have in mind. You will end up with too much of certain equipment (unnecessary duplication), not enough of other items, a conglomeration of food and menus, an itinerary that was supposedly satisfactory to everyone but which actually doesn't please anyone, and there will be other problems. Certainly in a small group of experienced backpackers the role of the leader is not as distinct or as involved as in a large group with varied and lesser experience, but someone still needs to "spearhead" the preparations. In a large group, intermittent preparation and coordination over a period of six weeks prior to takeoff is not unusual. You should have a few meetings of the group concerned, to plan your trip and to determine who is going to do what in getting ready for it. Following are some of the things that will need to be decided:

CHOOSING A LEADER. A leader for the group should be chosen to have general responsibility for planning and organizing the trip. He should also have overall responsibility for the welfare of the group and the conduct of the trip after it gets underway.

FOOD, COOKING GEAR. One person, hopefully someone skilled in cooking on the trail, should be in charge of menu planning, buying and packaging food, getting together cooking and eating gear, and distributing equal loads to each person in time to pack it with the rest of their equipment. In a small group the leader may also be the cook, but not necessarily. Someone in the group may be allergic to certain common foods or may have a strong dislike for some foods. It is best to find this out when the menus are being made up at home, rather than when the group is cooking in camp.

CHOOSING A ROUTE. Try to choose an area and a route into the area that some member of the party is familiar with. One or two persons should be responsible for getting together maps, compass, trail markers, outlining an itinerary, and providing all possible information on the route.

OTHER COMMON EQUIPMENT. Someone will need to assemble other items of common equipment, and distribute an equal load to each hiker, such as: fire making equipment, saw, toilet paper, wire, tape, first aid equipment, snake bite kits, salt tablets, and so forth. If it is agreed that one person carry a camera (or other item) for the benefit of all, then that person should be compensated accordingly in the weight of other common equipment that he is given to carry.

TRANSPORTATION. You will need transportation to the takeoff point. One approach is that those hikers furnishing vehicles get their gas and oil paid for by the others. An alternative is for riders to jointly pay the driver at the end of the trip for car or truck expenses, based on mileage driven (say seven cents per mile for passenger cars). Those furnishing vehicles should take special precautions to ensure that the vehicles are in good operating condition and not likely to break down on the way to the takeoff point. If a vehicle breaks down en route and the group has to wait at some remote crossroads while a fan belt or ignition coil is being brought out from the nearest town, it gets the trip off to a bad start. Preventive maintenance costs money, and a generous mileage allowance to the vehicle owner is essential.

Do the proper persons (drivers) have the full name and address of all the hikers they are to pick up? (There are a lot of Johns in the phone book.) Searching out street names and house numbers with a flashlight at four o'clock in the morning can be quite a chore, and phoning persons at that hour to ask them how to get to their home can lead to a certain amount of difficulty.

FUNDS. You will need to purchase foods and certain common supplies well in advance of the trip. If you are hiring a guide or arranging for special transportation at the roadhead, a deposit is usually made toward this service. Each member should make an advance deposit toward these costs. There also needs to be a clear understanding as to whether any of this advance payment is to be returned to a trip member who later cancels out. Generally such advance payments are not refunded, either in whole or in part. When supplies are purchased for the trip, or deposits made for a necessary service, the planning is already too far along to permit any refunds.

GENERAL PLANNING

There should be a trip plan, and every participant should understand it thoroughly. It is amazing how even very fundamental aspects, such as the length of a trip, can be misunderstood by some. It is not unusual to be far into the woods and then have an argument arise between some trip members as to whether the group was to return to the roadhead on a Saturday or on a Sunday. The date and the exact hour of the takeoff from home and the date and approximate hour of return to the roadhead are very important. There should also be a return date and hour, left with a responsible person back home, which will be a "cutoff" time. If you have not returned home by that time, it is to be understood that you have encountered a serious emergency or accident and that the responsible person at home is to take action accordingly. This is a very important and serious matter and should be treated as such.

There should be an itinerary for the trip, starting with the hour that the group leaves the trailhead, outlining the expected travel for each day and camping place for that day. After the group is on the trail, the itinerary can be as flexible or as rigid as you want to make it, but there should be a plan. On a well-conducted backpack trip a group does not go into a remote area and simply wander aimlessly about for a week. Be careful, however, not to try and crowd too many miles or too many activities into one day. Be particularly careful in your planning that you will have a suitable campsite, especially with respect to wood and water, when it comes late afternoon and it is time to camp.

Are you going to hire a guide? If you are going into a remote area, away from marked trails, and no one in the group is familiar with the area, a guide can save a lot of headaches. He need not be a professional guide. A local ranch boy of high school age may be an entirely satisfactory guide. If he knows where the trail is and can stay on it, he will be of more service to you than a Ph.D. who can speak seven languages (and doesn't know where the trail is).

Is there an automobile road all the way to the trailhead, or will special transportation need to be arranged for the last few miles of travel? If there is a road all the way to the trailhead, is it good in all seasons? Is a four-wheel drive vehicle required? If the road is dirt and an unexpected heavy rain makes it impassable, what alternate transportation is available? There has been more than one backpack trip that "never got off the ground" because the planners failed to recognize the possible need for special transportation for the last few miles of travel to the trailhead.

As you discuss and think through the proposed trip, you will find that there are many questions to be answered and some "rules" to be made. Some snapshots or color slides are an important feature of most backpack trips. However, if some trip member insists on a "commercial quality" shot every time he takes a photograph, it is going to mean some delays. There are types who like to have the entire "safari" trip by a certain spot two or three times so they can get just the right shot. Unless the trip is planned for this type of photography, most trip members will not want to go along with it. It is best to talk these things out beforehand. For example, you can make a rule that photographs can be taken freely as long as the photographer doesn't hold up the group. Those persons who need tripods and too much other paraphernalia every time they click the shutter may find that the rest of the group is a quarter mile down the trail by the time they get set up.

Have you carefully investigated the weather and minimum temperature that can be expected for the area (and altitude) that you will be in? Is rain to be expected at that time of year? At high altitudes don't overlook the possibility of snow and severe winds. These factors are important in planning your sleeping gear, clothing, and possibly the itinerary. A long distance phone call to a Weather Bureau, Chamber of Commerce, Forest Service Officer or rancher in the area, just prior to leaving for the trip, is a good idea. This will serve to determine whether there has been a sudden change in weather, floods, forest fires, or similar conditions that may call for postponement or a change in trip plans. State police in some states maintain radio contact with units in other parts of the state and will be glad to furnish information on local road conditions.

Try and get some reliable information on the prevalence of flies, mosquitoes, ticks, and other insects in the area where you are planning your trip. At certain seasons insects can be such a nuisance as to call for unusual protective measures or perhaps postponement of the trip. A few weeks earlier (or later) there may be no problem at all. Get advice on locally used insect repellents and protective measures, such as head nets, gloves, strong soaps, and mosquito netting.

Some trip member may be acquainted with the area where the group will be backpacking and may know the trails. He may recall where certain streams and springs are located and think that there is adequate water along the trail. Remember in such planning, however, that the flow of streams and springs may vary with the season of the year and that a spring that was flowing one year may be dried up the following year. If you write to the Forest Service or another knowledgeable organization for maps, this is a good time to inquire about the flow of certain streams and springs and other possible water supply along the trail. Never underestimate the seriousness of running out of water on a backpack trip.

One item of preparation is to determine what stream crossings are to be encountered on the trails you will be hiking. This in turn will dictate whether you should take one large pair of tennis shoes as an item of common equipment or whether each hiker should take his own, as an item of personal gear. If there are only a few scattered stream crossings, mild in nature, one pair of large tennis shoes to be shared by the group will probably do. However, if a given stretch of trail has, for example, four or more stream crossings in a mile of travel then it will be desirable for each person to have his own tennis shoes. For such stretches of trail the hikers will probably want to put the tennis shoes on and keep them on, even for the hiking between crossings. Then, when crossings are less frequent or the trail leaves the stream, each person will want to change back to regular hiking boots. Hiking for very long in wet socks or wet shoes invites blisters and sore feet. Wading streams in your hiking boots is definitely not recommended.

Should hikers take their own bag lunch for the first meal on the trail? Does the trail cross streams that will need to be waded? Are floods a possibility? If you are hiking along one of the big trail systems that "touches base" with civilization every few days, are certain supplies to be replenished along the trail? Are you going to allow smoking along the trail? Are you going to permit firearms to be carried? Are typhoid or tetanus shots recommended for trip members? Tetanus shots are recommended if pack stock are used on the trails you will be using.

If the takeoff point is more than several hours drive from your home, it may be desirable to drive there the evening before and camp at the roadhead. In this way you won't need to start hiking right after being fatigued by a long drive, and you can get an early start on the trail. When this is done, your breakfast the next morning at the roadhead should be planned with foods, utensils and cooking gear which are carried separately for the purpose. The only items you should need to unpack from your trip gear are your sleeping bag and mattress. Keep the breakfast simple. Otherwise it will take too long and you will probably start up the trail on too full a stomach, which is not good.

Are you going to allow any stops on the way to the trailhead, except for food and gas? Most hikers who have gotten up at three o'clock in the morning to meet an early takeoff hour will not appreciate sitting in a hot vehicle while some member trips gaily from store to store, shopping for camera film, sun tan lotion, fishing license, or some other item that he should have gotten weeks before. Are you going to allow shopping or sight-seeing stops on the return trip home? Once they are back at the roadhead, most hikers are anxious to return home. It's up to you, but it's best to have these things well understood beforehand.

After you have discussed all of these factors and made your decisions, it is a good idea to have the basic trip plan typed, and a mimeograph copy made for each member. Then there can be no misunderstandings. This particularly applies to large groups of six persons or more. The trip plan should outline the itinerary. It should also list common equipment which will be taken for the benefit of all members. It should list the basic "rules" that you have agreed to for the conduct of your trip.

THE LEADER'S JOB

The leader does not have an easy job. Except in very large and formally organized groups, the leader will be paying his way, along with other trip members, and the time that he has spent in planning and organizing the trip will be donated. Trip members should thus keep in mind that the leader is entitled to his share of fun from the trip and full participation in the various activities.

One of the most important tasks of the leader is to determine the hiking and backpacking capability of each member of the group, early in the trip planning that takes place at home. Probably most and perhaps all of the members will be well known to the leader and this may be no problem at all, but don't take too much for granted. A single newcomer to the group or an individual whose capabilities are not well known to other members can ruin a trip for the entire group. The newcomer to the group may overestimate his ability in the discussions and planning that take place in the living room at home. After a couple of hours on the trail he may throw off his pack, spread-eagle on the ground and doesn't want to or can't go on. Mr. Leader, you now have a problem — and a very serious one. The other members will see many weeks of their own planning and careful preparation going "down the drain," and they probably will not take kindly to you as a leader from now on.

Early in the planning at home, if there is any reasonable doubt about a trip member's capability, particularly his hiking ability and general stamina, you had best take some very specific steps to find out for yourself. If there are some mountain trails near your home, you can designate a particular trail and ask this individual to make a few hikes over it with a full pack. Or, you can spend an afternoon hiking with him over some rugged terrain. A few hours of reasonably strenuous hiking, with a full pack, should be sufficient to tell the story, and it will be a good investment for everyone concerned.

Someone has to make the decisions, and once the group is on the trail it is the job of the leader to decide on a course of action. There will frequently be differences of opinion. After the matter has been duly discussed, accept the leader's decision. If you are not willing to do this you should have stayed home. If the group is "honored" with a daredevil type of individual, it is a good idea to remind that person early in the planning phase that you (the leader) reserve the right to restrict his activities on the trail insofar as they may affect the welfare and safety of himself and the group.

If the group has found a leader who has had a lot of backpacking experience, as well as good leadership and management capabilities, take good care of him. There aren't too many of these types around.

PHYSICAL CONDITIONING

If you normally do considerable hiking and walking, you may be able to start a backpack trip with no special preconditioning and make out all right. For most persons, however, some special preconditioning is desirable to harden your muscles, toughen your feet, and check out your pack and pack load. Books or magazines, wrapped in towels or blankets, are good for simulating a loaded pack. Do not use rocks. Rocks are not a good simulation because the weight is concentrated in a small area, and carrying a load of rocks is hard on your pack sack.

PRETRIP HIKES. There is a lot of difference between hiking over level terrain and hiking through mountains, where normally there will be a lot of uphill and downhill travel. Try to arrange your preconditioning hikes in hilly country if there are no mountains nearby. Wear the same boots and combination of socks that you will be wearing for your backpack trip, and the same clothes, insofar as possible. This preliminary hiking should take place at least a month before your backpack trip and preferably longer. The situation is somewhat like studying for an exam in school. If you don't know the lesson thoroughly a week before, then you aren't going to be able to prepare yourself in a day or two. In preconditioning you should occasionally push yourself to where you are thoroughly fatigued to increase your endurance and to find out just what your limitations are. This will also give you confidence when on a real backpack trip and you are faced with a possible situation that calls for unusual exertion. For about a week before takeoff, however, take only moderate (but regular) daily hikes and exercise, never pushing yourself to the point of fatigue. Never prepare yourself for a backpack trip by taking another backpack trip just before the "big one." After any such trip you need a week of limited activity before you will be back to normal. For a week or more prior to a trip get plenty of sleep. Avoid late hours, as well as the exertion and concern that comes from waiting too long before getting your gear, clothing, and food ready and packed. Take extra precautions to avoid contact with persons having colds or other communicable diseases. In other words, give more than usual attention to good personal hygiene.

ALTITUDE CONDITIONING. If you are going on a backpack trip in the high mountains and you are not accustomed to exerting at high altitudes, it is very desirable that you take a number of short hikes in mountainous country prior to tackling a full-scale backpack trip. No person functions as well at high altitudes, but some are much more seriously affected than others. Don't wait until you are on a backpack trip to find this out.

FEET. It makes a sorry situation when a hiker develops blisters on his feet, usually in the first few hours of a backpack trip (if it develops at all). Besides taking preconditioning hikes, soaking the feet about fifteen minutes daily (for seven to ten days) in tannic acid just before a backpack trip will toughen them up significantly. Use one ounce of tannic acid (available from drug stores) to two quarts of water. You can use the same mixture over and over for any one trip. It will turn very dark but that doesn't matter. Wipe your feet on paper towels after soaking. Tannic acid will permanently stain a cloth towel, and this could conceivably cause certain members of the household to take a dim view of your backpacking activities.

Hours of walking over rugged trails can bring about sore spots and problems with your feet that will never show up in normal daily activity. A particularly vulnerable area is the toes. Trim your toenails straight across. If you round the outer corners the nails will dig into the skin, causing irritation and possibly infection.

For persons who experience foot problems, it may be desirable to carry a small bottle of rubbing alcohol. Apply this to your feet each morning and at night while on the trip. Foot powder may also be a help.

EATING. Serious and experienced backpackers will train and condition themselves for backpacking, just as an athlete trains. They will keep themselves in condition throughout the year by regular physical exercise. Just prior to a backpack trip they will exercise regularly but not excessively. If they are of normal weight for their body build, they may want to add two or three pounds to that normal weight over a period of a few weeks prior to the trip. On a strenuous backpack trip it is better to eat for energy rather than to try and maintain your precise body weight.

When undertaking heavy exercise which is not a part of your daily pattern of living, you will probably have more energy and feel better if you eat a bit less than necessary to maintain normal body weight. Strenuous, prolonged activity means fatigue. The prime remedy for physical fatigue is rest, or a change in pace, and a good night's sleep. Eating large quantities of food is not the cure for physical fatigue. When you are fatigued your body does not readily digest food.

You have to burn up about 3,500 calories to lose a pound of body weight. If you eat regular, reasonably well-balanced meals with generous amounts of high energy foods on a backpack trip, your energy will stay at a high level, even though you may burn up somewhat more calories than you take in. If you start a ten-day trip at two pounds overweight and finish two pounds underweight you have done yourself no harm if you were in good physical condition to start with. When you get back to the daily routine at home your weight will soon return to normal.

This approach results in a higher energy level for many experienced backpackers. It also means that weight of food in your pack can be several pounds lighter per person than if you started at normal weight and finished at normal weight. On a reasonably strenuous backpack trip you may use up to 4,000 calories per day or more. You do not have to replace that many calories each day during the trip, however, in order to feel well. This type of planning is not generally applicable to large groups, to mixed groups, or to teen-agers. It is primarily limited to small groups of adult sportsmen, who are accustomed to backpacking together and confident of their own ability and thoroughly familiar with the capabilities of the other members of the group.

Don't go "overboard" on your sugar intake during a backpack trip. Some backpacking literature advises that you not only eat more sugar at mealtime than you normally do, but that you eat a lot of candy between meals. This is wrong. Your body does not need that much sugar, and it may be harmful. Some increase in sugar over the quantity normally eaten at home is recommended, but certainly not the huge amounts that some literature indicates. It is recommended that you significantly increase your intake of fat and protein foods while backpacking. This will sustain your energy at a high level. Be reasonable on the sugar intake. There is some evidence that sugar increases cholesterol and some of the heart troubles associated therewith.

PRACTICE. You may have read all the books on lightweight camping and mountaineeering that are available. You may know them by heart. But when you climb your first mountain with a thirty to thirty-five pound pack on your back and the sun is blazing down, there will be an element of doubt in your mind. You will be wondering whether you will make it or not or whether you will hold up your companions who may be in better shape than you are. On the first time up that element of doubt will probably bother you just as much as the hot sun overhead. You won't have to say a word about it, it will still be there. After you have done it once, you won't be so worried. After you have

done it a dozen times, you won't give it a thought and you will really look forward to the climb. As for many other endeavors, advancement in backpacking techniques and added enjoyment comes largely from experience and persistent effort to improve. You should not attempt a week-long backpack trip until you have made a few trips that were several days in length. You should not attempt a trip of three or four days until you have made some overnight trips. Short trips are desirable in order to check yourself out and see how you do, as well as to check out your gear and to get thoroughly familiar with it.

WEATHER PROTECTION

A major decision in the planning of any backpack trip is to decide what is needed in the way of clothing and shelter for protection against the elements. This will largely depend upon the season, the particular area, and the altitude. Don't take this matter too lightly. To a lesser degree the planning will depend upon the individuals making up the party. For a mixed group, or a group of young persons, more protection would probably be planned under the same anticipated weather conditions than for a group of experienced men backpackers. The latter would normally be willing to take certain calculated risks that might not be advisable for some other group.

The difference of a few weeks in the time of the trip may dictate a difference in protective clothing and shelter. For example, the mountains of southern New Mexico are normally very dry in the spring of the year, through the month of June. Starting in early July, however, and extending through August, daily heavy rains can be expected in the afternoon. Therefore, a backpack trip in this area from April through June requires minimum rain protection. The same trip, taken in July or August, requires good personal rain gear and a good rain shelter at night.

Lightweight plastic sheets can be carried as emergency protection against improbable rain but never on a trip where frequent rain is expected. Further, don't take such a lightweight plastic sheet on a week-long trip without having had previous experience with it. You need to take time and patience with these lightweight sheets to handle them carefully and erect them properly. The heavier poly tube-type tents are available from many suppliers. If you use one of these, mark the area that goes next to the ground with a felt tip marker or with tape. Put the same section next to the ground each time the tent is used. That section will quickly

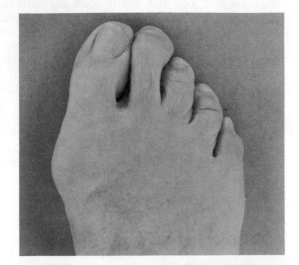

This picture shows the big toe of a hiker's foot folding under the second toe (a mild case). This is quite a common condition, often hereditary.

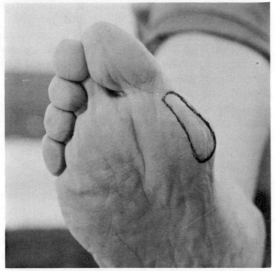

Although the "folding under" of the big toe as shown above is not severe enough to cause trouble in normal, limited walking, when on a hike a large and painful bunion will usually form in the area outlined in this photo.

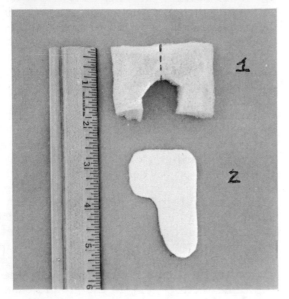

These items will alleviate the bunion and soreness caused by the above foot condition on a long kike. Item 1 is polyurethane foam, cut to about ½ inch thickness at center (half-moon) and tapered to about ¼ inch thickness at the outer edges. It is folded along the dotted line and wedged between the big toe and second toe as shown in the next photo. Item 2 is moleskin adhesive, placed over the potential bunion area as shown in next photo.

The polyurethane foam (after folding) is placed as shown. It is so light that you will soon forget it is there. Yet it does the desired job of holding the big toe in a more normal position. The moleskin adhesive can be left in place for the entire trip. When you wash your feet just wash over it. No problem.

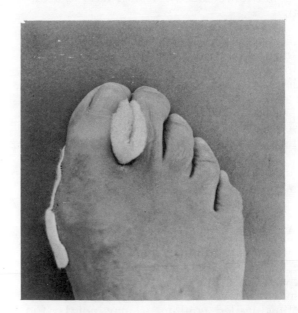

The moleskin adhesive in place. Use moleskin also on the top surface of certain toes, or any other places on foot where you have experienced soreness or chafing on past hikes.

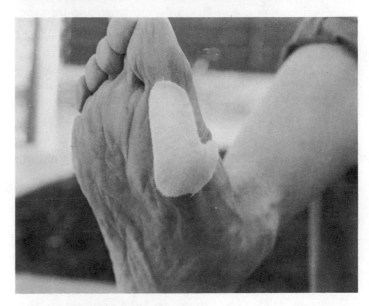

Such devices as this, which is a firm rubber form for accomplishing the job shown for the polyurethane foam, are not recommended. They are generally uncomfortable, and you will usually end up not using it, even though you may have one.

develop pin holes and will leak if used as a top section.

Polyethylene tarps (3 or 4 mil thickness) will provide protection against heavy rain, and a good tarp will last for a week or two of continued use. A better lightweight and more durable tarp is easily made from urethane coated nylon cloth and will be serviceable for many trips if properly cared for. Such cloth is available from some of the suppliers listed in Appendix A. For high altitude camping where rain, strong winds, and possibly snow may be encountered, a good lightweight mountain tent, with separate rain fly, provides the best protection.

USE A CHECK LIST

How many automobile trips have you been on where someone asked soon after the trip got underway, "Well, I wonder what we have forgotten?" When you are traveling by automobile, forgetting needed equipment may not be too serious. You can stop in some town and buy the forgotten item, if it is important enough. When you are in a wilderness or other remote area and find that you have forgotten something, it is a different story. Your money won't help there. If you think it isn't serious, try getting along without matches, toilet paper, soap, shortening, or some other essential item on a week-long backpack trip. It will make you a firm believer in check lists. Presumably, practically every item that you take on a backpack trip is essential, otherwise you would have left it at home.

Prior to doing any packing, make out a list of equipment, clothing, and other gear that you plan to take. If planning and packing the food and cooking equipment is assigned to another member of the party, you won't have to worry about that, but you will need to leave room in your pack for your share of this and other common equipment. As you make out the list of items that you intend to take, put down the weight of each one. Review the list a number of times, and be sure that you are not taking too many items of nonessential equipment or that there isn't some substitute item available that will do the job just as well and weigh less.

Check lists serve another important function in addition to serving as a means of reviewing every item of equipment that is to go in your pack and its weight. Hikers have left home on pack trips and forgotten cameras, canteens, fishing gear, food in the refrigerator, and other items that they planned to take. When you finally pack your gear for the last time, check off every item of equipment against your check list, as it goes in or on your pack. Then you will know absolutely that you have everything you

planned for. If some items are to be carried separately (in the car) from your pack until you get to the takeoff point, make a special note of this and fasten the note to the outside of your pack, where you won't overlook it.

After you arrive at the takeoff point you should very carefully go over the items on your check list that were not put in your pack or fastened to it (if any) when you left home. (Few hikers forget their packs.) In their anxiety to hit the trail, hikers sometimes leave canteens and other gear "safely" in the trunk of an automobile at the roadhead. To discover this after you are a few hours distant from the roadhead is very disconcerting, to say the least. Admittedly, it saves a certain amount of wear and tear on equipment to leave it at the car, but it is still not recommended.

There are a few items that should be left at the roadhead. For example, billfold, car keys, loose change and similar items are normally of no use on the trail. If you should lose your car keys while on the trail, you have a real problem, in addition to the nuisance of carrying them and keeping track of them while hiking. It is a good idea to have at least a spare ignition key hidden inside the car. One way of storing car keys is to wrap in foil and hide under a rock near the car at the roadhead. (Don't forget which rock.) If your fishing license is in your billfold, and you store your billfold at the roadhead, remember to remove the license and take it with you.

PACKING

Don't wait until the day before the trip to pack your gear. With some minor exceptions, everything can be packed a week or more in advance. After you have reviewed your check list a number of times and assured yourself that those items are what you need, you are ready to pack. Rather than having your pack a "jumble of gear" and having to turn it upside down to find some small item of equipment, most of your gear should be packed in heavy plastic bags, about nine by eighteen inches in size. Thus, except for large items, the contents of your pack should consist of a number of bags, which in turn contain the smaller items of equipment. Plastic bags are recommended because they are very light in weight and you can immediately see the contents without opening the bag. Only plastic bags that are new should be used. Do not see how much gear you can stuff into your pack sack. As stated in Part 2, you should choose as large a pack frame and pack sack as possible, commensurate with your body build. This is not so that you can carry a heavy load, but rather because any normal load that is carried will be more comfortable using a large frame and large pack sack.

In packing your gear, the usual tendency is to put heavy items in the bottom of the pack. This is wrong. The heavy items should be as high in the pack (without making it top-heavy) and as close to your back as possible.

Do not tie canteens, cooking pans, and similar gear to the outside of your pack or pack frame. Usually the only items that should be lashed to the pack frame are your sleeping bag (including small tent, if you carry one), contained in a suitable high tear strength, waterproof, cloth bag. Cooking pans and so forth will usually swing with each step you take if they are hung on the outside of the pack, and this is enough to drive most people crazy. If your gear is properly planned, there should be room inside the pack for such equipment. A probable exception is a fishing rod, and this deserves special mention.

The individual sections of most fishing rods are too long to go inside the average pack sack. There are fishing rods made especially for backpacking that have short, equal length sections, but many hikers will not have such rods. Some backpackers carry their rod sections in an aluminum case and lash or tape the case on one side of their pack frame. The case represents added weight and length, however, and is not usually necessary. Instead, it is recommended that you start by taping the rod sections together, simply lining up the sections in a parallel position, and then wrapping tape completely around the sections at several points. In addition, tie an eight or ten inch length of stout cord to one of the line guides of each section. Now lay the taped sections alongside one of the vertical outside frame members of your pack, so that the bottom of the rod sections is slightly higher than the bottom end of the pack frame member. Then wind some more tape completely around the sections and the frame member, at several points, taping them fast. The short length of cord fastened to the line guide of each rod section is a safety cord and should be tied to the frame member also. Then if the tape should come loose, you will not lose the rod section. Some rod sections will protrude up to six inches or more above the topmost part of the pack frame, but if you are careful in passing under overhanging limbs this should not be a problem. Fishing reels and detachable handles go inside the pack.

It will be desirable that one person, possibly the leader, carry many of the common equipment items, such as matches, first aid equipment, salt tablets, hand line, saw, toilet tissue, etc., in his pack. (He will then carry a corresponding lesser load of food.) If the person carrying such equipment has a pack with outside zippered pockets it will be helpful in making various common equipment items readily accessible and easily located.

An additional aid is to number the outside pockets on the pack, using a felt tip marker. Then when a party member asks for an aspirin or a Band-Aid, the leader can simply tell him to look in pocket No. 3 (or other numbered pocket) on the leader's pack, and thus save himself some detailed explanation, time, and steps.

Your canteen should go in an outside pocket of the pack sack (usually the large pocket at the back) where it will be readily available. Raincoats, tennis shoes for wading streams, first aid kits, and other items that may be needed while hiking should go in additional outside pockets or near the top of the pack.

Take care in packing food bags that items that may tear or rub holes in the bags are kept away from them. Wrapping a towel or an item of clothing around the food bag will help to protect it. In packing a flashlight, reverse one of the batteries, so that the light does not accidentally come on while you are hiking. Don't reverse both batteries because some flashlights will still work with both batteries reversed.

Some items, like matches, soap, toilet paper, and so forth, are best packed by dividing the total supply into two or more parts and packing in separate packs. Keep one supply as a spare until the other is totally used up. Then if the one supply is misplaced or lost you will have the spare. This is another reason for taking a few minutes to police each campsite and lunch site before you leave it. A supply of matches or soap left at the last campsite isn't going to help when you are ten miles down the trail.

If you are backpacking with a formally organized group, it is quite possible that the group leader will specify a maximum weight for packs. He does this for a good reason. He knows the trail and the terrain which lies ahead, and he knows the size of pack that an average person in good health can carry over that trail, at a moderate pace, without undue fatigue. By all means observe the limits for pack weights, as well as any other rules, that are specified. If the leader says the maximum pack weight is thirty pounds, he doesn't want anyone showing up with a thirty-five pound pack. If in doubt, get clarification from the leader well in advance of the trip. In a mixed group it is general practice for women to carry packs that are about ten pounds lighter than the men's packs.

If you are coming out of a remote area the same way you went in, you may want to leave a cache of food along the way. A cache or two of food, set aside for the last few meals, will save you from carrying that food all the way in and most of the way out again. If you plan to do this, put the food for the cache in a separate bag (or bags) when you are doing your packing at home. A cache (temporary) can simply be a heavy plastic bag containing the food for a particular meal or two, hung from a tree limb ten to fifteen feet off the ground. Select a tree that will not be readily visible from the trail, and mark the trail at that spot so that you will not pass by it on the way out. Pick a small diameter tree with no limbs close to the ground and a bear will not be so likely to climb it.

TOTAL PACK WEIGHT

In arriving at the total pack weight to be carried by each individual we will again assume a week-long trip for a group of three persons. The weight of the individual packs should be about as follows:

RECOMMENDED PERSONAL EQUIP-MENT. As outlined in Part 2, the weight of recommended personal equipment is 214 ounces, including pack frame and fitted pack sack.

RECOMMENDED COMMON EQUIPMENT. The recommended common equipment, discussed in Part 2, amounts to forty-two ounces for three persons or fourteen ounces per hiker.

OPTIONAL PERSONAL EQUIPMENT. Some items of optional personal equipment that may be desired are discussed in Part 2. A total of forty-four ounces of optional personal equipment is assumed.

OPTIONAL COMMON EQUIPMENT. A weight of twenty ounces per person of optional common equipment is assumed. This would provide sixty ounces of optional common equipment (3¾ pounds) in a group of three persons.

EXTRA CLOTHING. As discussed in Part 3, a total of twenty-six ounces of extra clothing (including duplicate socks) should be sufficient for temperatures down to 25°F. For a high humidity climate this may need to be increased a bit, and a total weight of thirty-four ounces of extra clothing is assumed in this case.

FOOD. Suggested menus are detailed in Part 5. The weight of food for a week-long backpack trip averaged out at 126 ounces per person (eighteen meals).

COOKING AND EATING UTENSILS. The weight of cooking and eating utensils, dishwash-ing equipment, plastic food bags and small food containers (Part 6) is fifty-eight ounces, or about nineteen ounces per person.

TABLE 11. WEIGHT SUMMARY

Category	Weight ounces
Recommended personal equipment	214
Recommended common equipment	14
Optional personal equipment	44
Optional common equipment	20
Extra clothing	34
Food	126
Cooking and eating utensils	19
Total	471

Thus, we have a total pack weight of 471 ounces or about 29½ pounds. For a group larger than three persons the weight would be slightly less because of additional sharing of common equipment. If you want to sacrifice some comfort and convenience, and eliminate sleeping pad, all nonessentials, optional equipment, etc., this weight can be reduced to twenty-five pounds or a bit under. That's up to you to decide. As the food is eaten the food load is reduced by about 1¼ pounds per day. Also, in a remote area you can leave a cache or two of food along the trail on the way in for a few meals on the way out, and this will further reduce the weight (after the food is cached on the way in).

TAKE THE INITIATIVE

Well, that's about it. Three or more persons can go into a wilderness or other remote area, each carrying a twenty-five to thirty-five pound pack, and live comfortably for a week, shut off from all outside communication. Backpacking is a sport with many challenges and many rewards. One of the challenges is to reduce the weight of the pack by another pound and still live comfortably and eat well. It's like taking another stroke off a golf score. Each one becomes a little harder than the one before, but it's fun trying.

Like a lot of other endeavors, it is one thing to talk about backpacking and another thing to do it. It is recommended that your first few backpack trips be short ones, primarily for the purpose of checking out and getting acquainted with your gear and to test your own capabilities. As your technique improves, you can lengthen the trip and get further from the roadhead. A good winter project is to make complete plans and preparations for a spring or summer backpack trip, getting all packs and equipment checked over, ordering necessary food, taking preliminary hikes to check out your gear and so forth.

If you like the out-of-doors, a well-planned backpack trip can be one of the outstanding experiences of a lifetime. So let's get going. We aren't getting any younger. The mountains were never more beautiful, and it would be a shame to let all of those trout die of old age. There are mountain summits to be climbed, intriguing canyons to be explored, winding trails to be pursued through pine forests, and meandering paths to be followed across mountain meadows and along rushing white water streams. As for any other sport, there will come a time in your life when you will be unable to participate because of physical limitations. Backpacking can provide some mighty fine memories for your old age. (It will also help to put off that old age, which can occur pretty young in some people.) Take the initiative! Use your ingenuity (and, hopefully this book). Good luck. May the good Lord smile upon you, may you have many campfires ahead, and may you have a light pack and a light heart as you go tramping along the mountain trails. Adios!

Appendices

APPENDIX A

SUPPLIERS SPECIALIZING IN BACKPACKING AND MOUNTAINEERING EQUIPMENT*

Name	Address
Alp Sport	P.O. Box 1081, Boulder, Colorado 80302
Cloud Cap Chalet	1127 S.W. Morrison Street, Portland, Oregon 97205
Highland Outfitters	3579 University Avenue, Riverside, California 92502
Sierra Designs	137 Tewksbury, Point Richmond, California 94801
The Smilie Company	575 Howard Street, San Francisco, California 94105
The Trading Post	86 Scollard Street, Toronto 5, Ontario, Canada
West Ridge Mountaineering	12010 West Pico Boulevard, Los Angeles, California 90064

*Also see Table 1.

SOME SUPPLIERS OF GENERAL CAMPING EQUIPMENT WHO CARRY SOME BACKPACKING EQUIPMENT

Name	Address
Eddie Bauer	1737 Airport Way South, P.O. Box 3700 Seattle, Washington 98124
L.L. Bean, Inc.	Freeport, Maine 04032
I. Goldberg	902 Chestnut Street, Philadelphia, Pennsylvania 19107
Herter's, Inc.	Waseca, Minnesota 56093
Morsan	#810, Route 17, Paramus, New Jersey 07652

APPENDIX B

GENERAL SOURCES OF SPECIAL FOODS FOR BACKPACKING

Name	Address
Chuck Wagon Foods	176 Oak Street, Newton, Massachusetts 02164
Dri Lite Foods	8716 Santa Fe Avenue, South Gate, California 90280
Durkee Famous Foods	900 Union Commerce Building, Cleveland, Ohio 44101
Oregon Freeze Dry Foods	Albany, Oregon 97321
Perma-Pak	40 E. Robert Avenue, Salt Lake City, Utah 84115
Richmoor	P.O. Box 2728, Van Nuys, California 91404
Ad Seidel & Son, Inc.	2323 Pratt Boulevard, Elk Grove Village, Illinois 60007
Stow-A-Way Products Co.	103 Ripley Road, Cohasset, Massachusetts 02025
Thunderbird	616 N. Robertson Boulevard, Los Angeles, California 90069
Trail Chef	1109 S. Wall Street, Los Angeles, California 90015
Wilson and Co., Inc.	Chicago, Illinois 60601

Note: Many of the suppliers of backpacking and mountaineering equipment listed in Appendix A and Table 1 also carry dehydrated foods, including some of the brands listed above. Also see Table 6.

APPENDIX C

ONE-MAN BACKPACK TENT

One primary reason for going backpacking is to be out-of-doors; that is, to live, cook, eat and sleep in the open. We are really not getting maximum benefit from our backpacking experience if we coop ourselves up in a tent each night. It is similar to the situation in which people go to the mountains to be out-of-doors and then spend much of the time inside of a cabin, with many of the conveniences of home. The fact that the walls are made of logs, in contrast to their normal home, is rather irrelevant.

Sleeping in the open, with nothing but the sky for a "roof," is one of the great pleasures of backpacking. To lie in your sleeping bag and watch the starlit skies overhead before falling asleep is an exhilarating experience. Yet there are occasions when flies, mosquitoes, ants, and other "peskies" can definitely detract from the pleasure of such a night. There may also be times when you want to be away from camp for brief periods but would like to leave your bed and some items of clothing or gear on the ground without having them accessible to bugs, rodents, snakes, birds, etc.

The "tent" described here is lightweight and will provide protection from the nuisances mentioned above. Yet you will still retain that pleasurable feeling of sleeping in the open and won't feel "cooped up" when using this tent. It is made essentially of nylon mosquito netting, which is a rather strong but lightweight material. For rain protection you simply cover the nylon netting "tent" with a plastic fly sheet or a fly sheet made of waterproof coated nylon. (It should be pointed out that the best commercially made mountain tents are not waterproof. For absolute protection against rain a separate flysheet must be used.) It is not difficult to make a nylon netting tent. The sketch below shows dimensions of the finished tent and paragraphs that follow describe the fabrication process.

MATERIALS

1. Nylon mosquito netting, about five square yards, required for top and ends of tent. Netting is sold in varying widths, so note the catalogue width and figure your requirements accordingly before ordering. Suggested sources are Recreational Equipment, Alp Sport, or Holubar. Dimensions of the floor, top and ends are cut about 1" larger than dimensions of the finished tent, to allow for overlap in sewing.

2. Cotton percale, nylon parachute cloth or other light weight cloth for tent floor, three square yards needed. You can use one of the special, light weight, waterproof tent fabrics if you wish, but this will make the tent more expensive. It is suggested that a cheaper material be used for your first tent. You can waterproof it with a waterproofing compound if you wish. You can easily cut out the floor and replace it with a more expensive one at a later date, if desired.

3. Two thirty inch zippers. A slip cover zipper, such as sold by Sears Roebuck Co., is satisfactory and inexpensive.

4. Use nylon thread for all sewing. Ask for the nylon thread that is made specifically for use in sewing machines. It has a relatively rough surface and is not shiny in appearance.

TOP. For the top you will need a piece of netting forty-seven inches wide at one end, sixty-seven inches wide at the other end, and ninety-seven inches long.

FLOOR. Using whatever material you have chosen for the floor, cut the floor piece to dimensions of thirty-three inches wide at the foot end, thirty-six inches wide at the head end, and ninety-seven inches long. If you expect to be doing much camping in wet weather it is suggested that you increase each of the floor dimensions so as to permit the floor to overlap the nylon netting top and ends about four to six inches. In such case the floor should be waterproofed or made of waterproof material.

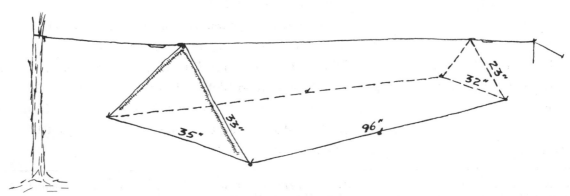

Backpack tent with plastic fly sheet for rain protection.

Backpack tent with coated nylon cloth (waterproof) fly.

Correct method of using shock cord in ridge line to provide "give."

ENDS. Make a triangular piece of netting which is thirty-six inches along the base (ground) edge and thirty-four inches along each of the other edges (about twenty-nine inches high). Sew the two zippers onto this front end piece so that the open ends of the zippers meet about one inch down from the peak of the triangle. One zipper should be sewn to open from the outside, the other from the inside. The foot end (before sewing) is a triangle thirty-three inches along the base and twenty-four inches along each of the other edges (about seventeen inches high).

A small hole, about 1/8 inch diameter, is needed at the peak of each end. The tent ridge line is installed inside the tent, passes through this small hole at each end, and is tied to cloth loops at the front and foot end of the tent.

SEWING. All of the sewing on this tent can be done on an ordinary household sewing machine. Sew a piece of cloth about four inches square to the netting at the top front of the tent and at the top foot end. Then sew small loops of cloth to these points for securing the ridge line. Sew three small loops for stakes, about one inch diameter, along each side of the floor (head end, foot end and center). Before sewing the loops you can sew on four inch squares of cloth at these points, if you wish, for reinforcement. Next, using straight pins or a basting stitch, fasten the floor loosely to the top. When that is done it is suggested that you take the tent to a level spot in your yard, install it on a ridge line of proper slope, and stake out the ground edges. When you are satisfied that your pins or basting stitches are properly located, take the tent back to the sewing machine and sew the floor securely to the top.

Next sew the foot end to the tent, then the head end. If you want to be cautious, use the straight pin or basting stitch procedure, with another trial setup in the yard.

THE RIDGE LINE. It is recommended that you use parachute cord or an avalanche cord for a ridge line. Use a piece about twenty feet long and leave it permanently attached to the tent. It is secured by a knot to the cloth loops at the front top and foot end top of the tent. Erect the tent in the yard, and with some trial and error secure the ridge line so that when it is pulled taut the ridge of the tent material is smooth (free of wrinkles) but not stressed.

It is also recommended that you install about a one foot length of 1/8 inch diameter shock cord in the ridge line, adjacent to the front and foot ends of the tent (outside). Install the shock cord by first tying one end of it securely at the desired point in the ridge line. Shock cord does not tie easily. Pull each part of the knot tight with pliers. Next, tie the other end of the shock cord into the ridge line at such distance from the first point that when the shock cord is stretched to the desired degree the ridge line will have a definite sag in it between these two points. However, if the shock cord is stretched very much further, the ridge line becomes parallel to it and the ridge line takes the stress.

USE. Many tents require poles to be carried or cut at the site or two trees ten to fifteen feet apart, with a level area between. The latter are frequently difficult to find at the particular spot where you decide to camp. This tent only requires a tree or good sized bush near the head end for fastening the ridge line. A short stick, near the foot end, will keep that end at the proper height. It is best to erect the rain fly on a separate ridge line, about one foot higher than the tent ridge line, so cut the width of the plastic fly sheet accordingly. The length of the fly should be such that it will extend about two feet out over the front edge of the tent and about one foot past the foot end. Secure the ground edge with round, smooth rocks. Have all of the rocks ready and in place before trying to put up the fly. A slight breeze may blow the plastic fly into a tree or bush and tear it, so use caution at this stage. Once it is up there is normally no danger of tearing. If a heavy plastic fly sheet is used, you may be able to insert grommets along the ground edge and hold the sheet in place with stakes. The best and most rugged fly is, of course, waterproof nylon cloth.

The writer has used such a rig as described above on many wilderness backpack trips and, in emergencies, has weathered hard driving rain storms, sleet storms and snow storms. This is a good outfit for most mild weather backpacking.

APPENDIX D

ONE-WHEEL DUFFEL CARRIER

Some time ago I gave a talk and demonstration on backpacking to a Scoutmaster's round table group at Las Cruces, New Mexico. Afterward there was the usual question and answer session. One Scoutmaster raised the question, "How do I take a deserving and qualified Scout who happens to have such a small body build that he cannot possibly carry a pack of sufficient size to hold his gear on a full-scale backpack trip?" My answer was that I frankly did not know. However, for some time afterward I gave the matter some very serious thought. Why should such a Scout, or any other person for that matter, be denied the pleasure of a backwoods trip simply because his physical size and strength do not permit him to carry a large enough pack?

My first thought was that pack animals could be used. However, I have had considerable experience with pack animals, pack mules in particular, and I quickly realized that many persons would not have the knowledge and experience to successfully manage pack animals. I do not like to see mechanized equipment of any kind used on pack trips. However, after much deliberation and planning, I designed and built a one-wheel pack carrier or duffel carrier, which will be briefly described in the following paragraphs.

The chassis or main structure of this carrier consists of a two-by-four wood member mounted to a bicycle wheel. A new sixteen inch bicycle wheel was purchased and a semi-pneumatic "flat-proof" tire mounted to the rim. The tires are heated in hot water and forced onto the rim.

There is no inner tube or valve stem. Strap iron members then were used to mount the two-by-four to the axle of the wheel. A "superstructure" was added to the two-by-four main member to provide a load-carrying surface eighteen inches wide and seventy-two inches long. "Handles" were added front and aft.

I will readily admit that I have not used this one-wheel carrier for any full-scale backwoods trips. However it has been used for trial runs on nearby mountain trails. It will do the job of transporting gear over mountain trails, where a reasonably good trail is available. It will readily carry 125 to 150 pounds, and this is enough for four persons.

While working on this device another thought occurred to me. There are many outdoorsmen with families who would like to take the members of their family on a backwoods trip. However, there are often small children involved. The children can frequently do the necessary hiking but simply cannot carry a pack. Also, some outdoorsmen have had their future backpack activities permanently damaged by strapping too large a pack on the wife and taking off into the woods. Speaking from experience, some of the most pleasurable and memorable pack trips I have taken have been with my family. More families would do well to give it a try, and such a one-wheel carrier may help them to do so. Many times I have observed that suitable, attractive areas for a backwoods outing lie only a day's travel from the road head. Yet, much of the hiking population only penetrates the woods to the extent that they can travel to a given area and back to the roadhead in a single day. They are missing a lot by not having the means and technique to stay for a day or two.

1

2

3

Stages of fabrication

1. Wheel assembled to chassis (two-by-four)
2. Top view, wheel and chassis
3. Finished carrier, with load carrying superstructure mounted on chassis.

Carrier in use

APPENDIX E

WILDERNESSES AND PRIMITIVE AREAS IN THE NATIONAL FORESTS

State	National Forest	Headquarters	Total Acreage
ARIZONA			
Blue Range (also in N. Mex.)	Apache	Springerville	180,139
Chiricahua	Coronado	Tucson	18,000
Galiuro	Coronado	Tucson	52,717
Mazatzal	Tonto	Phoenix	205,137
Mount Baldy	Apache	Springerville	7,106
Pine Mountain	Prescott	Prescott	16,399
	Tonto	Phoenix	
Sierra Ancha	Tonto	Phoenix	20,850
Superstition	Tonto	Phoenix	124,117
Sycamore Canyon	Coconino	Flagstaff	49,575
	Kaibab	Williams	
	Prescott	Prescott	
CALIFORNIA			
Agua Tibia	Cleveland	San Diego	25,995
Caribou	Lassen	Susanville	19,080
Cucamonga....................	San Bernardino	San Bernardino	9,022
Desolation	Eldorado	Placerville	41,343
Dome Land	Sequoia	Porterville	62,121
Emigrant	Stanislaus	Sonora	97,020
High Sierra	Sierra	Fresno	10,247
	Sequoia	Porterville	
Hoover	Toiyabe	Reno, Nev.	42,779
	Inyo	Bishop, Calif.	
John Muir.....................	Sierra	Fresno	503,258
	Inyo	Bishop	
Marble Mountain	Klamath	Yreka	213,363
Minarets	Inyo	Bishop	109,484
	Sierra	Fresno	
Mokelumne	Eldorado	Placerville	50,400
	Stanislaus	Sonora	
Salmon Trinity Alps	Klamath	Yreka	223,340
	Shasta-Trinity	Redding	
San Gabriel	Angeles	Pasadena	36,137
San Gorgonio	San Bernardino	San Bernardino	34,644
San Jacinto	San Bernardino	San Bernardino	20,564
San Rafael	Los Padres	Santa Barbara	142,722
South Warner	Modoc	Alturas	68,507
Thousand Lakes	Lassen	Susanville	15,695
Ventana	Los Padres	Santa Barbara	52,769
Yolla Bolly-Middle Eel	Mendocino	Willows	108,451
	Shasta-Trinity	Redding	
COLORADO			
Flat Tops	White River	Glenwood Springs	102,124
Gore Range-Eagle Nest	Arapaho	Golden	61,101
	White River	Glenwood Springs	
La Garita.....................	Gunnison	Gunnison	48,486
	Rio Grande	Monte Vista	
Maroon Bells-Snowmass	White River	Glenwood Springs	71,060
Mt. Zirkel....................	Routt	Steamboat Springs	72,472
Rawah	Roosevelt	Fort Collins	26,674
San Juan.....................	San Juan	Durango	238,407

State	National Forest	Headquarters	Total Acreage
Uncompahgre	Uncompahgre	Delta	53,252
Upper Rio Grande	Rio Grande	Monte Vista	56,600
West Elk	Gunnison	Gunnison	61,412
Wilson Mountains	San Juan	Durango	27,347
	Uncompahgre	Delta	
IDAHO			
Idaho	Boise	Boise	1,224,733
	Challis	Challis	
	Salmon	Salmon	
	Payette	McCall	
Sawtooth	Boise	Boise	200,942
	Challis	Challis	
	Sawtooth	Twin Falls	
Salmon River Breaks	Nezperce	Grangeville	216,870
	Bitterroot	Hamilton, Mont.	
Selway-Bitterroot (see also Montana) .	Clearwater	Orofino	988,655
	Nezperce	Grangeville	
	Bitterroot	Hamilton, Mont.	
MINNESOTA			
Boundary Waters Canoe Area	Superior	Duluth	747,128
MONTANA			
Absaroka	Gallatin	Bozeman	64,000
Anaconda-Pintlar	Beaverhead	Dillon	157,803
	Bitterroot	Hamilton	
	Deerlodge	Butte	
Beartooth	Gallatin	Bozeman	230,000
	Custer	Billings	
Bob Marshall	Flathead	Kalispell	950,000
	Lewis & Clark	Great Falls	
Cabinet Mountains	Kootenai	Libby	94,272
	Kaniksu	Sandpoint, Idaho	
Gates of the Mountains	Helena	Helena	28,562
Mission Mountains	Flathead	Kalispell	73,340
Selway-Bitterroot (see also Idaho) ...	Bitterroot	Hamilton	251,930
	Lolo	Missoula, Mont.	
Spanish Peaks	Gallatin	Bozeman	49,857
NEVADA			
Jarbidge	Humboldt	Elko	64,667
NEW HAMPSHIRE			
Great Gulf	White Mountain	Laconia	5,552
NEW MEXICO			
Black Range	Gila	Silver City	169,356
Blue Range (see also Arizona)	Apache	Springerville, Ariz.	36,598
Gila Wilderness	Gila	Silver City	433,690
Gila Primitive Area	Gila	Silver City	130,637
Pecos	Santa Fe	Santa Fe	167,416
	Carson	Taos	
San Pedro Parks	Santa Fe	Santa Fe	41,132
Wheeler Peak	Carson	Taos	6,027
White Mountain	Lincoln	Alamogordo	31,171

State	National Forest	Headquarters	Total Acreage
NORTH CAROLINA			
Linville Gorge	Pisgah	Asheville	7,575
Shinning Rock	Pisgah	Asheville	13,350
OREGON			
Diamond Peak	Deschutes	Bend	35,440
	Willamette	Eugene	
Eagle Cap	Wallowa-Whitman	Baker	220,416
Gearhart Mountain	Fremont	Lakeview	18,709
Kalmiopsis	Siskiyou	Grants Pass	76,900
Mt. Hood	Mt. Hood	Portland	14,160
Mt. Jefferson	Deschutes	Bend	99,600
	Mt. Hood	Portland	
	Willamette	Eugene	
Mount Washington	Deschutes	Bend	46,655
	Willamette	Eugene	23,071
Mountain Lakes	Winema	Klamath Falls	33,003
Strawberry Mountain	Malheur	John Day	196,708
Three Sisters	Deschutes	Bend	
	Willamette	Eugene	
UTAH			
High Uintas	Ashley	Vernal	237,177
	Wasatch	Salt Lake City	
WASHINGTON			
Glacier Peak	Mt. Baker	Bellingham	464,219
	Wenatchee	Wenatchee	
Goat Rocks	Gifford Pinchot	Vancouver	82,680
	Snoqualmie	Seattle	
Mount Adams	Gifford Pinchot	Vancouver	42,411
Pasayten	Okanogan	Okanogan	518,000
	Mt. Baker	Bellingham	
WYOMING			
Bridger	Bridger	Kemmerer	383,300
Cloud Peak	Bighorn	Sheridan	137,000
Glacier	Shoshone	Cody	177,000
North Absaroka	Shoshone	Cody	351,104
Popo Agie	Shoshone	Cody	70,000
South Absaroka	Shoshone	Cody	483,130
Stratified	Shoshone	Cody	203,930
Teton	Teton	Jackson	563,500

APPENDIX F

SOURCES FOR MAPS, TRAIL INFORMATION, AND BACKPACKING INFORMATION

Adirondack Mountain Club
Gabriels, New York 12939

Appalachian Mountain Club
5 Joy Street
Boston, Massachusetts 02108

The Appalachian Trail Conference
1718 N Street N.W.
Washington, D.C. 20036

Direccion de Geografia
Y Meteorologia
Tacubaya, D.F., Mexico

Federation of Western Outdoor Clubs
201 S. Ashdale Street
West Covina, California 94590

Greb Hiking Bureau
1 Adams Street
Kitchener, Ontario, Canada

Green Mountain Club
108 Merchants Row
Rutland, Vermont 05701

Mazamas
909 N.W. 19th Avenue
Portland, Oregon 97209

New York-New Jersey Trail Conference
G.P.O. Box 2250
New York, New York 10001

The Sierra Club
1050 Mills Tower
San Francisco, California 94104

U.S. Forest Service
Washington, D.C. 20240
(and Regional Forest Service Offices)

U.S. Geological Survey
1028 General Services, Administration Building
Washington, D.C. 20240

U.S. Geological Survey
Federal Center
Denver, Colorado 80204

Wilderness Society
729 15th Street N.W.
Washington, D.C. 20005

APPENDIX G

ORGANIZATIONS WHICH PROMOTE CONSERVATION OF NATURAL RESOURCES

The following is a partial list of some well-known organizations that are fighting the uphill battle of conservation, from one standpoint or another. You are urged to take an active interest in the programs of one or more of these organizations. If nothing more, you can at least become a dues-paying member. Don't delay! Write to them today!

American Forestry Association
919 17th Street N.W.
Washington, D.C. 20006

American Planning and Civic Association
901 Union Trust Building
Washington, D.C. 20005

American Recreation Society
1404 New York Avenue N.W.
Washington, D.C. 20005

Appalachian Trail Conference
1916 Sunderland Place
Washington, D.C. 20036

The Conservation Foundation
30 E. 40th Street
New York, New York 10016

Defenders of Wildlife
731 Dupont Circle Building
Washington, D.C. 20036

General Federation of Women's Clubs
1734 N Street N.W.
Washington, D.C. 20036

The Izaak Walton League of America
1326 Waukegan Road
Glenview, Illinois 60025

National Association of Soil and Water
    Conservation Districts
1424 K Street N.W.
Washington, D.C. 20005

National Audubon Society
1130 Fifth Avenue
New York, New York 10028

National Parks Association
1300 New Hampshire Avenue N.W.
Washington, D.C. 20036

National Parks and Conservation Association
1701 18th Street N.W.
Washington, D.C. 20009

National Recreation Association
8 West Eighth Street
New York, New York 10011

National Wildlife Federation
1412 16th Street N.W.
Washington, D.C. 20036

The Sierra Club
1050 Mills Tower
San Francisco, California 94104

The Wilderness Society
2144 P Street N.W.
Washington, D.C. 20037

Wildlife Management Institute
709 Wire Building
Washington, D.C. 20005

APPENDIX H

SURVIVAL

The aspect of survival usually implies that you have had an emergency of some sort in the woods or other remote area. Yet, when one starts thinking and talking about survival, the discussion almost invariably centers on precautions to take so that actual survival circumstances are not encountered. When we get right down to fundamentals, your knowledge and experience in backwoods travel (under various conditions) are the most important tools at your disposal for either preventing circumstances from developing into a situation that calls for survival techniques or for successfully getting out of an emergency situation if one does occur. A situation that might cause one individual or a group to go into semipanic might cause a more experienced individual or group only mild concern. Or, the latter might simply look upon the situation as an interesting challenge. So if you want to avoid a serious emergency in the woods, take every opportunity to add to your knowledge and experience. This especially concerns travel and living in foul weather, staying oriented at all times, knowing where the next water supply is, first aid, and preparedness for emergencies.

As your knowledge and experience grow, you will become more sure of yourself. This in turn will lead to a "frame of mind" and an "attitude" toward the backwoods that can save your life in an emergency. Panic has caused more persons to lose their lives under emergency situations than any other single factor. Many people who take to the woods are fine as long as the sun is shining and the birds are singing. But let a little foul weather move in or a slight emergency occur, and they start seeing hidden dangers behind every rock and tree. This is due to lack of knowledge and experience. There is nothing in the woods that can or will hurt you if you take reasonable precautions. You are in far less danger there than in traveling around in a big city. That statement is made with full knowledge of a number of accidents that have involved campground bears, as well as certain other so-called "hazards" of the woods.

So, take every opportunity to increase your knowledge and experience of the woods. If you are a beginner, when you go on a backpack trip try to go with persons who are knowledgeable. If this is not practical, go in an area which has well-marked and frequently used trails and don't get more than one or two days' travel away from the roadhead. Give some frequent thought to emergency situations that could occur, and

mentally plan, step by step, what you would do about them. Do this often enough that if the emergency does occur your reaction to the situation will be somewhat automatic, and it will not be such a shock to you.

Probably the most frequent mishap among backpackers that is likely to call for some survival techniques is to get lost. When you enter a remote area, you should not only have a good map but also a good mental picture of the area. Is the overall area bounded on one side by a road? How many hours' travel is it from the vicinity that you will be in? Perhaps there are one or more streams in the area. Do they eventually lead to a small town or other habitation? In what general direction do they lie with respect to your planned route and, again, how many hours' travel would be required to reach them? What are the most prominent unmistakable landmarks of the region? Are there occupied fire spotting towers or survey stations in the area, and could you find your way to them if you had to?

A most important factor is water. If you were lost you might not be able to find your way to a spring or small lake, unless they were marked by very prominent landmarks. However, if you knew that a stream lay parallel to your general route of travel and about how many hours it would take to reach it, that could be extremely important information to your survival. You can live a long time without food, but your days are few if you don't have water.

Survival, under the conditions that most backpackers would encounter the need for survival techniques, would probably be for a period of a few days or a week, at the most. Let's say that in a party of two or more backpackers one member gets sick or hurt. If the injured or sick person could not travel you would ordinarily make him as comfortable as possible and go for help. You would leave him in the care of a third member of the party, if there is a third member. There is nothing in the woods that will hurt him and, unless he is dying, he will be all right until you return with help. You would make certain that the injured person had ample water and, preferably, some food within reach.

You can backpack for years and never get lost. Most of our wilderness areas and National Forests have well-marked main trails. If you stay on or close to those main trails there is no reason to get lost. Backpackers being what they are, however, you will eventually want to push further into the backwoods, away from the main trails. (I admit to being temporarily lost in the wilderness quite a few times.) When you leave the main, well-marked, frequently used trails, that is when you need to be alert to the possibility of getting lost, be especially meticulous about keeping yourself oriented. Know where you are at all times with respect to major landmarks. As soon as you realize you are lost, try to backtrack if you can. That is, try to find your way back to a known trail, stream, or other landmark rather than to keep pushing ahead. Frequently a party will be "lost" with respect to where they are going but not in regard to where they are. That is, they have an objective in mind that lies somewhere ahead, but the trail has "vanished" and they don't know where to find it. Yet, if they face the truth in time, they will be able to find their way back to where they came from. The answer is — BACKTRACK! Forget the objective for this particular trip. Wait until you can arrange for some assistance from someone who is familiar with the area.

Let's assume, however, that you not only are lost with respect to the way ahead, but you aren't too sure of the way back. When you know you are really lost, make a firm and immediate resolution that you are going to pay particular attention to your "frame of mind" or mental attitude until the ordeal is over. Act slowly and very deliberately. Don't move hastily or do anything else hastily. Haste often leads to panic under such circumstances. Remember that the human body has far more mental strength, as well as physical endurance, than most people have ever put to test. The "old woodsman" books say to sit down on a log and smoke your pipe. OK, if that's what it takes, do it. (Check your match supply first.)

One of the first things to consider when you realize you are lost is water. How much water do you have with you? How far must you go in a certain direction before you are fairly certain of coming to a water supply? Do you recall passing a stream, spring, or other water supply during the past few hours? If possible, head back for it now. When you have found a water supply, stay with it until you have developed a positive plan for getting out of your predicament. Your water supply is always a foremost consideration when backpacking. When you are lost, it should be constantly considered.

Do you have any kind of container, aside from perhaps a one or two quart canteen? If not, unless you are in an area where water is abundant, you had better plan to camp awhile near the water supply you have found. Set up your "headquarters" there. From that headquarters you should carefully make short trips out in straight lines of travel in the most likely directions of picking up familiar landmarks. Mark your path out from your "headquarters"

WATER CONTAINERS. The one gallon plastic jug and 2½ gallon plastic bag make good containers for an emergency water supply. They weigh (empty) 4 oz. and 8 oz., respectively.

or base camp very carefully so that there will be no doubt in finding your way back again. Spend several days or more in making these reconnoiter trips if necessary. A little elevation can sometimes be a big help in orienting yourself. Try and find some higher ground from which you can scan the area you are in. If you can find a tree in a favorable location that isn't too hard to climb, give that a try. In the meantime try and make some additional water containers. A sheet of plastic, a waterproof garment or a ground cloth can be fashioned into a water pouch holding one to three gallons and carried on the end of a stick over your shoulder (like a "hobo"). If you have a water supply and have fashioned a means of carrying more water, you now have the most important single item necessary to your survival.

Your knowledge and experience in backwoods travel are also very important, as stressed earlier. Hopefully you have substantial amounts of both; otherwise you should have stayed with the main, well-marked, frequently used trails. Other things to consider soon after you realize you are lost are protection from the elements and various ways of attracting attention, particularly from possible passing aircraft. There are very few areas in the United States these days that do not have an occasional passing aircraft. If you are in a National Forest or wilderness area, it is quite likely that there will be aircraft within view almost daily, primarily Forest Service patrol planes.

Now, how do you attract their attention? Hopefully, your normal backpack gear or your survival kit (which we will discuss later) contains a steel mirror. It is a very important item. A mirror is the most reliable means of attracting attention from passing aircraft. There are heavy glass mirrors, with sighting holes, made especially for signalling. However, with a little practice an ordinary steel mirror can be used and will be just as effective. (Do your practicing at home or on a routine hike, before the need for emergency use comes up.) The steel mirror will be lighter and will not be subject to breakage. The universal distress sign is three of a kind; a volley of three gunshots, three fires or three billows of smoke from one fire, three flashes of a mirror, etc. Lacking a mirror you can use a knife blade or the shiny surface of a cooking utensil, metal container, etc. These are not nearly as dependable, however.

Another good "attention getter," especially in a forest, is smoke. Forest Service planes make regular patrols for the purpose of spotting forest fires. Fire towers are scattered throughout many of our forests for the prime purpose of locating forest fires and fixing their position. If you can build a fire and make enough smoke for them to

see (it doesn't take much), you can be reasonably sure that the fire will be investigated. One problem, in the case of aircraft, is having the fire going and enough "greenery" available to make the necessary smoke at the particular moment that a plane comes into view. A solution to this is a smoke signal cartridge, of the type shown in part 7 of this book. With such a cartridge you have instantaneous smoke in good quantity when you need it. Such a smoke cartridge (or several) is recommended as an item for the survival kit of every party that ventures into the remote sections of the forests or wilderness areas.

By this time you are probably wondering, "When do we eat?" For the most part, forget it. You can go a long time without eating. It is unlikely that the average survival situation which a backpacker would encounter would be of such duration that food would be a great problem. If you have some food with you it should be rationed from the beginning of your emergency. One substantial portion of food per day is better than three smaller portions or frequent "nibbling" under such conditions. Also, it is sometimes possible to eat off the land to some extent. Berries or nuts in season are obvious foods.

Hopefully, your normal gear or survival kit included fishing line and hooks. Catch yourself a fish if you can. In shallow streams fish or minnows can sometimes be driven into very shallow pockets and clubbed or beached. A log or stick entrance way or "funnel" to the shallow area will help keep them there. Minnows are eaten whole.

Deadfalls and snares for the trapping of animals are usually associated with survival

CATTAIL ROOTS. These are a good survival food. They occur over a large area of the country and cattail is easily recognized. The roots can be eaten raw or cooked (boiled).

periods of weeks in extremely remote areas and would not normally be applicable. However, if you should come across a porcupine take the time to "do him in" and take him along as a food supply. Also, snakes (including rattlesnakes) are a good source of food and can usually be easily killed if you see any. The best way to kill a rattlesnake is to use a stick four or five feet long and to strike him sharply just back of the head. It is very difficult to kill a rattlesnake by throwing stones at it. Also, don't follow a rattlesnake into dense cover. (You already have enough problems.) Frogs are a possibility, but don't eat toads. A rabbit will sometimes "freeze" in position hoping you don't see him, and you may be able to get one if you carry a stick or stone. Lastly, insects are an important source of food under such circumstances. Grubs (from rotted stumps or logs), grasshoppers, etc., are good food. Practically all flying insects are satisfactory food, and a small light or fire at night, in season, will attract large numbers. They can be eaten as is or roasted on a flat stone after the stone has been heated in a fire.

Let's say that after three or four days of living in your "headquarters" camp you have been unable to attract attention of aircraft, and you haven't been found by any surface-operating search parties. You have made regular reconnoitering trips out from your camp in straight line patterns like the spokes of a wheel. You have been unable to establish your position and pick up any firmly defined landmarks, although there are perhaps possibilities. You now have another decision to make. That is, whether to stay at your camp and make like Robinson Crusoe or to pack up all the water you can carry (along with a few other essentials) and strike out for "civilization."

Hopefully, in your "mind pattern" of the general area you will remember that there is a road paralleling the north-south border which should lie perhaps 20 miles about due east. Or, it may be a railroad. Perhaps there is a logging area bordering the National Forest you are in that is operating, and you are reasonably certain you can find it. Or your best way out may be a stream in some other direction that you know will lead to habitation some 30 or 40 miles distant. So you are ready to "pack up and head out." Avoid the choice of destination that, if you miss it, will simply take you deeper into the woods. A long stretch of road, a river, or a railroad are good places to head for because your chances of missing them are not nearly so great as a pin-point objective such as a logging camp or small town. In packing up, forget the luxuries. Take all food, all the water you can carry (up to three or four gallons per person), your survival kit, and necessary clothing. If the weather is hot conserve your energy by traveling as soon as it is daylight and resting during the heat of the day. If the weather is hot, it is just as important to keep your body cool as it is to ration your water. Avoid hurrying and any excessive exertion. Especially if your water is in short supply, take every precaution to avoid sweating (and loss of body water). Utilize shade when possible to save a few degrees in temperature (and, water). Every time you come to a water supply fill up your water containers. Have your signalling mirror and smoke cartridges handy. If you are following a river you can of course dump most of your water supply while you are traveling with the stream. As soon as you leave the river, however, fill up all water containers.

Whether to follow mountain ridges or canyons in traveling is a question of terrain. Although there are exceptions, a lot of backpacking is done in fairly high country. To leave the country you will want to go down. If there is a canyon with a stream (or a trickle) of water at the bottom it will be very wise to stay with it, if it goes in the general direction you are heading. "Staying with it" does not necessarily mean walking in the bottom of the canyon. The canyon may be fairly wide at the bottom and provide relatively easy going, or it may be quite narrow, with possibly dangerous cliffs to be negotiated. In such cases it will be better to stay on higher ground, probably the first ridge on one or the other side of the canyon. Canyon bottoms may also have almost impenetrable thickets and undergrowth because the bottom gets more rain runoff. So, whether you travel the ridges or the canyon bottoms, or some of both, will depend upon the particular terrain. Again, if there is a trickle of water in that canyon bottom, keep it in sight as long as possible. You may also strike out through more "open" country. However, traveling through heavy timber without a trail to follow can be next to impossible. Down timber and thickets will frequently be so dense as to simply rule this out. Also, attempting to travel in such a forest will probably get you "more lost" than you already are.

If you come to a trail and you are sure it is not a game trail, it will probably be best to follow it. That will depend on your knowledge of the area and where the trail may lead. Certainly if it is a well-used trail you would definitely follow it, rather than to cross it and plunge into the woods again. The same applies to a road or a railroad, or a power line. You would follow it with the probability that it would lead to habitation. Which way to follow it would, again, depend upon your knowledge of the area. Normally, however, you would follow

TRAIL MARKER. Lightweight cloth strips, made up at home and numbered with a felt tip pen, make excellent trail markers. They are tied to a tree limb or bush at conspicuous places along the trail, using a simple overhand knot. A note on the back trail is made on a 3 X 5 inch card, or in a small notebook. The note is numbered to correspond with the number on the cloth strip marker.

in the direction that takes you to predominantly a lower elevation. When you come to such a trail or road, it would be a good idea to impale a three by five inch note card (another item for the survival kit) or tie it on a branch with a string in plain view of persons who may travel the trail or road. The note card should give your name, address, phone number, and the fact that you are lost. Specify the date and the direction you are headed on the trail or road. Ask the reader to get in touch with certain family members or authorities, or both.

By following these procedures you may arrive back at civilization. It cannot be stressed too strongly that, before going into a remote area, some responsible person or persons should be notified in advance that you are going, the general area you will be in, and the date you will be back. They should also be told that if you are not back by that date you have met with an emergency and they are to notify authorities to start a search for you. This immediately makes it apparent that the most favored choice for survival is to set up camp very near the point you became lost and make like "Robinson Crusoe." Then the searchers will have perhaps a ten or twenty square mile area to search for you instead of 100 or 200 square miles. You should

only try to travel out if, for some reason, the odds are all against your being found where you are. If you are embarrassed by being lost and that is about to cause you to strike out into unfamiliar country, forget it. That too could cost you your life. Statistics have proven time and time again that if you are thoroughly lost your best chance for survival is to "stay put." Find the best place for a "camp" in the area you are in, make yourself as comfortable as possible, and wait for rescue. Try to make camp in an area where there is open terrain nearby. In addition to a smoke signalling fire, stamp out a pattern in the snow (if there is snow), use fire ashes to make a pattern, stake out a bright colored tent or ground sheet, and use all other available means to aid aircraft in spotting your location.

And now some word about that survival kit. Some of the items mentioned are simply those that you would normally carry as part of your routine backpacking gear and they will be carried in a packsack pocket or wherever you normally carry them. However, a few items are "special," and it is recommended that you actually carry them in a small, separate kit, to be used only for survival purposes.

The following are items that are generally carried as a part of your normal backpacking gear. If not, they should be when you venture off the main trails of a Wilderness or Forest area:

1. Matches (several supplies stowed in different places in your pack(s) and more than normally carried).

2. Long-burning candles. Two or more candles that will burn six hours or longer. Save your match supply by lighting a candle and using it for starting a fire each time you need fire.

3. First aid kit (the more remote the area, the more complete it should be).

4. Extra water container(s). Several collapsible plastic, one gallon containers are good. During "normal" travel they will possibly be carried empty.

5. Heavy plastic or coated nylon (waterproof) tarp.

6. Cold weather clothing if there is a possibility of low temperatures.

7. Map. Also a good "homemade" sketch of the area that has been drawn with the aid of a person who is thoroughly familiar with the area. It should show all important trails, sources of water and recognizable landmarks that may not be included on a commercial map.

8. A good compass.

9. Canteen for each member of the party.

10. A good knife, a saw and such items of cooking gear, equipment and clothing as are nor-

mally carried by an experience backpacker.

11. Good flashlight(s) and extra bulb. At least one flashlight in party should be a "C" or "D" size. Extra batteries.

12. Small sewing kit.

The following additional items should be carried and many of these might be contained in a special, specific "survival" container:

1. Three or more smoke cartridges for signalling (see part 7 for photographs).

2. Some survival foods. Meatbars, jerky, pemmican, and nuts are good (concentrated and rich in protein, with some fat). Carry extra salt.

3. Note cards, three by five inches (fifteen or twenty cards). A good wood pencil. Enough transparent, plastic map covering material to cover ten or fifteen of the note cards and make them waterproof, after the note is written. Some stout cord for hanging note cards (with a written message) in a prominent place along your trail or at "camps" to aid a search party in finding you.

4. Trail markers. Strips of very light weight cloth, with a number added.

5. About one square yard of nylon mosquito netting, preferably about two feet wide by four feet long to use for fashioning into a net to catch insects for food and for seining minnows or fish for food.

6. Some fish line, a few hooks and some split shot (sinkers).

7. Some "picture frame" wire to possibly use for an animal snare.

8. Water purification tablets. (Iodine tablets are somewhat preferable to halazone.)

9. Whistle (shrill and loud, for signalling).

For a final bit of advice, don't let your pack get lost. (It has happened.) A hiker may throw off his pack and maybe walk to a certain vantage point for a better view, perhaps only a short distance away. He then returns for his pack and finds it isn't there. (It is still there but he didn't return to the exact spot where he left his pack.) Obviously this is a serious situation. Your pack is your "house" when you are in the woods, and keeping it with you may very well decide the difference between surviving and not surviving.

APPENDIX I

SUB-ZERO CAMPING

James (Gil) Phillips of Albuquerque, New Mexico, a good friend of the author, is one of the foremost experts in the United States on camping in sub-zero weather. When temperatures plunge to 30 or 40° below zero, Gil heads for Wolf Creek Pass in southern Colorado. For a number of years, Gil has taken groups of interested persons into that area in January to instruct them on camping out in sub-zero weather and thoroughly enjoying it. He has developed a complete line of clothing and cold weather gear for this type of camping, based on a unique approach to the problem of staying comfortable in cold weather, that many outdoorsmen are not familiar with. The purpose of the next few pages is not to make you an expert on cold weather camping but rather to briefly describe Gil's techniques and equipment, and perhaps spark your interest so that you will want to look into the subject further. Before describing the equipment in some detail, let's first briefly discuss some basic concepts that Gil has developed, largely through his own learning process of trial and error.

FIRE

You do not need a fire or any source of artificial heat to keep warm at 40° below zero. As Gil says, suppose there was a blizzard or you could not find fire wood. You would be in real trouble if you had depended upon fire to keep you warm. The Eskimo never depends upon fire for warmth. Under certain conditions you may want a fire, but look upon it as a luxury, never as a necessity.

FOOD

You do not need hot food for such camping. Your body derives no more energy from hot food than it does from cold food. That doesn't mean you can't have some hot meals but, again, look upon hot food as a luxury, not a necessity.

BODY MOVEMENTS

The concept that you must work fast and move fast in such temperatures, in order to keep warm, is taboo. In such temperatures you move very slowly and deliberately. It takes five to seven times as long to perform simple camp jobs in such weather as it does in normal temperatures.

SLEEP

Some outdoorsmen consider it a fact that if you go to sleep in sub-zero weather you may never wake up. Gil Phillips claims this is essentially impossible to do. He says if you get cold enough you will wake up — shivering — just as you do in normally cold temperatures.

FEET AND HANDS

The extremities of the body, the feet and hands, are usually the first to get cold. The head usually gets cold last. To prevent heat loss from the body you need to protect all areas from exposure. The saying "If your feet are cold, put your hat on" is not at all farfetched. Another point, if your hands, ears, or another part get frostbitten, you do not rub them with snow. You rub the affected part with your hands to restore circulation. Or, you place your feet (for example) against someone else's bare chest or stomach for warmth.

PLASTIC FOAM AND PLASTIC SHEETING

A basic part of Gil's approach to keeping warm in sub-zero temperatures involves the use of plastic foam (polyurethane foam) and plastic sheeting. The polyurethane foam is the basic thermal insulation and moisture remover. The plastic sheeting is the wind stop and vapor barrier at the bottom of the bed. He wraps a plastic sheet completely around his bed, as will be described later. He says if you should get low on air to breathe you will wake up — fighting. He claims that only babies who lack the strength to work their way free from such an enclosed plastic sheet are in danger of suffocation.

SLEEPING BAG

The sleeping bag which Gil uses for sub-zero camping, as for articles of clothing, is made of polyurethane foam. The right thickness for the sleeping bag is about one to one and one-half inch. For some years Gil took Boy Scout troops on winter camping trips into the Pecos Wilderness of northern New Mexico. He taught the Scouts to make their own sleeping bags, as well as various articles of clothing, from polyurethane foam. Sleeping bags are always of mummy shape to conserve heat. The foam is glued together with automobile trim cement. A complete large-size sleeping bag weighs about 3½ pounds. In sub-zero temperatures you sleep with all clothes on and at 40° below zero such a sleeping bag will be comfortable. The manner in which this sleeping bag is made into a "bed" is quite unique and will be described in some detail.

A twelve foot square plastic sheet, of about 4 mil thickness, is a basic part of the bed. A polyurethane pad (without cover), twenty-four by seventy-two by one inch thick, is also needed. Lastly, you need a piece of nylon cloth about the same size as the poly pad, or slightly larger. The polyurethane pad is not for the purpose of bone comfort but rather moisture comfort. It carries the ice forming moisture away from the sleeping bag. The nylon cloth is placed beneath this pad and will be frozen stiff in the morning. It can be shaken out, hung in a breeze, and it will soon be dry — even in sub-zero temperatures.

The order of events in making up your bed for the night is as follows:

1. Lay the twelve by twelve foot plastic sheet down on the snow. The purpose of the plastic sheet is to form a waterproof barrier between your bed (sleeping bag) and the snow. It is also part of your wind barrier.

2. Lay the piece of nylon cloth down along one side of the plastic sheet.

3. On top of the nylon cloth goes the one inch thick polyurethane pad. On top of this you place your sleeping bag.

4. You now fold the free side of your plastic sheet over the top of the sleeping bag and tuck it under that part of the same plastic sheet which is already beneath the sleeping bag.

5. Next, that part of the plastic ground sheet extending out from the foot end of the sleeping bag is tucked underneath. The sleeping bag is now completely enclosed in the plastic sheet, with the plastic sheet tucked under one side and the foot end of the overall bed. There is still a slip-through "tunnel" formed by the plastic sheet extending beyond the head end of the bed. You "maneuver" through this end and slide into the sleeping bag when you are ready to go to bed, tucking the plastic sheet back under the bed at the sides, where it probably came "untucked" while you were getting into bed. Your supply of breathing air for the night comes through the "tunnel" of plastic extending out from the head end of the bed.

6. When you get into one of these beds for the night, you really get "all the way" in. Head, face, mouth and nose go inside the hood of the sleeping bag which is then drawn completely shut with the draw string, the string held by a simple knot or drawstring clamp. Air can pass freely through the foam as you breathe and there is no necessity of providing an opening at your face or nose.

Much of this procedure and technique seems contrary to the principles that many outdoors-

PREPARATION OF BED. A twelve foot by twelve foot plastic sheet is first laid on the ground (snow). A sheet of nylon cloth, slightly larger than the sleeping bag goes next. A one inch thick polyurethane pad goes on top of the nylon cloth. The sleeping bag is placed upon the foam pad. The free side of the plastic sheet is then folded over the top of the bed and tucked under at the side and foot end.

men, including the author, have long adhered to in using conventional sleeping bags of down, sleeping in small tents (if any shelter is used), fighting the problem of condensation, etc. A good goose down bag loses much of its insulating value when damp. The polyurethane sleeping bags apparently "eat up" the moisture. Gil Phillips explains the process like this:

"Moisture given off by your body during the night will pass into and through the polyurethane sleeping bag. The moisture from the sleeping bag then passes into the poly pad beneath the sleeping bag. The nylon cloth beneath the poly pad will soak up this moisture and may be frozen "stiff" with frost in the morning. This is easily removed by "beating" it out. It is dry "water dust," or sublimated evaporation. Also, the moisture that travels upward from your sleeping bag condenses on the inside surface of the cold plastic sheet. All of this moisture is "dust" in the morning and is simply shaken from the plastic sheeting."

BOOTIES

Your daytime footwear, the mukluks, are of course removed when you get into your sleeping bag. A foot "mitten" or "bootie" made of the polyurethane foam is worn at night to help keep the feet warm. Socks are not usually used, either for daytime use or at night.

CLOTHES

At temperatures below zero, one inch thick polyurethane foam is a basic part of the clothing. It is worn as underclothing next to the skin. You can use very large, loose fitting mesh underwear to hold in place the panels of foam which are wrapped around the trunk of the body and around the thighs. The arms and legs are also wrapped in sheets of foam. Wool or synthetic (nylon) trousers and wool shirts are recommended rather than cotton. Again, they should be very large and loose fitting, because of the builkiness of the foam to be worn underneath. Now for a few remarks on outer clothing.

WATERPROOFING

For temperatures below freezing, clothing should not be waterproof. Our bodies require that moisture be emitted even at 50 degrees below zero. If the clothing is waterproof this moisture is forced to stay in the clothing insulation. The moisture then reduces the effectiveness of the clothing in retaining body heat. You should use clothing that permits the continuous passage of moisture to the outside air as it is being formed. Poly foam has this characteristic, if it is not enclosed in a waterproof cover.

COAT

The coat should be large, loose fitting, and preferably long enough to reach well below the hips. Gil Phillips favors a quilted dacron type of coat with nylon outer cloth shell. A most important part of the coat is an attached hood. The hoods that you will normally find attached to such coats, if you find them at all, will be too light in weight (one layer of cloth) and too small. They must be large enough to accommodate a foam hat and possibly a face tunnel, which will be discussed in a moment. A suitable coat is so seldom found with a satisfactory hood that Gil finds it desirable to make his own hood and attach it to the coat after the coat is purchased. A quilted type of hood is best. A draw string is very important, to fit the hood around the face. The coat and the arms of the coat must be large enough that you can pull both arms out of the coat sleeves and cross them over your chest.

HAT

The hat is made of one inch polyurethane foam. It is to come well down on the forehead in front and to completely cover the back and sides of the neck.

FACE TUNNEL

The face tunnel might be considered part of the head gear. It is simply a piece of one inch poly foam shaped into an essentially cylindrical form. Clothes hanger wire is used to give "shape" to the tunnel.

MITTENS

Gloves are never used in sub-zero camping, always mittens. Your fingers need "companionship" to keep one another warm. The mittens are made of the one inch poly foam, with generous gauntlets covering the cuffs of the coat. A very important part of the mittens is a substantial cord which goes around the neck and shoulders to connect with the mittens. Losing one or both mittens in sub-zero temperatures can be disasterous. You never lay your mittens in some "convenient spot" while working. They stay with you constantly. In doing various camp chores, eating, etc., you will slip your hands out of the mittens for a few minutes at a time, then back into the mittens when they start getting cold. They are like a portable pocket.

MUKLUKS

As for any other type of backpacking, your feet and the "shoes" that you put them in are of the utmost importance. In sub-zero hiking and camping, a new dimension is added (compared to normal backpacking) — the requirement to keep the feet warm. Thermal socks, leather boots, rubber boots, rubber boots with leather uppers, etc., are all left at home when camping in sub-zero temperatures. Gil Phillips has found that the only satisfactory footwear are mukluks. He makes his own mukluks from a pair of over-size galoshes, with attached canvas uppers reaching almost to the knees. The galoshes are lined with one inch thick polyurethane foam. He does not use socks. He takes a piece of one inch polyurethane foam which is 29½ inches square and wraps each foot with this foam before inserting it in the mukluk. After a period of hiking the foam which is wrapped about the foot will tend to compress and wear in the area beneath the foot. Therefore, the foam is wrapped about the foot so that a different area falls beneath the sole of the foot each time the mukluks are put on.

EQUIPMENT SOURCES

It is possible to make your own polyurethane foam sleeping bag, hat, mittens and your own mukluks, and you may want to do this. The Ocate Company of Santa Fe, New Mexico, is now manufacturing these items on a commercial basis. Gil Phillips is a consultant to the company. One of the retail outlets of these products is "Camp and Trail Outfitters, 21 Park Place, New York, New York 10007

POLYURETHANE FOAM HAT AND FACE TUNNEL.
Gil Phillips is shown here with a poly foam hat and face
tunnel of the type he designed and has used for many
years in his sub-zero backpacking and camping. Other
articles of clothing, and sleeping bag, are made of the
same polyurethane foam.

FACE TUNNEL. The face tunnel is used in this manner.
The hood of the coat must be of generous size to accommodate the poly foam hat and face tunnel. The snow
goggles, being worn here, are very important as a preventive measure against snow blindness. Note the heavy
cord connecting the mittens. Loss of one or both
mittens could be a disaster.

MUKLUK. The mukluk is the only satisfactory footwear
for sub-zero temperatures and deep snow, according to
Gil Phillips. This is the chosen footwear of the Eskimo.

MOISTURE CONTROL

Whether you are hiking, working in camp, or in your sleeping bag, you should take the necessary precautions to avoid perspiring. Whether you perspire will depend primarily on the weather temperature, amount of wind, and your level of exertion. If you find you are starting to perspire, slow down in your exertion, open up your clothing a bit, or remove some of your clothes (or do all of these). Remember to move very slowly and deliberately at sub-zero temperatures.

SHELTER

Gil never uses tents in his sub-zero camping. He frequently makes his bed right out in the open on the snow, using the procedure described above under "Sleeping Bag." When he does build a shelter it is most frequently a snow house. His course of instruction in sub-zero hiking and camping techniques always includes a considerable amount of time spent in building snow houses, which the students then live in. The snow houses are made with snow blocks, cut from the snow with an ordinary household saw. However, he does not consider a snow house or other such shelter to be really necessary, provided you are thoroughly trained and experienced in the other basic techniques. A snow cave can also be built and will provide a very adequate shelter. Gil sometimes builds igloos but he says that, in general, these take too much time. Incidentally, Gil is an electrical engineer and his work frequently takes him to the Aleutian Islands, off the coast of Alaska. A few years ago he took time off from his duties to instruct the Eskimos of the Barrow area on the building of igloos. (The use of igloos is primarily an art of the inhabitants of Nova Scotia, not Alaska.) He and his son then lived in the igloo for two weeks. He has on many occasions, after building an igloo or snow house, slept outside on the wind swept snow, just to prove the adequacy of his clothing, sleeping bag, and technique.

TRAVEL

A conventional backpack is carried for winter camping, and Gil states that it need not weigh more than thirty to thirty-five pounds. All traveling is done on snowshoes. He particularly warns against use of skis unless you are very expert with them. There is too much danger of a twisted ankle or knee — or worse. About five miles per day is all that should normally be counted on in winter camping. The question of using a sled or toboggan for hauling gear is frequently brought up by his students. Gil does not recommend these except where it is known that the terrain will be open and level. Snow goggles are an important item of gear and are worn almost constantly when traveling and working about camp. Snow blindness can be very serious.

WATER SUPPLY

With snow covering the landscape one would think that water supply would be no problem. Yet there are difficulties in obtaining a water supply from snow, and Gil has a solution for this. In sub-zero temperatures all streams will probably be solidly frozen. Also, when the snow is several feet deep or more, the approach to a running stream, if it does exist, can be hazardous. You cannot "eat" enough snow to replace the water that your body uses every day. This amounts to a minimum of about 1½ quarts of water per day, and that is a lot of snow. To pass that much snow through your mouth in the form of snow is essentially impossible. It will cause your lips to swell and crack, and you will have a terrible time. You could melt snow in a pan over a small stove used for backpacking, but Gil does not like to depend on fire or mechanical aids. His solution to the problem involves a large plastic bag with a wide mouth opening. An ice bag with a large opening would be satisfactory. He stuffs this full of snow and puts it next to his body. The body heat causes the snow to melt as you hike along or work about camp. He stresses that it is important to put more snow into the bag before you pour out the water that is already in the bag. Carrying a bag of snow inside your shirt or close to your skin may not sound very comfortable, but Gil says that you soon get used to this.

FOOD

The choice of food is more important in winter wilderness travel than in the summer. When you cannot depend upon fire for cooking, your choice is narrowed considerably. The food chosen should be high in protein and fat. Sugar and starch base foods are poor sources of lasting body heat and energy. Gil considers unprocessed foods to be best. The food should be cut in bite-size chunks before leaving home. It is terrible to be hungry and to try and bite or cut a piece of cheese at 20 below zero. (It makes excellent structural material at this temperature.) Cheese and dried fat beef are good foods. (Most commercial jerky is too lean for this usage.) Raisins, nuts, bacon, "Tang," dried milk, and shredded coconut are good. Fresh frozen fish and frozen beef can be eaten "as is" with some "practice." Soup and other common backpacking foods which require cooking should be considered "luxury" foods, rather than essential.

WHERE TO GO

A good place to go for your sub-zero backpacking and camping activity is to a ski area. In the dead of winter, in areas where sub-zero temperatures will be found, many roads will be hazardous or impassable. However, roads into ski areas will usually be kept open. After some persuasion, Gil frequently convinces a ski lift operator to haul him and his equipment to the top of a ski lift and he takes off from there. For those just starting to learn the sub-zero hiking and camping techniques it is a good idea to stay fairly close to "civilization," such as an operating ski resort. As for other backpacking activity, you can increase the duration and distance of your trips as your knowledge and experience grow.

That, very briefly, is a description of the unusual techniques, clothing and accessories that Gil Phillips uses in his hobby of backpacking and camping in sub-zero temperatures. In closing, Gil asked that I stress the fact that, for the most part, he has simply adapted the principles that the Eskimos have used for many years, and to be sure and give the Eskimos their due credit. He is a most unusual and interesting person and you will be hearing more about him, I am sure. He is constantly experimenting, testing, and perfecting his gear and methods. If you would like to learn more about his techniques and equipment and have fun doing so, he will be glad to meet you at Wolf Creek Pass in southern Colorado — next January.

OTHER LITERATURE

Following is additional reading material, dealing with some of the various aspects of backpacking with which you may want to become familiar.

1. "American Red Cross First Aid Textbook." The American National Red Cross, Philadelphia, Pennsylvania, 1957.

2. "Appalachian Trailway News." A magazine published three times yearly by the Appalachian Trail Conference, 1718 N Street N.W., Washington, D.C. 20036.

3. "Carters' Map and Compass Manual." Published by Carters Manual Co., P.O. Box 186, Estacada, Oregon 97023.

4. Cunningham and Hansson. "Light Weight Camping Equipment and How to Make It." The Highlander Publishing Co., Boulder, Colorado 80302.

5. Darvill, Fred T., Jr., M.D. "Mountaineering Medicine." The Skagit Mountain Rescue Unit, Inc., P.O. Box 2, Mount Vernon, Washington 98273.

6. "Going Light With Backpack or Burro." The Sierra Club, San Francisco, California, 1956.

7. Lathrop, Theodore G., M.D., "Hypothermia: Killer of the Unprepared." Booklet published by Mazamas, 909 N.W. 19th Avenue, Portland, Oregon 97209.

8. "Lightweight Equipment for Hiking, Camping, and Mountaineering." The Potomac Appalachian Trail Club, 1718 N Street N.W., Washington, D.C. 20036.

9. "The Signpost." A newsletter for backpackers and mountaineers, published at 16812 36th Avenue West, Lynwood, Washington 98036.

10. "Summit." A mountaineering magazine published ten times yearly at Big Bear Lake, California 92315.

11. "Trail Walker." A newsletter published six times yearly by the New York-New Jersey Trail Conference, G.P.O. Box 2250, New York, New York 10001.

12. "Wilderness Camping." A magazine published six times yearly. Subscription address is P.O. Box 1186, Scotia, New York 12302.

Index

Accidents, 7-1 to 7-3
Achilles tendon, bruised, 3-3
Air mattress, 2-4
Altitude, 10-6
Animals, 7-7
Antivenin kit, 2-11, 7-7
Applesauce, 4-3, 4-9

Bacon, 4-2, 4-3, 5-3, 5-5, 5-6 to 5-10
Band-Aids, 2-10, 7-10
Batteries, flashlight, 2-7
Bears, 7-7, 7-8
Bed, 2-1, 2-4, 9-3
Beef, 4-3, 4-4, 4-5, 5-3 to 5-10
Belt pack, 2-13
Belts, for trousers, 3-2
Beverages
    bouillon, 4-7
    cocoa, 4-3, 4-8
    coffee, 4-7
    gelatin, 4-8
    lemonade, 4-3, 4-8
    tea, 4-7
Blisters, 2-11, 3-3, 3-7
Boots, 3-3 to 3-5
Bread, 4-9
Bread substitutes, 4-3, 4-9
Breakfast, 5-3, 5-5, to 5-10
Bulb, flashlight, 2-7
    camera, 2-15

Campfire (see Fires)
Campsite
    choosing, 9-1
    setting up, 9-2
Camp spirit, 9-5, 9-6
Candy, 4-3, 4-11, 5-3, 5-5 to 5-10
Canned meats, 4-3 to 4-5
Canteen, 2-6
Carrier, one-wheel duffel, A-7
Caves, 7-9
Cereals
    cooked, 4-6, 5-3, 5-6, 5-8, 5-9
    dry, 4-6, 5-6
    oatmeal, 4-6, 5-3, 5-6, 5-7, 5-8, 5-9
Check list, 10-10
Chicken, 4-4, 4-10, 5-6
Chili, 4-11
Chow mein, 4-3, 4-10
Cleanliness, 2-8, 7-11
Clothing, 3-1 to 3-8, A-21, A-22
Clothesline, 2-7
Compass, 2-10, 8-3
Condiments, 4-13
Conservation of natural resources, A-13
Containers
    food, 6-1, 6-2
    water, 2-6, 2-7, 2-15, A-15, A-16
Cooking, 6-1 to 6-11
Cooking fire, 6-9, 6-10, 9-4
Cooking utensils, 6-3 to 6-8
Corn, 4-3, 4-9
Cups, 6-6

Dehydration, prevention of, 7-9, 8-1, 8-2
Desserts, 4-3, 4-11, 4-12, 5-3
Dingle stick, 6-8
Dishwashing, 6-10, 7-11
Ditty bag, 2-9, 2-10
Dried and dehydrated foods, 4-1
Duffel carrier, one-wheel, A-7, A-8
Duplicate clothing, 3-8

Eating, 7-10, 10-6
Eating utensils, 6-6
Eggs, 4-3, 4-5, 4-6, 5-3, 5-6 to 5-10
Equipment, 2-1 to 2-16, 6-10, 10-2
Extension handles, 6-6

Fatigue, 7-10
Feet, care of, 7-10, 10-6, 10-8, 10-9
Fireplace, 9-4, 9-5
Fires
    camp, 9-4, 9-5
    cooking, 6-9, 6-10
    equipment for making, 2-6
    precautions, 9-4
    starting, 6-9, 7-2, 9-5
    wood for, 9-5
First aid, 2-10 to 2-13, 7-11
Fish, 4-4, 5-3
Fishing rod, packing, 10-11
Fishnet clothing, 3-6, 3-7
Fly sheets, 2-6
Foam rubber pad, 2-5
Food, 4-1 to 4-13, A-17, A-24
Footwear (see Boots)
Forest Service (see U.S. Forest Service)
Freeze-dried foods, 4-1, 4-3, 4-6, 4-7, 4-9
Fruit, 4-3, 4-5, 4-7, 5-3, to 5-10

Garbage, 6-10, 9-6
Geological Survey (see U.S. Geological Survey)
Grate, 6-8
Groundcloth, 2-4

Handkerchief, 3-7
Hash, 4-11
Hats, 3-2
Hatchets, 7-4
Headgear, 3-2
Hiking, 7-9, 8-1, 10-6
Horses, 1-2
Hunting, 1-1

Improvising, 2-1
Inner soles, boots, 3-5
Insect repellent, 2-9
Insects, protection against, 2-6, 7-5

Jackets, 3-7
Jerky, 4-3, 4-5, 5-3, 5-4, 5-8, 7-10

Kindling, 6-9, 9-5
Knapsacks (see Packs)
Knives, 2-7

Labeling, food bags, 6-2, 6-3
Laxatives, 2-11, 7-10
Leader, 10-2, 10-5
Lemonade, 4-3, 4-8
Lightning, danger from, 7-5
Liner, sleeping bag, 2-3
Litter, 9-6
Losing gear, 9-5
Lunch, 5-3 to 5-10

Macaroni, 4-10
Main dishes, 4-9 to 4-11
Maps, 2-9, 2-10, 8-6, 8-7
    care of, 2-10, 8-8
    sources for, A-12
Margarine, container for, 6-2
Matches, 2-6
Meals (see Menus and Food Lists)
Measuring units, food, 4-12
Meat, 4-2 to 4-5, 5-3
Meats, canned, 4-3 to 4-5
Menus and food lists, 5-1 to 5-10
Milk, 4-13
Milk of magnesia, 2-11, 7-10
Mittens, A-22
Moleskin patches, 2-11, 7-10
Mountain backpacking, 3-1
Mountains, walking in, 7-2
Mukluks, A-22
Mummy bags (see Sleeping bags)
Muscle ointment, 2-11

National Forests, Wilderness primitive areas,
    A-9 to A-11
Needles and thread, 2-9
Notebook, 2-9, 8-5
Note cards, 2-9, 8-5, A-19
Nylon
    air mattresses, 2-4
    cord, 2-7, 2-14
    pack bags, 2-13
    ponchos, 2-5
    rope, 2-7, 2-14
    tarp, 2-5, 10-10
    tents, 2-6, A-4

Organizing a backpack trip, 10-2, 10-3
Orientation, 8-3

Pace, 8-1
Pack bags, 2-13
Pack frames, 2-11 to 2-13, 10-10
Packing, 6-1 to 6-3, 10-10 to 10-12
Packs, 2-11 to 2-13, 8-3, 10-10 to 10-12
Pancakes, 4-6
Pants, 3-2, 3-3
Peas, 4-3, 4-9
Pens and pencils, 2-9
Pepper, 4-13
Photography, 1-1
Physical condition, 1-2, 10-5
Plants, poisonous, 3-1, 7-6
Plastic
    air mattresses, 2-4
    canteens, 2-6

groundcloth, 2-4
ponchos, 2-5
tent tarp, 2-5, 10-7, 10-10
Plastic bags, 2-9, 3-5, 4-5, 6-1 to 6-3, 10-10
Plates, 6-6
Pliers, 2-8
Pockets
    in clothes, 3-2
    in pack bags, 2-13, 3-2
Ponchos, 2-5
Popcorn, 4-12
Potato salad, 4-3, 4-8, 5-9
Potatoes, 4-9, 5-6
    sweet, 4-3, 5-6, 5-8
Pots and pans
    cleaning, 6-11
    packing, 10-11
Practice, 10-7
Predator traps, 7-8
Preparation, 6-1, 10-1 to 10-13
Protective clothing, 3-7
Protection from weather, 2-5, 10-7

Rainstorm, 7-5
Rainwear, 2-5
Rattlesnakes, 3-1, 7-6
Recommended reading, A-26
Repairs, 2-4, 2-8, 2-9
Recipes, 4-8, 4-10, 4-11
Rests, 8-2, 8-3
Retailers, mail order, 2-2, A-3
Rope, 2-7, 2-14
Routine, daily, 8-1

Safety, 7-1 to 7-11
Safety pins, 2-9
Salad, 4-8, 5-3, 5-9
Salad dressing, 4-8
Salami, 4-4
Salt, 4-13, 7-10, 8-1
Salt tablets, 2-11, 2-13, 7-10, 8-1
Sausage, 4-4
Saws, 2-7, 2-8
Sewing kit, 2-9
Shaving gear, 2-9
Sheath knives, 7-4
Shelters, natural, 7-5, A-24
Shirts, 3-2, 3-7
Shoes (see Boots)
Shoelaces, 3-5
Shortening, 4-13
Skillet, 6-4
Sleeping bags, 2-1 to 2-4, A-20, A-21
Sleeping gear (other than sleeping bags), 2-4, 2-5
Snakebite kit, 2-10, 2-11, 7-6, 7-7
Snakes, 3-1, 7-6
Soaking jar, 6-4
Soap, 2-8
Socks, 3-5, 3-7
Solo trips, 7-3
Soup, 4-7, 4-8, 5-3, 5-4, 5-6 to 5-10
Spaghetti, 4-10, 5-5, 5-7
Spoons, 6-4, 6-6
Stebco air mattress, 2-4
Stream crossing, 10-4

Storms, 7-2, 7-5
Stoves, 6-10
Sub-zero camping, A-20 to A-25
Sugar, 4-13
Sunburn, 2-9, 3-1, 7-10
Sun protection, 2-9, 3-1, 3-7, 7-10
Supper, 5-4 to 5-10
Suppliers of equipment and food, 2-2, A-3, A-22
Survival, A-14 to A-19
Suspenders, 3-2

Tape, 2-8, 2-10
Tea bags, 4-7
Tent tarps, 2-5
Tents, 2-5, 2-6, A-4 to A-6
Ticks, 7-6
Toilet articles, 2-8, 2-9
Toilet stops, 8-3
Toothbrush and paste, 2-8
Toothpaste, substitutes for, 2-8
Topographical maps, 2-10, 8-3, 8-6, 8-7
Towels, 2-8
Trail
    information, sources, 8-6, 10-4, A-12
    leaving the, 8-5
    markers, 8-4, 8-5, 8-6, A-18
    organizations, 8-6, A-13
    stops, 8-2, 8-3
Transportation, 10-3
Traps, predator, 7-8
Trousers, 3-2
Tumpline, 2-13

Underclothes, 3-6, 3-7
Utensils
    cooking, 6-3 to 6-7
    eating, 6-6
U.S. Forest Service, 2-10, 8-3, 8-6, 10-4, A-12
U.S. Geological Survey, 2-10, 8-6, 8-7, A-12

Vacuum-dried fruits, 4-3, 4-7
Vegetables, dehydrated, 4-8, 4-9
Vest, 3-6, 3-8

Wading, 3-5
Wading shoes, 3-5
Waistbelt, trousers, 3-2
Walking, 7-9, 8-1
Wash basin, 7-11
Washcloth, 2-8
Water
    containers, A-15, A-16
    purification of, 7-9
    supply, 7-9, A-24
Weather, 7-2, 7-3, 10-4, 10-7
Weight
    general considerations, 1-2, 1-3, 4-1, 6-11, 10-12
    of food, 4-1, 4-3, 5-4 to 5-10, 6-2
    of pack, 1-2, 10-12
Well-being, 7-9 to 7-11
Wind chill factor, 7-3
Wire, 2-9